ALL AMERICAN BOYS

ALL AMERICAN BOYS

---■---

Draft Dodgers in Canada from the Vietnam War

Frank Kusch

Westport, Connecticut
London

Library of Congress Cataloging-in-Publication Data

Kusch, Frank, 1959–
    All American boys : draft dodgers in Canada from the Vietnam War / Frank Kusch.
      p. cm.
    Includes bibliographical references and index.
    ISBN 0–275–97268–2 (alk. paper)
    1. Draft resisters—United States—History—20th century. 2. Canada—Emigration and immigration—Social aspects. 3. United States—Emigration and immigration—Social aspects. 4. Americans—Canada—History—20th century. 5. Vietnamese Conflict, 1961–1975—Draft resisters—United States. I. Title.
    UB342.U5K87   2001
    355.2'24'09730904—dc21   2001021161

British Library Cataloguing in Publication Data is available.

Library of Congress Catalog Card Number: 2001021161
ISBN: 0–275–97268–2

First published in 2001

Praeger Publishers, 88 Post Road West, Westport, CT 06881
An imprint of Greenwood Publishing Group, Inc.
www.praeger.com

Printed in the United States of America

The paper used in this book complies with the
Permanent Paper Standard issued by the National
Information Standards Organization (Z39.48–1984).

10 9 8 7 6 5 4 3 2

For Jo

Contents

Preface

Patriotism and individualism are difficult terms to rectify. Where does loyalty to the state end and loyalty to one's self begin? Few of us ever have to examine these ideas during our lives; they are often the esoteric motifs left to historians, philosophers, and political scientists to ponder. For thousands of young American men who evaded the draft and went to Canada in the 1960s, however, these were not abstract arguments, but decisions that affected the balance of their lives. Their actions as draft dodgers raise some fundamental questions about loyalty and duty. The idea that these men could turn their back on their country and still embody the essence of Americanism may seem implausible. However, one's condemnation of the nation and one's embrace of the founding principles of that nation need not be mutually exclusive. A central question arises when looking at this issue: Is America a nation or a collection of ideals, unbound by borders? Indeed, arguments such as these run through the history of American thought.

Today, there is little agreement on what the various conflicts of the Sixties really meant, or achieved. Decades after the last shot was fired in Southeast Asia, debate about the war continues. Vietnam grips the imagination. Captured in film, words, and memory, the images have endured time. While the decade's politics, music, fashion, drug use, alternative lifestyles, sexual revolution and women's movement continue to reverberate in public life, it is the war that echoes loudest. Vietnam, and America's reaction to it, more than any single event, represented a break in America's Cold War consensus and created a rift between generations. People disagreed then, and they disagree now. Simplifications about the decade, the events of the war, and the war at home are not easy to make. Nevertheless, the prevailing assumption about the men who evaded service in Vietnam is that they were cut from the same cloth. Yet Muhammad Ali and Bill Clinton no more resembled each other in their actions as draft resisters than the many involved in the counterculture or the anti-war movement did each other. Perhaps the only indisputable point one can make about the Vietnam War is that its supporters and detractors cannot be pigeonholed.

The draft evaders interviewed for this book, along with the deserters and Vietnam veterans encountered along the way, arrived at middle age from radically different directions. They share, however, one unfortunate commonality: they are all, in some manner, condemned for their role in the Vietnam saga. Neither those who served nor those who avoided service are spared criticism. This was strikingly evident with the firestorm of controversy over Robert McNamara's book *In Retrospect*, as he tried in vain to reconsider his role in the lengthy and futile war. The opposition to the restoration of diplomatic relations with Vietnam and perennial questions over MIAs reveal a nation's endless struggle to deal with the past. Veterans even jeered their commander-in-chief, President Bill Clinton, during his 1993 Memorial Day address for his avoidance of service in Vietnam. These events reveal that the scars from the war have not faded.

Today, the Vietnam Veterans Memorial sits in Washington, D.C. like a dark gash in the earth—a wound unhealed. Names of the dead mix with reflections of the living, who gaze silently into the smooth, raven stone. Reflected images from the wall accuse, implicating all, sparing no one.

Acknowledgments

There are many who helped to make this book possible, and who deserve my sincere thanks. First, I am indebted to the draft dodgers for their willingness to speak about their lives. Many thanks to the historians who provided me with their wisdom, constructive criticism and guidance. They not only displayed their love of the past, but their love of people and ideas. Sincere thanks go to Dr. Alonzo Hamby, Dr. Katherine Jellison, Dr. Steven Miner, and Dr. Donald Richter from the Department of History at Ohio University, and Dr. Dave De Brou, Dr. Martha Smith-Norris, Dr. R.C. Grogin, Dr. Michael Swan, and Dr. Brett Fairbairn from the History Department at the University of Saskatchewan. Thanks also to Professors Don Kerr and Peter Stoicheff from the Department of English at the University of Saskatchewan, who teach people every day to love the written word. I extend my much belated gratitude to my Grade 11 social studies teacher, Mr. Bone, who single-handedly salvaged my early education, and allowed me to pursue this work in ways he will never really know.

To the patient library staff from Ohio University, the University of Saskatchewan and the University of Wisconsin at Madison, who provided their valuable research assistance, I extend my appreciation. To my fellow graduate student cohorts, and the staff, past and present, at the Department of History at Ohio University in Athens—thank you; you're the best. To the fine people at Praeger Publishers, and to my editor Heather Staines, my sincere gratitude for your support in making this project see the light of day. To my brother Larry: many thanks for your keen eye during the final proof of the manuscript. There are also those, too numerous to mention, who through their kind words, tips, ideas, and their help in locating interviewees, made the project a rewarding experience.

I extend a special thank you to my family, and especially to my mother, who has always had a strong sense of family history and has patiently listened to my own unique take on it.

And finally, to Jo, who has heard more about draft dodgers than many historians, and for whom words alone will not suffice in expressing my gratitude.

Selective Service Classifications

1-A Available for military duty.

1-AO Conscientious objector (CO) status. Available for non-combat military duty.

1-C Current member of the U.S. Armed Forces, public health service taking military training and aviation cadets.

1-H In holding status—not subject to processing for induction.

1-O Conscientious objector, public service, civilian work for maintenance of national health, safety, and interest.

1-S Student deferment. Until completion of high school, or age 20, or until end of academic year of college.

1-W One who has completed service as CO performing civilian work in national health, safety, and interest.

1-Y Available for military service only in time of war or national emergency.

2-A Special occupational deferment, other than student or agriculture.

2-C Agriculture deferment.

2-S Student deferment available upon request for continuing college students.

3-A Extreme hardship deferment, or with dependent children.

4-A Person with prior military service or sole-survivor of a parent killed in action.

4-B Official exempt by law.

4-C Alien resident, not liable for military service.

4-D Divinity student or minister of religion.

4-F Permanent deferment—not qualified for any military duty.

5-A Over the age for military service.

Chronology

1945

- United States drops atom bombs on Hiroshima and Nagasaki
- Second World War ends—demobilization begins
- Beginning of post-war baby boom
- Peter Dewey of the Office of Strategic Services (OSS) is killed—the first U.S military official to die in Vietnam

1949

- Soviet Union detonates its first atomic weapon
- Chinese Communists take over mainland China; Mao Tse-tung establishes Peoples Republic of China

1950-1953

- Korean War
- U.S. grants the French $15 million in military aid in Indochina

1955

- United States begins to directly aid the government in Saigon, and begins to train Vietnamese army

1956

- France pulls out of Indochina
- Rosa Parks is arrested after refusing to give up her seat and move to the back of the bus in Montgomery, Alabama
- Martin Luther King, Jr., leads bus boycott lasting 381 days
- United States increases military presence in Southeast Asia

1957

- Soviet Union launches Sputnik
- American military advisors enter Vietnam

1959

- Fidel Castro takes over in Cuba
- July 8, first U.S. serviceman is killed in Vietnam

1960

- Black students stage a sit-in at a Woolworth's lunch counter in Greensboro, North Carolina
- Student Nonviolent Coordinating Committee (SNCC) organized
- Students for a Democratic Society (SDS) forms
- John F. Kennedy is elected as the thirty-fifth president of the United States
- Hanoi forms National Liberation Front for action in South Vietnam

1961

- Bay of Pigs invasion
- Freedom Rides begin in the South
- Kennedy meets Khrushchev at Vienna summit
- Kennedy increases number of military advisors in Vietnam

1962

- The Cuban Missile Crisis
- Port Huron Statement released by the New Left and SDS

1963

- March on Washington—Martin Luther King, Jr. gives his "I Have a Dream" speech
- President John F. Kennedy assassinated in Dallas

1964

- Lyndon Baines Johnson elected president
- Freedom Summer
- Harlem riots
- Assassination of Medger Evers
- Three student civil rights workers killed in Mississippi
- Civil Rights Act is passed in Congress
- Gulf of Tonkin Resolution is passed
- Students in New York burn draft cards chanting "We Won't Go"
- China detonates first atomic bomb

1965

- Draft card burning becomes criminal offense, punishable by five years in prison
- U.S. Marines land in South Vietnam
- September—Selective Service calls 27,500 men into service, the most since the end of the Korean War; in December, 40,000 are called.
- Assassination of Malcolm X
- The United States begins bombing North Vietnam
- Watts Riots
- Civil rights march from Selma to Montgomery, Alabama

1966

- Sit-ins against the war and the draft begin at universities across the United States
- Stokely Carmichael, president of SNCC, begins Black Power Movement—encourages young blacks to refuse the draft
- 400,000 U.S. troops are in Vietnam

1967

- Draft deferments for married men and most graduate students end
- Muhammad Ali sentenced to five years in prison for refusing induction
- October 15-21—Stop the Draft Week. Thousands of draft cards burned
- Baltimore Four burn draft files
- Hundreds arrested in New York and Oakland in anti-draft riots

1968

- Martin Luther King assassinated in Memphis
- Over 500 U.S. servicemen are killed in action during one week in May
- Tet Offensive
- LBJ chooses not to seek reelection
- Robert F. Kennedy assassinated in Los Angeles
- Rioting outside Democratic national convention in Chicago
- Pierre Elliott Trudeau elected prime minister of Canada
- Milwaukee Fourteen destroy 10,000 draft records
- Richard Nixon elected president of the United States
- General Creighton Abrams replaces Westmoreland in Vietnam
- More than 500,000 U.S. troops in Vietnam

1969

- Draft lottery begins
- Americans land on the moon
- Fight for the People's Park at Berkeley
- Woodstock
- 500,000 protest the Vietnam War in Washington, D.C.
- Nixon begins secret bombing in Cambodia, gives his "silent majority" speech

1970

- Four students killed by National Guard at Kent State University
- Students killed at Jackson State
- Nationwide student strikes
- U.S. invades communist sanctuaries in Cambodia
- U.S. troops down to 280,000 by year's end

1972

- Nixon reelected as president
- Amnesty hearings begin in Washington

1973

- The last servicemen is sent to Vietnam
- Watergate scandal erupts in Washington, D.C.

1974

- Nixon resigns

1975

- Last Americans leave Saigon

1977

- President Jimmy Carter grants amnesty for all draft offenders, including draft dodgers in Canada

Introduction

Who are those who are really disloyal? Those who inflame racial hatreds, who sow religious and class dissensions. Those who subvert the Constitution by violating the freedom of the ballot box. Those who make a mockery of majority rule by the use of the filibuster. Those who impair democracy by denying equal educational facilities. Those who frustrate justice by lynch law or by making a farce of jury trials. Those who deny freedom of speech and of the press and of assembly. Those who demand special favors against the interest of the commonwealth. Those who regard public office merely as a source of private gain. Those who would exalt the military over the civil. Those who for selfish and private purposes stir up national antagonisms and expose the world to the ruin of war. . . . It is easier to say what loyalty is not than what it is. It is not conformity.[1]

On a winter day in 1968, a young man stood outside a government building in Winnipeg, Manitoba, with the collar of his thin jacket turned up against the January wind. After checking an address on a crumpled piece of paper, he climbed the steps and disappeared through the doors of the plain brick building. The sign on the CRYPT offices within provided little comfort from the weather outside. It stated: "Yankee Dodgers and Deserters. Welcome to Canada. Don't crash in the office. See someone at the desk. You better dig it here, you're stuck!" CRYPT stood for the Committee Representing Youth Problems Today, which provided legal counseling, food, accommodations, and free medical care. His destination was the office of the Winnipeg Committee to Assist War Objectors. The young man was a Vietnam draft dodger. It was his first day in a country he would from then on call home.[2]

From the mid-1960s to the early 1970s, thousands of young American men crossed the border into Canada to avoid war in Vietnam. Untold numbers never returned.[3] Although they comprised one of the largest migrations to Canada from the United States—rivaling the hordes of British Loyalists who fled north during the War of Independence—they have been relegated to a footnote in the history of the 1960s and the Vietnam War.[4] The scant attention paid to this topic in scholarly works leaves us with little understanding of the draft evaders who chose to remain in Canada following President Jimmy Carter's amnesty in 1977—the subjects of this book.[5] It is often assumed that these draft dodgers were either anti-war radicals, or traitors and cowards—products of a decadent society. But were they?

What sort of young Americans would not only refuse service to their country, but flee the nation, never to return? While the decision to go to Canada to avoid the draft was the biggest decision they had made in their young lives, for the majority of these expatriates it does not appear to have been one that required much deliberation. Most made their decisions quickly, long before their absence would have caught the attention of their draft board or the long arm of the law. These young Americans left their country with little hesitation or remorse. What is apparent is that from the moment these men left the United States they had no intention of returning. What emerges is that the expatriates' motivations for leaving their country of birth permanently lay not solely with the Vietnam War, but with their experiences, influences and expectations growing up as Americans in the 1950s and 1960s.

These findings are based, in part, on interviews with more than 30 draft dodgers conducted by this author, as well as an examination of the published testimonies of other draft dodgers in books, journals, magazines and newspaper articles stemming from the mid-1960s to the present. This research is augmented by the findings of David Surrey and the Vietnam Era Research Project (VERP); the Notre Dame Survey conducted by Lawrence M. Baskir and William B. Strauss; and a wide range of secondary literature on the draft, the protest to it, and the Vietnam War.[6]

ALIENATED AMERICANS

The expatriates who dodged the draft became disaffected from their nation of birth at an early age. They never developed a sense of community or belonging to the United States in their formative years. This early detachment led not only to a deep sense of alienation from the country, but underlay their decisions to evade conscription and make permanent moves north. In contrast to stereotypical images of long-haired drifters, cowards or radicals, the majority of the Canadian-bound draft dodgers tended to be stable, conservative in behavior, highly individualistic, and resolute to pursue higher education and careers free of interference from the state. The expatriates also tended not to be involved in anti-war activities as most were interested primarily in completing their studies and focusing on their futures. It is easy to argue that leaving the country to avoid the draft is protest's ultimate act. The draft dodgers' overall behavior, however, indicates that Vietnam was the final straw, and their reasons for leaving—and staying in Canada—stem more from attitudes about the United States, and not simply or primarily a protest against conscription. Most were not interested in struggling to reform a country that they felt was intractable—and more important, the majority no longer cared. This explains why, when the war ended and amnesty made it safe for their return, they declined. Successful assimilation in Canada does not by itself explain adequately their refusal to return.

Interestingly, the vast majority of these expatriates did not have to go to Canada to avoid the war. They were the sons of the white middle- and upper middle-class, a fact supported by all scholarship to date.[7] Their parents were three times as likely to be professionals, executives, managers and business owners than the average rate in the U.S. population. The expatriates came from "relatively elite family backgrounds," with parents "educated well beyond national levels," and with children well informed about the world. These draft evaders were from a class that, more often than not, went to Vietnam by choice or did not go at all.[8] Education and connections made it possible to circumvent the draft in the 1960s. While some deferments, including those for graduate students, were phased out as the war progressed, there were numerous methods for these men to avoid conscription without going to Canada. Even when all avenues had been exhausted to avoid military service, only 8 percent of combat troops in Vietnam came from their class-background, and at least half of that number had actually requested combat placements.[9] This class advantage, combined with a strong economy, gave them options to the military that previous generations did not enjoy. Unlike those who served in uniform in the Second World War, and even Korea, these young men had choices with higher education, professional careers, and deferments allowing them to remain in the United States without going to Vietnam.

These draft evaders, however, showed neither interest nor obligation to embrace forced military service with affluence and a strong economy at their wait. They resolved to continue with their future plans in Canada, where their skills and training were welcomed and they were free of government interference. Interestingly, by heading north they did not feel that they were turning their back on the promise of America, but rather they realized that they were free to live "The American Dream" in Canada.[10]

The irony is that despite their alienation from the United States, these expatriates are, in many respects, quintessential Americans. They are products of the society in which they were raised. With thought and deed, they personified the Jeffersonian ideals of freedom and individual liberty, as they were determined to let no intervening authority dictate their lives. As such, they appear as ardent individualists who disavowed incursions on their freedom of choice by the state—an American trait since colonial times. By dodging the draft for the Vietnam War, these young American men unequivocally displayed their refusal to sacrifice personal autonomy to demands of state.

This book does not intend to speak for all expatriates; there are sure to be individuals with differing opinions on the United States, the reasons why they left, and their perceived role in activism against the war (although all the men interviewed for the book found the war to be morally reprehensible). What this book does suggest is that for most expatriates there appears to be considerable evidence that the Vietnam War was not the main cause of their alienation from America, their draft evasion, or their refusal to return to the United States following amnesty. These young Americans believed they had the right to decide their course in life, a path, which, for convenience sake, led across the border to Canada. It was a country where they were generally welcomed, and they could resume their lives in the manner they wished with a minimum of trouble or interference.[11] These findings speak to the common misconception that everyone who crossed the border to avoid conscription was an anti-war activist. Indeed, it appears that a sizable number of those who came north simply wanted to resume their lives free of the clutches of the draft, and the demands of their nation, and were not interested in the struggle to "reform America," unlike the draft evaders and deserters who planned to return home.[12] While they were generally more left than right of center, politically, what sent them across the border as young men was not that they were liberals or conservatives or Republicans or Democrats, but their individual experiences and expectations about life and about America. They were, in fact, part of a much larger exodus from the United States during the Vietnam era for whom Vietnam played only a secondary role to feelings of alienation from the country.[13]

One of the purposes of this study is to determine what caused these young Americans to behave as they did. To explain their motivation, the expatriates' formative years must be placed in a historical context. Their decisions on the draft had their origins in childhood.

AMERICA AFTER WORLD WAR II

The expatriates were among the first wave of the post-war baby boom. They were born into middle- and upper middle-class families, and their parents prospered in the economic expansion that followed the cessation of hostilities. Their early years were spent in the 1950s—a decade that's often portrayed as a tranquil, placid time of middle-class bliss. Low crime and consumer abundance helped create the illusion of happy families. This image is reinforced in television programs of the era such as, *Leave It To Beaver, The Adventures of Ozzie and Harriet,* and *Father Knows Best.* While these images partly reflected reality, the decade was also a time of private family turmoil and palpable public discontent. American society was changing and those changes shaped these future draft dodgers.[14]

They were children at the height of the Cold War, when battles for civil rights raged in the South, gender and social norms were challenged, and a fragile post-war consensus waned. They came of age when the problems of the outside world, for the first time, came home through television. Several of the expatriates interviewed for this study belonged to families embroiled in the social strife of the 1950s and early 1960s. This, on occasion, resulted in families at odds with their communities, and is apparent especially for those raised in the South.

Several of the future expatriates were school-aged boys during the early civil rights movement and the rise in anxiety concerning communist infiltration. Sixty percent of the draft dodgers who were interviewed for this book grew up in the Southern United States. Most of these "Southerners," however, were actually from the North—they had moved South with their parents at a young age. Seen as outsiders and "Yankees," they were caught in the social upheaval of Southern communities at a time when blacks were fighting for civil rights. And if their parents happened to be activists, they were further marked. Some became outcasts in their neighborhoods. Because of their situation, they became much more sensitive to issues, such as racism in the South, but it also made them targets of the forces that were attacking the civil rights movement. Such difficulties were not confined to the South. Disrupted family life, parental activism, racism, Cold War tensions and the awareness of these social and political issues are a pattern present in the lives of many expatriates. They speak of a general disaffection, alienation, and detachment from community and country.

The expatriates belonged also to the first generation to grow up under the threat of nuclear annihilation. Several interviewees have vivid recollections of air-raid drills at school and the possibility of nuclear doom. Some attached significance to the launch of the satellite Sputnik by the Soviet Union, and recall growing up with a sense of dread concerning the nation's future; they began to question their country's direction. It also led to a belief that they needed to get the most out of life before it was too late. They had a sense of urgency in their adolescent years.

The 1950s and early 1960s were also a time of tremendous economic growth and opportunity. As they matured, the future expatriates envisioned lives of choice and prosperity. The advantages and opportunities for them far outweighed anything experienced by their parents or grandparents. The economic prospects facing the previous generations were grim in comparison. The crippling Depression and the struggles and challenges of the onset of the Second World War made the prospect of joining the military much more acceptable for those born in the inter-war period than for those born following the war. It is not surprising that the percentage of potential conscripts dodging the draft in the Second World War, and even the Korean War five years later, was much lower than for Vietnam. The young men born after 1945 inherited a world of unmatched opportunity.

The draft evaders' childhood experiences fostered in them a heightened independence which flourished when they became teens and young adults. Some found diversions in the growing counterculture emanating from San Francisco and New York's Greenwich Village. They became attracted to some aspects of Beatnik culture and related to figures, such as Jack Kerouac and Allen Ginsberg, who became voices for countless individuals who found themselves out of step with mainstream views.[15] Yet they were not part of "the crowd," and tended to be very independent thinkers. They immersed themselves in influential American writers and philosophers, such as Thomas Jefferson and Henry David Thoreau, whose writings not only validated their sense of individualism and individual liberty, but helped shape their character. Most believed that they had much in common with core American values and ideals.[16]

As they reached physical maturity and left their parents' homes in the early 1960s, the mood in the country, and especially on college campuses, validated their feelings. An important factor was the climate of anti-war and anti-American protests that (according to the draft dodgers themselves) gave them the level of support they needed to make their dramatic moves to avoid the draft. This was a factor absent from both world wars and the Korean War. The majority of these young men had become so disenchanted with their nation's direction that, when drafted, they often neglected to investigate or accept legitimate options available to them to avoid induction, let alone combat.[17] Their behavior suggests that they did not care enough about their country to find ways of avoiding service while remaining in the United States.

While these draftees were young in years, they were not young in experiences. The two decades following the Second World War to the eve of the Vietnam War were among the most tumultuous in American history— they were also among the most prosperous and promising. It was from this paradoxical post-war era that these young men emerged to face the draft, and those experiences were not secondary, but central to their decisions on Vietnam.

THOSE WHO RETURNED

This book does not deal with the draft dodgers who returned to the United States after the amnesty in 1977. According to VERP, and to other draft dodger accounts, the majority of those who returned had planned to do so before leaving for Canada. They were a close-knit group of self-imposed exiles who claimed to be working to change America and stop the war—an assertion hotly challenged at the time by anti-war activists in the United States. A number of American activists were perplexed and angry with some of the draft dodgers in Canada who believed their actions would help end the war in Vietnam. Folk singer and activist Joan Baez, for example, remarked: "These kids can't fight the Vietnam madness by holing up in Canada. What they're doing is opting out of the struggle at home. That's where they should go, even if only to fill up jails." This sentiment was echoed by others including Stokely Carmichael and Students for a Democratic Society (SDS) president Tom Hayden, who questioned the usefulness of going to Canada as a means of protest.[18] Nonetheless, these draft dodgers claimed sincerity in their feelings about reforming their country and wished to return as soon as it was possible.

Many of these evaders followed the well-traveled path created by earlier draft dodgers and realized that Canada might be a good place to "hide out" until the war's end. Several became active in Canadian-based protest action against the war, centered in Toronto. Organizations, such as the Student Union for Peace Action (SUPA), counseled dodgers and potential draft dodgers on the Canada option. This more radical group, however, remained relatively small. Indeed, scores of journalists from the United States who traveled to Canada to cover the draft dodger phenomenon were surprised when they met few left-leaning radicals and activists. Edmond Taylor of *The Reporter*, for example, who traveled to Toronto to interview draft evaders, tried to label those he met as anti-American subversives who where more interested in attacking American society than protesting against the Vietnam War. Even in his virulent tirade against the dodgers in Canada, however, he admitted that most of those he met were not radicals, and actually there was only a "small hard core of revolutionary fanatics among them." Furthermore, Anthony Hyde of SUPA told *The Detroit News* that out of the three distinct groups of draft dodgers he saw, the largest by far was that of "ordinary Americans from middle-class backgrounds, who don't want to take two years out of their lives [to serve in Vietnam]." Hyde said that the two smaller groups consisted of a few conscientious objectors and those who opposed the Vietnam War. The majority of these Americans had melded into Canadian society so quickly, that there was not a great need for extensive exile centers. This was the case with SUPA, which ceased operations in 1967.[19] As Surrey found, "members of this community chose not to establish deep roots in Canada" and worked to gain amnesty for themselves back in the United States. The majority of this group returned to the United States when they became immune from prosecution in 1977. Among the others who returned were a small number of black Americans for whom assimilation into the predominately white culture in Canada in the late 1960s and early 1970s was difficult. VERP's research also concludes that draft dodgers with less education and less advantaged backgrounds more readily returned as there were fewer job opportunities north of the border.[20] Baskir and Strauss' Notre Dame Survey suggests that many of those who returned were those who went to Canada as a last resort, after exhausting all other options to avoid the draft. These men worked eagerly for amnesty and planned to return when possible.[21] Those who did return in the first few years following amnesty, however, consisted of a "small core" of activist exiles. Surrey also found with VERP that "the actual numbers [of those who returned] were relatively small."[22]

Perhaps the most salient point is Surrey's conclusion that deserters (the largest percentage of exiles and the most radical of those in exile organizations), who were not completely covered in Carter's amnesty, "were more likely to return to live in the U.S." than draft dodgers, "who could return to the United States with a clean slate [but] usually elected to remain in Canada." Baskir and Strauss point out that while one in four exiles (including deserters and draft dodgers) stayed in Canada, at least one-half of the total number of returnees were deserters. Four out of five deserters returned to the United States following amnesty.[23]

It is to those who chose to remain—the *expatriates*—that this study restricts itself; it is an examination of those for whom evading the draft was merely a symptom of their desire to separate from their country of birth.

The American expatriates in this book were raised in a culture which taught them that they could become anything they wanted in life. They believed that liberty in thought and deed was their national birthright, rather than a creed of unquestioning obedience to a country they believed was increasingly unworthy. Conscription to serve in what most believed was an immoral war, simply validated their beliefs. Instead of traitors to the ideals of America, these men, as draft dodgers, embodied those ideals. In the spirit of their revolutionary forefathers, their behavior in refusing state servitude and their *practice* of individual liberty was quintessentially American.

The purpose of this work is to judge not the actions of these men concerning the draft, but to explain those actions within the historical context of the 1950s and 1960s. This book looks at the United States as these young Americans perceived it to be and shows how this perception led to their decisions. These men are referred to throughout as "dodgers" or "evaders" because that is how they refer to themselves. It is clear, however, that they were more than draft dodgers evading the Vietnam War. They were American boys evading America.

1

The Draft in American History: Balancing Liberty and Necessity

If we are made in some degree for others, yet, in a greater, are we made for ourselves. It were contrary to feeling, and indeed ridiculous to suppose that a man had less rights in himself than one of his neighbors, or indeed all of them put together. This would be slavery, and not that liberty which the bill of rights has made inviolable, and for the preservation of which our government has been charged. Nothing could so completely divest us of that liberty as the establishment of the opinion, that the State has a perpetual right to the services of all its members. This, to men of certain ways of thinking, would be to annihilate the blessings of existence, and to contradict the Giver of life, who gave it for happiness and not for wretchedness. And certainly, to such it were better that they had never been born.[1]

Since the Declaration of Independence, duty to country in the donning of military uniform has been the requisite of generations of Americans. In a nation born in war and revolution, the call to arms has recurrently raised the question of who shall serve, and who may justly order service. The pages that follow provide a summary of conscription from colonial times to the eve of the Vietnam War. What emerges is that the draft's legacy in America is the arduous balance of protecting the liberties of the many, while preserving them for the few called to serve. The conundrum of state obligation and individual liberty has shaped national policy and public attitude concerning the draft throughout the republic's history. While conscription has on occasion achieved wide public acceptance, this acceptance was always conditional. For the draft to succeed, Americans need to be convinced that there exists a clear, national threat. It has always been necessary for citizens to view conscription not as an infringement upon individual liberty, but as a measure necessary to ensure liberty. Americans also have needed to see their military as a citizen-based volunteer army, one that reflects the will of the people and not the whim of government. American citizens have to agree that a cause is just before they are willing to commit to arms. Moreover, even when the draft was used successfully in both world wars, it never surpassed the people's willingness to volunteer despite the use of conscription.

That delicate balance, which served the nation well in two world wars, slowly eroded as the draft became more permanent following Korea, and it disappeared altogether during the Vietnam era, when many young Americans began to question their nation's direction and purpose, and others of draft age believed their freedoms as individuals were usurped by induction. Viewed as a regional conflict of little threat to the country, the Vietnam War lost public legitimacy. The war's disastrous conclusion coincided with a time when the draft was viewed increasingly by Americans as not only unnecessary, but unfair and intrusive to liberty. In the wake of Vietnam, the government's provisional privilege of drafting citizens for the military was supplanted by the move to an all-volunteer military—one that reflected traditional American values. For the expatriates in Canada, their feelings about service and individual liberty mirror attitudes that have existed in America since colonial times.

THE COLONIAL ERA

The idea of a large standing army and a draft in support of one was never palatable in early American history. In 1784, following the Revolutionary War, the entire Continental Army was discharged, save fewer than 100 veterans who were retained to guard military supplies at West Point and Fort Pitt.[2] Given the traditions and attitudes of early Americans, a large military force, supported by conscription, was unacceptable. The colonies faced the question, however, of how to raise an adequate army if needed. Most colonial legislatures required able-bodied males between 17 and 60 with property holdings to be members of their local militias. The idea was that the militia was an unobtrusive entity in American life. This belief held sway and gained strength in the mid-to-late 1700s as hostilities with London escalated. The opprobrious behavior of the British army in 1763 convinced many Americans that large standing armies curtailed individual liberty and republicanism. In the prevailing climate, the ideal soldier was the local militia, citizen soldier.[3]

Not only did most early Americans feel an ideological resistance to standing armies, but war was sporadic, and financial resources to support one were scarce. When the Revolution began in 1775, colonials successfully faced the dilemma of how to raise a force with the ability to repel the British, without creating one that would eventually threaten colonial independence. What the revolutionaries had in their favor was that the conflict was viewed by many not as an effort to create a new country, but as a method to protect local autonomy. In this climate of self-interest, it took little to convince colonialists that it was worth the fight. Since local militias were already sizable, there was no need to conscript men into service. Buttressing state militias were the well-trained and equipped Minute Men. Formed from select groups of volunteers, the Minute Men were designed to come together in a moment's notice, and prepared in advance for duty. Other than Virginia—where there were some brief and sporadic calls for a general militia—no widespread or effective implementation of conscription occurred. During the War of Independence, state militias were joined by the Continental Army, consisting of volunteer enlistees from each state, joined together loosely by the Confederation Congress. These volunteers were inducted and paid for two three-year terms. The states maintained units of the Continental Army, as well as their own short-term militias. Even this multi-state army raised considerable controversy, as it ran against the republican ideal of citizen soldiers, and threatened to expand the federal government.[4]

While both the state militias and continental forces were initially composed of propertied white males, their numbers swelled when many poor whites, blacks, and women in support capacities—and some pretending to be men—joined the war effort. Of the approximately 200,000 Americans who served sporadically in the Continental Army throughout the war, most served in local militias. In 1778 the full strength of the army stood at only 16,800.[5]

When the Continental Army demobilized in 1784, Congress created a small, permanent regular army and a permanent national unit. The 1st U.S. Regiment was the initial unit of the U.S. Army and was used to guard the Indian Frontier, ensure internal order, and provide national defense. This of course brought new rounds of controversy, with calls to keep the local militias strong to provide the bulwark against the tyranny of centralized power. Although Congress attempted to create a uniform militia, there was no agreement on implementation or uniform national standards.[6]

While volunteers remained as the main source of personnel for the army for several more decades, Congress allowed itself to progressively swell its size during successive conflicts in the late 1700s. The Army grew to 5,000 in the 1790s during the defeat of Indian forces in the Ohio Valley, and then to 12,000, temporarily, during the undeclared naval war with France in 1798–99. By the beginning of the nineteenth century, under President Thomas Jefferson, the regular army was 9,000 strong, but all remained volunteers.[7]

The first serious attempt to establish a national draft came during the War of 1812. President James Madison was convinced that the state militias could not prevail against the British, nor succeed in the plan to invade their colonies in Canada. Madison sought the creation of a large regular army—a national force picked from each region. The president attempted to establish national conscription, drawing from state militia units, creating an army of 80,000 men. These men were to serve under nationally appointed generals. The push for the draft came on the heels of two years of military setbacks and low turnouts at recruiting offices. Madison broke with past traditions and did not encourage the volunteer militias to join. Instead, he moved to increase the size of the regular army. By using cash incentives (three months of pay in advance) and promising soldiers 160 acres of land, Madison was able to raise the size of the regular army from 7,000 to 15,000. The president obtained the authority from Congress to raise 62,000 regulars, but he never managed to recruit even half that number. The war was generally unpopular, and Federalists in New England opposed the declaration of war with Great Britain. There were also many who were against the plan to invade the Canadian colonies as it was perceived by them not to be a defensive act, but one of an aggressor. Madison also faced difficulty with the idea that the militia should be used to fight outside the continental United States. Opposition came primarily from strict constitutionalists who argued that the U.S. Constitution did not permit such a use of military force. As some historians have observed, however, it wasn't just that some members of the militia were unwilling to fight, but that they were unprepared to fight. Madison feared also that the militias were not prepared sufficiently to challenge the British Regulars, as they were often short of weapons and shoes and lacked proper clothing, blankets, camp equipment, and other basic necessities.[8]

The war was so unpopular that despite a British invasion in 1814 and the burning of Washington, the army still had not been able to achieve the strength authorized by Congress. The attempts to launch national conscription began in October 1814, when a plan was submitted to Congress to draft 40,000 men into the regular army. The conscription bill died, however, on the Senate floor in December when the two sides could not agree to amendments. The debate over the draft soon became moot, as the Peace of Ghent was signed on December 24, ending the war.

The U.S. Army remained relatively small for the next three decades. By mid-century, following the conclusion of the Mexican War, the permanent, peacetime army stood at a mere 11,000 men. It was small compared to the ever growing population.[9] Until the 1860s, there were in reality two armies—one was composed of a small number of peacetime regulars, the other of wartime citizen soldiers; it was a balance maintained without the need for conscription. Since the Revolution, this reality balanced nicely the need for ready soldiers with the republican ideal of decentralized power. It was not until the Civil War that the two philosophies came to loggerheads, when the Union and the Confederacy turned to conscription.

THE CIVIL WAR

The American Civil War was by far the nation's worst constitutional crisis, and what was demanded of citizens on both sides of the conflict is unmatched in the history of the republic. Conscription also faced its first test as citizens were called to battle each other. No conflict before or since has cost the lives of so many Americans, even outmatching the carnage suffered by U.S. troops in the Second World War. By the end of the war's first year in 1861, the North had more than 600,000 men in the field.[10] Initially, the forces were composed of regulars, militia men, and volunteers. But because of the war's long duration, reports of irregular pay, unsanitary conditions, poor food, and high casualty rates, the numbers of volunteers dropped off greatly. In 1861–62 there was no clear indication of when the war would end, and no real sign or promise of victory.

The North, however, was not alone in its difficulty to raise men for the protracted conflict, and not the first to resort to the draft. The Confederacy ushered in compulsory term enlistment with the Conscription Act of April 16, 1862. While the act was proposed initially to help retain enlistees until war's end, it was soon used as a method to conscript.[11] Considerable resistance followed, especially among the poor and the middle class, as the price for substituting money for service went as high as $6,000 Confederate dollars, or $600 in gold. Other exemptions were also seen as class-based, as middle-class professionals and skilled artisans were exempt from service. In 1864, in some desperation, the Confederacy went as far as to conscript all white males aged 17 to 50. While 21 percent of the 1,000,000 men who served in the Confederate Army were drafted, conscription was most effective in keeping the original volunteers in the ranks.[12]

To meet state quotas in the North, President Abraham Lincoln created the first national conscription law in the Union with the Enrollment Act of March 3, 1863.[13] Before the act, there was mounting pressure from citizen soldiers and officers to provide more recruits. Veterans voiced their resentment of "shirkers" who avoided duty. The draft's unofficial motto was "fight, pay, or emigrate."[14] Even though evading the draft was a federal crime punishable by two years in prison, the first ever national draft was met by fierce resistance and some of the worst rioting in the republic's history. Riots and other civil disturbances erupted in various parts of the North, including Albany, Boston, and Rochester, as well as in rural areas from the Midwest to the eastern seaboard. Thirty-eight federal enrollment officers lost their lives. The worst draft riots occurred in New York City, where the death toll was in the dozens. Much of the violence was caused by those who were angry because the wealthy were able to avoid service by paying a $300 fee to the government. Draft headquarters were burned, and the homes of draft officials were broken into and looted, along with the homes of prominent Republicans. Among the worst aspects of the rioting was the targeting of blacks. Many were severely beaten, and others lynched from street lamps. The disturbances were so serious that six regiments, fresh off battles at Gettysburg, had to return to restore order.[15]

Draft resisters came from various backgrounds including urban immigrants, rural poor, the lower middle class—many who were native born—as well as a good number of Protestant Americans. Some were Jeffersonian democrats who believed in states' rights and limited government, and saw the war as assaulting those ideals. Others in the North feared the increased competition for jobs from freed blacks from the South. Out of 300,000 men drafted, 40,000 failed to respond, an additional 165,000 were granted exemptions due to physical disability, or dependency, while another 52,000 with means paid the $300 sum to avoid service.[16]

The first ever draft was a failure. The goal of mass conscription was not achieved as less than 8 percent of the army was made up of draftees, and many of those were viewed as unreliable and unpatriotic in the field. Volunteers constituted 92 percent of the Union army.[17] What the Civil War did achieve, as far as the draft was concerned, was to introduce the idea of "national forces" into the military vocabulary, while conspicuously avoiding mention of the militia. It also constituted the first significant growth of the federal military bureaucracy, and the national government as a whole. President Lincoln and Secretary of War Edwin Stanton, for example, used the Union army to quell civil disobedience and enforce the draft. In Boston, the Union army was used to subdue a crowd of 1,000 demonstrators who were attempting to sack the National Guard Armory. Two dozen citizens were killed in the melee.[18]

Lincoln believed the federal government had the right to draft citizens and to uphold this right unconditionally. The President wrote:

The case simply is, the Constitution provides that the Congress shall have the power to raise and support armies. This is the whole of it. . . . The power is given fully, completely, unconditionally. It is not a power to raise armies if state authorities consent; nor if the men to compose the armies are entirely willing; but it is a power to raise and support armies given to Congress by the Constitution without an if.[19]

Following the war, revitalized state militia units called the National Guard became popular. In 1891, the guard had 100,000 part-time citizen soldiers, compared to 27,000 who served in the regular army. While volunteers remained the main source of manpower for the Spanish-

American War in 1898, from 1899 to 1901 under Theodore Roosevelt, the army expanded to 80,000 regulars. At the turn of the century, the U.S. government became increasingly concerned that the size of its military did not match its growing role in foreign affairs, and believed it was time to expand its military capability overseas. With the wane of the British Empire, America assumed a greater international role and began to consider the need for larger reserves. The Militia Act of 1903 designated the National Guard as the nation's ready reserve. In the threat of war, numbers of the guard were to be called up before volunteers; it signified not only the beginning of federal control, but the final transformation from citizen soldier militias, to the modern-day American military.[20]

THE WORLD WARS

While conflict plagued the initial attempts at widespread conscription, it was not the case for the world wars. Never a popular institution, the draft, nevertheless, was quite successful when used over the next 40 years. Although conscription was flirted with on a national basis, it was not needed to any great extent until the coming of the Great War. With America's emergence on the world's stage in the new century, it was thought that the U.S. military had to adapt to meet the needs of a modern military in a modern world. Contributing to this belief was the outbreak of war in Europe. America's entry into the First World War formed the basis for the country's first comprehensive national draft. The draft was established under the auspices of the Selective Service System. The new system prohibited inductees from volunteering, calling the practice inefficient and unmanageable. It was thought that a U.S. Army composed of volunteers was much too small to compete effectively with rival powers on the international stage.[21] The draft followed on the heels of a massive campaign to enlist men into universal military training (UMT&S). The goal of this program, which began in 1915, was to have a pre-trained mass army of citizen reservists. The men would train for six-month terms and would constitute a large, ready-trained force of national reservists for quick call-up in the event of war. As President Theodore Roosevelt once explained, "A democracy must do its own fighting." The president and others continuously emphasized the integral relationship between military obligations and citizenship rights; the idea was to make conscription appear as a democratic responsibility and necessity, while making the older tradition of paying volunteers to serve only in wartime seem archaic. Induction and training through Selective Service was made to fit the idyllic picture of citizens doing their duty, rather than the tyranny of a too powerful central government.[22]

The effort to raise a large army through Selective Service, while balancing localist dissent, turned out to be quite effective. When America entered World War I in 1917, public acceptance of the draft was strong. No doubt helping matters was President Woodrow Wilson's threat of one year in prison for anyone avoiding conscription. By June 5, 1917, 10 million men had reported for the draft. There was little protest or disturbance, and the army had no difficulty in reaching its goal of an additional 1.5 million recruits. Key in the success of the draft was that 40 percent of servicemen had already volunteered before Selective Service prohibited the practice in December 1917. The reason why there was no widespread negative reaction to conscription was that the American public generally supported U.S. involvement in the war. This shift, however, from volunteers to draftees and insisting that they *be* draftees, more than any event in the draft in World War I, represented a clear break with past military tradition.[23]

Conscription in the First World War was a success for several reasons. Absent in 1917 was the practice of purchasing draft exemptions, a factor that caused class and racial conflict during the Civil War. The United States was also a very different country than in the 1860s. Waves of immigrants from Europe transformed both urban and rural areas. Many newcomers, not wanting to be branded as anti-American during a wave of wartime nationalism and increased xenophobia, kept their peace, or fell in step with their native-born cousins. Contributing to the fall-in-line mentality was the constant rumors of German spies and espionage, which helped to keep dissenting public opinion in check. No one wished to be branded a German sympathizer or, worse yet, a traitor. Most opposition was suppressed under the pressure to conform to America's new global posture. While poor whites, Southerners, blacks, women's organizations, peace groups, organized labor, as well as religious pacifists, such as the Quakers, were involved in the anti-draft movement, there was little organization, cooperation, or sustained voice; much of the protest was muted in the surge of nationalism and sense of national duty and obligation that swept the country and dominated public opinion.[24]

Perhaps the primary reason for the draft's success in the First World War was that the Selective Service System, unlike the draft in the Civil War, was able to meet the need for ready manpower while maintaining treasured American ideals of individualism, localism, and the appearance of civilian control of the army. Viewed as a patriotic, democratic, and, more important, as a temporary policy, conscription was not only politically acceptable, and militarily successful, but in this light, palatable to much of the American public. Underpinning it all was the idea that President Wilson and others promoted so well: that military duty was part of a person's obligation as a citizen.[25] Americans also did not face the prospect of fighting each other on their own territory as they did in the Civil War.

Ultimately, the draft succeeded because there was little need for it. One-half volunteered before receiving their draft notices, and the countless others who would have volunteered were prohibited because the government deemed the practice too inefficient. Essentially Americans, as they had in the past, had drafted themselves.

While the first national draft had come to America and was widely, if not totally, accepted, it ended abruptly on Armistice Day, on November 11, 1918, when a massive demobilization began. The war's end ushered in once again the traditional American opposition to a large standing army in peacetime. After prolonged debate in Washington, the number agreed to for the regular army was 298,000, while the status of the National Guard remained intact.[26] The National Defense Act of 1920 contained no reference to a national draft,[27] but for the first time in U.S. military history, there were three individual components that would from then on share in the duties of war: the U.S. Army, the National Guard, and the organized army reserves.[28]

The tide toward the draft turned again in the autumn of 1940. With the German Blitzkrieg rampaging across Europe, Americans found themselves again on the cusp of a world war. But unlike before, the nation was about to debate and experience the first peacetime draft in the republic's history. The conscription controversy followed President Franklin Roosevelt's policy of gradual retreat from isolationism to internationalism and increased aid to the Allies already at war in Europe. Roosevelt realized that the U.S. military as it stood was no match for the Axis powers. He also had an early understanding of the need for massive recruitment before any direct American entry into overseas hostilities. The army had dwindled to 120,000 in the inter-war period and the United States had dropped to a lowly 17th among military forces in the world. While Chief of Staff George C. Marshall recommended the need for an army of 1,000,000 men by the end of 1941, and an even more ambitious 4,000,000 by 1942, the administration was reluctant to raise the conscription issue with Congress. With vocal isolationist forces both in government and throughout the nation, there was a belief that no draft could be ordered without a declaration of war. Pacifists and religious organizations were also against a draft as many believed it would lead to unnecessary foreign conflicts, and that present volunteer forces were sufficient. The military command was convinced, however, of the inadequacy of the current volunteer system and pushed the White House for compulsory training and service. Conscription stalwarts from the First World War again came to the fore, and they lobbied Congress for a pre-war draft of recruits. Led by Grenville Clark, a determined group of civilian conscriptionists gained the ear of Secretary of War Henry Stimson and, ultimately, Roosevelt and General George C. Marshall.

While the majority of Americans had been against the passing of a draft bill, by late summer, 1940, with the war going badly for the Allies in Europe, public opinion grew in favor of conscription. Tough debate followed in Congress, with the Senate voting 58 to 31 in favor of the draft and the House approving the measure by a 263–149 count.[29] President Roosevelt promised the American public that its sons were not being conscripted to fight in foreign wars, although he understood that the Selective Service was the most efficient method of gaining recruits for the armed forces, and war overseas, if needed. Roosevelt, however, was a political animal. He had his own delicate balancing act to perform: one of keeping the isolationists at bay by not appearing to lean too heavily toward drafting American boys, especially before a federal election. As in the First World War, peace groups, women's groups, and religious pacifists refused to cooperate with the conscription effort. Pacifist groups worked to expand the scope for the conscientious objector (CO) position to include non-religious objectors. Most of these issues, however, became moot with the Japanese attack on Pearl Harbor on December 7, 1941. The vast majority who had refused the draft, including conscientious objectors, nevertheless served the war effort in either the medical corps, or in the civilian public service camps. Fifty thousand COs served in non-combat support roles. Another 12,000 refused to aid the military in any manner, but agreed to work without pay in civilian public service camps for agriculture and soil research. Five hundred allowed themselves to be human guinea pigs for medical experiments.

Along with those drafted through Selective Service, 5,000,000 men volunteered before the military prohibited the practice as inefficient in December 1942. By that time, draft calls reached almost 500,000 a month. During the Second World War, 10,000,000 men received draft notices, and 5.4 million of these served overseas. It was a massive and highly successful effort.[30] Key to the success of the draft, as it was in the First World War, was that most Americans rightly perceived the building dangers in Europe and understood that a call to arms was necessary. After Pearl Harbor, there was no question. While it is safe to assume that the draft aided in increasing the numbers of men in the war effort, the reality is that millions volunteered prior to receiving draft notices, and most assuredly more would have continued to have volunteered in even greater numbers had the government not again prohibited the action as inefficient. The draft, as in the First World War, was a success because it did not conflict with either the majority opinion of those of draft age, or the general population.

In 1946, following the end of the Second World War, the draft was terminated, over the objections of the military. The armed forces, however, continued to expand in the immediate post-war years as the West faced the new threats of communism and the Cold War. Following mounting tensions with the Soviet Union and events, such as the Berlin Blockade in 1948–1949, the military was allowed to resume the draft on a "temporary" basis, using the WWI Selective Service arrangement.[31] The legislation enabled conscription to be used in renewable four-year periods, as required—a system utilized in the Korean conflict.[32]

KOREA

The draft under Selective Service proved successful in the Korean War (1950-1953), receiving considerable public acceptance even though the hostilities were regional, with no direct threat to the United States. The war was seen as a necessary measure to stop the spread of communist influence in Southeast Asia. Unlike World War II, however, to make the draft appear more temporary and palatable to the public, draftees were required to serve for no more than two-year terms, and were rotated through the combat zone.[33] Following the invasion of South Korea by the North, President Harry Truman called up 56,000 inductees, up from the 10,000 originally scheduled for compulsory duty. Before the end of the war, the monthly draft rate had reached 90,000. In 1951 alone, 600,000 draftees entered the U.S. forces, and the total manpower of the army had risen from 593,000 to 1,531,000. Large numbers of the National Guard and reserve units were also called during the Korean War. A total of 140,000 guardsmen and 290,000 reservists were called. Many of these were veterans of the Second World War, and were sent to the battle-lines for nine-month rotations. Despite this, there was growing resentment and dissent over the draft as Selective Service prosecutions for draft offenses rose considerably between 1950 and 1954. The war ended, however, before it became a serious problem for draft boards. Most opposition to the draft deflated with the armistice on July 27, 1953.[34]

While the size of the army was reduced by a third after the war, the draft had expanded in dramatic fashion. By Korea, the draft included prewar mobilization, use in local, limited, undeclared expeditionary wars, and had become a source of extra reserves to maintain large overseas garrisons for Cold War purposes. U.S. politicians and the military assured the public that conscription was both temporary and necessary to prevent the spread of communism and insure the survival of liberty. While the draft remained in effect it was used sparingly for the remainder of the decade. During the Eisenhower administration the numbers of draftees steadily declined, and none lost their lives in battle.[35] The low-key peacetime draft to ensure military readiness against the Soviet threat was tacitly approved by the American public as part of the general Cold War consensus. This fragile consensus, however, was broken in the Vietnam era. While Selective Service prosecutions rose during the Korean War, the number of serious violations was not significant until Vietnam.[36] In the Vietnam War, of the approximately 27,000,000 draft-eligible males, 16,000,000 never served in the military in any fashion due to deferments, exemptions, and disqualification, while an additional 500,000 committed draft violations.[37] The interminable American struggle to balance national duty with personal freedoms and liberty exploded during the Vietnam era. The Vietnam War, as well as U.S. policy in Southeast Asia, became anathema for Americans from various backgrounds and political persuasions, including draft resisters. Never before had so many refused the call to duty; never before had so many others protested a war's very existence.

VIETNAM

French Indochina was created in the nineteenth century from remnants of the old kingdoms of Laos, Cambodia, and Vietnam. The Vietnamese had been under one form of foreign rule or another dating back 1,000 years. It was a French colonial possession for most of the twentieth century, and came under partial Japanese control during the Second World War. The struggle for independence from Imperial Japanese and French colonizers took form under the communists led by Ho Chi Minh. At the end of the war, Ho and his communist forces held the north. With a capital established in Hanoi, Ho proclaimed the territory the Democratic Republic of Vietnam on September 2, 1945. Ho had courted the assistance of the United States, and had received some aid against the invading Japanese during the war. After 1945, the Truman administration declined requests for further aid. Ho's allegiance to communism did not win him any consideration from the new president.[38]

In 1946 France recognized Ho's government as a "free" state, but their relationship quickly went sour with French efforts to install a separate entity in Vietnam's southern provinces, culminating in the First Indochina War. In 1949, the United States and Great Britain backed the French puppet government in the south, led by Bao Dai, who was reinstated by the French as head of state. Ho turned to Red China and the Soviet Union for assistance. There was increasing U.S. concern for regional security and the fear that Southeast Asia would fall to the communists. This was especially true after Mao Tse-tung established the People's Republic of China in October 1949. Full-scale material support was given to the French by the United States for the war against the communist forces. At a meeting with the French in Paris in May 1950, Secretary of State Dean Acheson outlined the administration's attitude toward its growing commitment in the region. Acheson said, "The United States recognizes that the solution of the Indochina problem depends both upon the restoration of security and upon the development of genuine nationalism and that United States assistance can and should contribute to these major objectives."[39] Following the Korean War, U.S. aid to the French continued and intensified. By 1953, the United States was carrying the bulk of the French effort at a total of nearly

$1 billion per year. The French, however, faced a series of military setbacks, including a crushing defeat at Dien Bien Phu, which coincided with the Geneva Accords in the summer of 1954. Efforts to divide Vietnam at the 17th parallel, with Ho's government in the north and the French in control in the south until an election could be held in 1956 to reunify the country, failed. The Americans and the South Vietnamese refused to sign the final accords.

The result was that Ho consolidated his forces in the north, while the formation of a pact for mutual regional defense began under new U.S. Secretary of State John Foster Dulles. In September 1954, the Southeast Asia Treaty Organization (SETO) was created. It pledged that Australia, France, New Zealand, Pakistan, The Philippines, Thailand, Great Britain, and the United States come to each other's aid, and to the aid of Cambodia, Laos, and the free territory under the jurisdiction of the State of Vietnam. None of these latter states signed the agreement.[40] The groundwork had been laid for American intervention. Dulles enunciated the ideology of preventing the region from falling under the domination of the communists. "Sometimes it is necessary to take risks to win peace just as it is necessary in war to take risks to win victory."[41] Vice President Richard Nixon gave further voice to the need for U.S. military commitment. Nixon said that the United States "as a leader of the free world cannot afford further retreat in Asia. It is hoped that the United States will not have to send troops there, but if this government cannot avoid it, the Administration must face up to the situation and dispatch forces."[42]

At the urging of both the French and the Americans, Ngo Dinh Diem became premier in the south, a move that was imposed on head of state Bao Dai. Diem's regime was increasingly backed by the CIA and military advisors ostensibly there to train Diem's forces. While the United States hoped that Diem would begin political and economic reforms, his regime descended into political corruption. During the Geneva negotiations in 1956 he refused to participate in elections set up to unify the country, arranged the ouster of Bao Dai, and proclaimed himself president. Such actions only created more opposition and resistance grew under the National Liberation Front, with the outbreak of civil and guerrilla warfare throughout the country. In backing Diem the United States had painted itself into a corner; the choice in the Eisenhower administration was reduced to "sink or swim with Diem."[43]

The situation in the south disintegrated under Diem's leadership. The Kennedy administration came to the reluctant conclusion that Diem had to go, and did not stand in the way when dissident generals lobbied for his ouster. Diem, however, was not merely ousted but was assassinated on November 1, 1963. The assassination of Diem did not stabilize the situation. Even Kennedy, who had appeared in favor of continued U.S. involvement in

Southeast Asia, showed signs of reluctance in the face of mounting confusion and chaos among the South Vietnamese. American commitment, however, had grown considerably under his administration, with thousands of U.S. military advisors in the south. While historians debate whether or not Kennedy was going to pull out of Vietnam, the young president's plans remain a mystery as he was assassinated on November 22, 1963, in Dallas, Texas.

The number of inductees through Selective Service in 1963 was 119,265. By 1965, under the administration of Kennedy's successor, Lyndon Johnson, that number had almost doubled to 230,991.[44] American involvement in Southeast Asia expanded rapidly under the new administration, and so too did the need for manpower. But by the spring of 1965, when Johnson sent the first ground troops into Vietnam, protests against the war had also expanded and grew as the war progressed. By the end of the decade, the Selective Service System, which in the past had served the nation so well, was finished.

COLLAPSE OF THE DRAFT

Why did the draft face massive opposition for Vietnam and not during the Korean War? Remarkably, protests against the war in Vietnam began early, long before there were significant numbers of casualties and at a time when far fewer soldiers were committed to the military effort than had been to the Korean peninsula. Also remarkable is that the Vietnam War could not have appeared substantially different to most Americans in 1965, when the first combat troops were deployed: both Korea and Vietnam were efforts to support southern governments against northern communist regimes, and were in the same region of the world—far from American shores. By 1965, however, protests against U.S. involvement were greater than at any time during the Korean conflict—a war in which more than 30,000 American servicemen lost their lives. In contrast, U.S. casualties in Southeast Asia numbered only in the hundreds when protest movements against U.S. involvement grew across the country.[45] This resistance also began long before anyone could have known of the toll it would take, or the disaster it would become; no one at the beginning of the war had a crystal ball. Protest also occurred despite a lack of conflict in Congress over American involvement in Vietnam. Although there was never any declaration of war, the vote in Congress was virtually unanimous for the Gulf of Tonkin Resolution. Additionally, there was, for the most part, bipartisan support for U.S. involvement for much of the first half of the war, and thus little opposition to the Vietnam War in the House or the Senate before 1967.[46]

It appears that the crucial variable was not the war, but the disposition of the generation that was called to serve. In many respects the Sixties generation was quite different than the one which fought the Second World War and in Korea. The generation that came of age in the 1950s and 1960s had markedly different experiences and expectations, including much more access to information than those who were called to serve in the previous two wars. The generations differed also in their attitudes toward America as a nation. Those born before World War II not only had less affluence than those of the Vietnam era but were more trusting of their government. They were less likely to challenge requests for military service. Those called on to fight in Vietnam were more worldly, more mobile, and enjoyed a higher rate of college education than their parents and grandparents. These were young people who had cut their teeth on images from the civil rights movement, a decade and a half of Cold War, and the excesses of anti-communism. This generation witnessed violent events in their nation on a scale not experienced since the Civil War, and much of it was displayed on their television screens. Many of their childhood and adolescent experiences culminated in the assassination of President John F. Kennedy. The event came at a time when they were beginning to take a hard look at society. Perhaps most important, they, like the rest of the nation, saw it all on TV. With television, the Sixties generation not only had greater access to information than any before them, but it was the *type* of information that was unmatched. It was information that challenged orthodoxy. What defined this generation came home to roost on college campuses across the nation in the mid-1960s.

Contributing to the ire of the anti-war movement was that Vietnam broke with a tradition of military volunteerism that had existed since the birth of the republic. Throughout the nation's history, conscription has worked only when Americans were willing to fight *before* the implementation of the draft, as was so clearly demonstrated in both world wars. It's been said that the reason America "was not allowed to win" in Vietnam was that the administration never had the support of the American people. This point was articulated well by the last U.S. commander in Vietnam, General Fred Weyand, who stated that "the American army is really a people's army in the sense that it belongs to the American people, who take a jealous and proprietary interest in its involvement. When the Army is committed the American people are committed; when the American people lose their commitment, it is futile to try to keep the Army committed."[47] Key is that the military did not have the support of enough of the *right* people—the ones who would be called on to fight, and those who had the energy to protest loudly on the streets of America. The United States had not only parted from a tradition of military volunteerism but this coincided with the emergence of a generation that was predisposed to reject the sort of war its country was waging.

The combination of a break with historical tradition, an unpopular war, and a wary and idealistic young generation explains much of the intense opposition against Vietnam. It is likely that the Selective Service System would have faced the same resistance in gaining conscripts for Korea had that war prolonged. It should be remembered that the numbers of draft violations began to rise near the end of the Korean War. Americans, as they had in the past, were not willing to support an effort that did not fit with their national interests. Had the Korean War dragged out, it may well have produced a scene strikingly similar to what took place on the streets and campuses of America during Vietnam.

Young Americans during the 1960s reacted in numerous ways to conscription. Many accepted their draft notices out of a sense of duty, or because of a family tradition of military service. Some went because they were afraid to say no. Others, with little education and few job skills, served their country in uniform because it was a chance to do something with their lives. Others protested vigorously on the streets of America, and burned their draft cards in open defiance. Although they were opposed to the war they remained committed to the country and its reform. Some deserted from the military, went underground, or fled the country, choosing temporary exile in Canada, Sweden, and Mexico, waiting for an opportunity to return home after the war. And others had more long-range plans when faced with the draft and crossed the Canadian border permanently.

CANADA BOUND

For thousands of young Americans who fled to Canada, the Vietnam War severed what were already tenuous ties to their country. While the expatriates' opposition to the war was a factor, it did not by itself cause them to leave the country. The tugs of patriotism and the sense of duty and obligation to the nation were not strong enough to bind them to a country that went to war and demanded their service in uniform.

The draft—as it had in the past for other Americans—came to them as a particularly unpalatable prospect. They were not willing to be drafted to fight in a war in which they did not believe, nor did they feel that their country had the right to demand of them what they were unwilling to give on their own accord. In their decision to evade, these draftees, in essence, reflected the ideals of their forefathers: personal liberty, autonomy, and individualism. They embodied an ideology which has existed since colonial times, an ideology that has played a significant role in the history of the military draft in the United States. They proclaimed with their actions that there are limits to what a nation can demand of its people, and that the state cannot supersede the inalienable rights of individual citizens, even in the defense of the nation.

2

Childhood: The Origins of
Disaffection

[We] see groups of boys and young men disaffected from the dominant
society. . . . They are failing to assimilate much of the culture. . . . [T]he
authorities explain it by saying there has been a failure of socialization.
They say that background conditions have interrupted socialization and
must be improved. . . . But perhaps there has not been a failure of
communication. Perhaps the social message has been communicated
clearly to the young men and is unacceptable.[1]

In *Growing Up Absurd* (1960), noted sociologist Paul Goodman
examined the difficulties of late adolescence in the 1950s. He wanted to
show how "desperately hard" it was for the "average child" to grow into
adulthood in a modern, organized society. What, however, was it really like
to come of age during this time? It is difficult to reach a consensus on the
era. For some, the Fifties have become the favorite whipping boy,
explaining everything that "went wrong" in subsequent decades, while
others claim America has become a more base society since the beginning of
the Sixties, one mired in cultural decay. The latter group's remedy is to
return to the world of the 1950s where the nation, in their view, still retained
basic American morals and principles. Such commentators drape the Fifties
in utopian garb—painting it as a time that was essentially free of crime,
homelessness, pornography, and violence. It was a time, their narrative goes,
when people enjoyed unlocked doors and were free of today's coarse youth
culture. Teen violence, pregnancy, and drug addictions were nonexistent.
More recent commentators, such as Pat Robertson and former U.S. Supreme
Court nominee Robert Bork, argue that this benchmark of civility and
morality has eroded and America has been "slouching towards Gomorra"

ever since.[2] Few accept this as a complete or accurate picture of the era, although this view was embodied in television programs of the time. While the Fifties *was* a time of general peace and prosperity, it was also a time of extreme Cold War politics, waged in both the public and private spheres. America in the 1950s faced the anticommunist excesses of Joseph McCarthy and fears over nuclear war. Interestingly, the public worried then, as some do now, about the rise in juvenile delinquency "caused" by the influence of radio, television and the "evils" of rock 'n' roll music (today video games and the Internet are added to the list). The Fifties and early Sixties were also characterized by the civil rights movement and its struggle against racism and segregation throughout the South. While the shortcomings of the era are not in and of themselves responsible for later unrest, the decade's conditions did contribute to people's perceptions and actions. Unlike the previous generation, which served generally without complaint in the Korean War, those raised in the shadow of the bomb and the growing civil and social unrest had a markedly different set of experiences. What they experienced shaped their world views before they reached maturity and witnessed their nation's involvement in Vietnam.

The mid-to-late 1950s and early 1960s childhood experiences of the expatriates now living in Canada were the seeds of their disaffection and alienation from the United States. The pages that follow offer an examination of the expatriates' home lives, neighborhoods, and interactions with family and community. Examined are the events in the country as these individuals saw them and how their perceptions led to their later decisions. Their testimonies reveal a predisposition to evade not only induction, but the country when draft boards called. In their early years they were taught about American history and the sacrifices of their forefathers. They were raised to believe that their birthright as Americans offered them the opportunity to be anything they wished to be in a country that offered unlimited opportunity. They were also raised to be individuals and think for themselves. America taught them freedom of thought and action. Conversely, they were raised during a time that challenged fundamentally their feelings about community and country. Their experiences as children, while welding them to certain axiomatic American ideals, succeeded in alienating them from their nation and caused them to question and mistrust its direction from their earliest memories.

'WHERE IN THE NAME OF CONSCIENCE IS THEIR SENSE OF HISTORY?'

By late 1965 the protests of young American men and women against the Vietnam War and the draft had become commonplace on university campuses. On the weekend of October 16, violent demonstrations broke out across the country resulting in numerous injuries and arrests. There were disturbances in states, such as Oregon and Vermont, demonstrations in the cities of Philadelphia and Boston, and student protests at Cornell and Johns Hopkins universities. In Berkeley, members of the Hells Angels (known for their patriotism and protection of core values) broke through police lines and attacked students on their way to demonstrate at the Oakland army base. In New York, an estimated 10,000 to 20,000 students marched down Fifth Avenue while hecklers from The Young Americans for Freedom and other conservative organizations pelted them with eggs, red paint, and tomatoes. The protesters carried pictures of burned Vietnamese children and bloody Uncle Sams. It took more than 1,000 city police officers to keep the sides apart. That weekend, the state commander of the Veterans of Foreign Wars threatened to make a citizen's arrest of 22-year-old David Miller, who had publicly burned his draft card, unless the authorities did so within 24 hours. James Reston's editorial in *The New York Times* left no doubt on how he felt about the weekend events. Reston blamed the protesters for "postponing peace" and playing into the hands of communists. The demonstrators' ranks, Reston argued, were full of "hangers on, intellectual graduate school draft dodgers and rent-a-clown boobs who will demonstrate for or against anything."[3]

The beginning of protests and violations against the draft sent tremors through Capitol Hill. The numerous mainstream press accounts of demonstrations against American military involvement in Southeast Asia were not ignored. On the heels of Reston's fiery column, members of Congress voiced their outrage and disgust at those attempting to avoid the draft. On the Senate floor Republican Senator Thomas H. Kuchel of California remarked: "Over the weekend in Berkeley, a dirty little sheet has been distributed which is entitled: 'Brief Notes on the Ways and Means of Beating the Draft.' " Kuchel seemed especially insulted that this was taking place in his state: "People have thrown themselves on the railroad tracks in my state in an attempt to prevent passage of troop trains and railroad cars carrying military supplies to the docks for transshipment to Southeast Asia. A few contemptible youths have publicly torn up their draft cards in great glee."[4] Kuchel was not alone in his observations. Republican Senator John Duncan of Tennessee realized that demonstrations were spreading: "Whether you live in a big city, in a small town, or even in the wide open country, you are never far from a lively demonstration."[5]

There was bipartisan condemnation of the character of the protesters. Senate Majority Leader Mike Mansfield of Montana believed those trying to avoid service were a "discredit and a disgrace to the country in which we live. . . . [A]s citizens of this country, they have a responsibility, and they should act with maturity. . . . [W]hat they have done has been a disservice to this country."[6] Democratic Senator Frank Lausche of Ohio was even more harsh. He called anti-war demonstrators "long-whiskered beatniks, dirty in clothes [who] do not have the backbone to stand up for their country. They want to go into some hiding place completely devoid of the attributes and character of true-blooded Americans."[7] Senator Richard Russell of Georgia was more prophetic: "These boys do not know what they are doing. . . . They will go through life dishonored and die unsung. . . . Where in the name of conscience is their sense of history?"[8]

Russell asks an interesting question. What sense of history did these young men have—many of them not even of legal drinking age—when faced with fighting in a far-off war? What conditions and factors shaped their views and perspectives as America moved headlong into Vietnam? One obvious starting point is the brief two decades of their childhood and early adulthood. For the majority of the draft evaders who went to Canada, their earliest clear recollections began in the early-to-mid-1950s.

CHILDHOOD

One of the distinct groups among the expatriates consists of transplanted Northerners in the Southern United States. One of the more typical draft dodger stories of childhood in the South comes from Carroll Obline. Born in 1946, a year after his father returned from the South Pacific, Obline spent the first 10 years of his life with his parents on a small dairy farm in Wisconsin. His father and mother ran the operation with the help of a relative who had dropped out of school; Obline's father had lost part of a foot to a land mine in the war and needed extra help with the farm work. Obline describes his parents as conservative, politically and socially, "but not to any extreme." His father voted for Harry Truman in 1948, believing that his decision to use the atomic bomb was justified. His dad was not as pleased with that "bastard, coward Ike." He thought something had to be done about the Russians, and his son concurred: "I agreed with him as a kid. . . . When you're a kid, you're much more militaristic. . . . I wanted us to drop the big one on Moscow. I called Eisenhower a communist.[9] Mom told me I didn't know what a communist was." Obline's father talked incessantly about an eventual nuclear war with anyone who would listen: "He kept telling me and my mother that 'any day now we would all be roach fricassee.' " Obline says that his father lost more than just his foot to the war. His father suffered from psychological problems after returning from the Pacific, but denied the fact and refused treatment. The turmoil resulting from his father's "dark moods" and his occasional outbursts of violence resulted in his parents' separation in 1956. His mother took him and his 4-year-old sister to live with their aunt in Rock Hill, South Carolina. Trouble began early for the 10-year-old Obline, as he tried to fit into a new town and school. On his first day he was asked by his teacher to introduce himself to his new class. After a few words, several students began chanting: "Sit down, Yankee." The boy did not take part in many school activities, and had few friends. Instead he read books and internalized his feelings. He thought of himself as "another victim of what was going on around [him] in society." He remembers that his family was thought to be "Northern white niggers who did not belong in *their* town." Obline grew up with practically "no sense of community or feeling part of anything."[10]

Another transplanted Northerner was Ron Needer. In 1954, when Needer was 8, his parents moved south from Illinois. His father had lost his job and found a management position in Little Rock, Arkansas, through a family friend. While they tried to adjust to their new surroundings, Needer learned to fight in schoolyard brawls because he was considered the "token Yankee." His mom and dad were not welcomed with open arms in their new Southern home. Their cat was killed and left on their window ledge, and their garage was spray-painted: "Go home job-stealing Yankee noodle." Needer believes: "They thought that people like us, from the North, were the cause of all the beginnings of civil unrest taking place there with segregation . . . and we [they thought] were part of that." Needer recalls that he never felt like he was a part of any community: "I was more than an outsider. I was an alien."[11]

Michael Fischer echoes some of Ron Needer's experiences. Fischer's family moved from Fort Wayne, Indiana, to Gadsden, Alabama, when his father landed a lucrative engineering job. Fischer's grandparents were financially secure, putting his father through college and supplying the down payment on his first home in Fort Wayne. But Fischer recalls the resentment from his peers as he began the 5th grade in Gadsden: "We lived in a fairly upscale neighborhood, and the other kids were well off, but they seemed to particularly resent me and my family for doing well. It was like, because we were from the North, we were rubbing it in their face—which wasn't the case." Fischer, like others, isolated himself with books, television, and science projects at home. He remembers some of his teachers were not terribly open or helpful with him, causing him to keep his thoughts and ideas to himself: "It was an odd, backwards place to grow up. There is an attitude in the South that probably hasn't changed much since I was a kid, that is very inward looking, suspicious, resentful. I'm really not sure exactly what it is, but I experienced it as a child, and I tell you it makes you think about your society when you grow up with that environment." Fischer always felt estranged from his community. "We lived on the outside of the community. My parents were prosperous, but in our interactions with society, we were paupers."[12]

Aston Davis was yet another transplanted Northerner. Born in Connecticut, he moved with his family to Houston, Texas, as his father and uncles were breaking into the oil business. Davis had just turned 9, and began the 4th grade in a new suburban Houston school. He remembers that his new classmates already realized that his family was from outside the state: "Some of them seemed to take it as a personal insult that Northerners were in their state taking their resources. I faced that nonsense most of my years there. And it wasn't just that I faced it, some was directed at me, but it was more of the total attitude of Texas. And if you think it is backwards and redneck now, just imagine what it was like in 1960. . . . Texas was a nightmare." Davis tried out for his high school football team, but never made it "even though [he] was as fast or faster than anyone else there." He felt that there was no sense of community or anything that bonded him to his home. The friends that he made felt similarly about life in Texas—most wanted out. With these early experiences, Davis began to withdraw from those around him and was someone who tended to keep to himself as a child: "It was clear that I was not wanted, and I certainly never wanted them."13

Brian Linton was born in Dearborn, Michigan, in 1946. His father was a ship contractor and moved the family to Shreveport, Louisiana, in 1953 to take advantage of lucrative business opportunities. Linton recalls that life was much the same as in the North until he turned 10 or 11 and civil rights became an issue in the South: "The fact that I was from the North never seemed to mean much until civil unrest with blacks. And all of a sudden, I was a meddling Yankee. . . . I was guilty by association with Northern civil rights workers." One of the factors contributing to this situation was that the Linton family opened their home to visiting Northern student civil rights workers. They soon became a target of hostile feelings from the community. He was suspended twice from school for sticking up for his parents: "I was suspended for being an unhealthy influence on the other students. I was a 'bad example' since, according to the teachers and the school principal, I was the son of parents who were 'soiling the fabric of Southern society.' " He recalls being out of step from an early age: "We were not wanted, and I just wanted to move to a town where I could have a normal childhood, but I didn't have any say in that, of course." Linton wished to fit in but gave up before he reached his teen years: "I was in over my head and it wasn't my fault. It was really a terrible feeling, a cultural and moral depravity that you have to experience to really understand. Please don't get me wrong—there are some very good people in the American South, but there was, and perhaps still is, an underlay of decay and contempt for anything or anyone that is considered an outsider." Linton grew up dreaming of the day when he would leave home and the South for university, and never return.14

This type of alienation was not restricted to Northern-born draft dodgers. Southern-born expatriates found themselves on the outside of their communities if their parents were involved in political activism. Bill Warner was one of this group of Southern liberal families. Although born and raised in Knoxville, Tennessee, he too felt like an outsider in his community. His mother's work in establishing a local chapter of the Congress of Racial Equality (CORE) put him on the defensive at school. Warner remembers: "I was called a 'white nigger' and a 'commie'. . . . I think I was even called a communist by one of the teachers."[15] Warner's mother was a somewhat representative figure. In the mid-to-late 1950s, a growing number of whites began to join with blacks in their quest for civil rights. Women, often motivated by their desire to gain equal rights with men, joined and initiated various groups such as CORE. In the South, during the early years of the civil rights movement, it was not Northern whites, but Southern-born white women who entered the cause through church organizations.

Southern Activists

There is a long history of Southern white women involved in various forms of social activism, civil rights work, and bucking the trend of their communities. In the early-to-mid-nineteenth century, sisters Angelina and Sara Grimke rejected their South Carolina upbringing and culture, and spoke openly against slavery. They did so not only from the standpoint of devout Quakers, but as members of a prominent Charleston slave-holding family. Their activities soon made them outcasts in their state and throughout the South. While unique in their day, their actions paved the way for other women as the century progressed. As the battle over slavery became a national issue, the early women's movement was able to piggyback on the growing abolitionist movement in the 1840s and 1850s. This development did not end with the abolition of slavery in 1863, but continued into the next century, with a number of white Southern women becoming active in the campaigns against lynching. Many joined the Commission on Interracial Cooperation (CIC) in the 1920s and 1930s. This constituency was based on a close network of women's church organizations and auxiliaries throughout the South. In the 1940s and 1950s these groups worked to oppose church segregation in several Southern states. It was this tradition that made its way into the early civil rights movement of the 1950s. As historian Sara Evans points out, there were a number of church groups involved with ending racial intolerance in the South. Evans writes, "Most white women who participated in the early years of the civil rights movement tended to be Southerners, and virtually without exception all the white Southern women who joined the civil rights movement, came to it through the Church."[16]

Bill Warner's mother was part of the movement in the South, and the family, as others involved in civil rights, came under harsh criticism in the community. Warner remembers an incident at a local grocery store in 1957 or 1958:

I was about 10 or 11, shopping for groceries at the store a few blocks from where we lived. Two women approached my mother and me and insinuated that she was causing trouble where there was no trouble, and unless she wanted trouble—to that effect. . . . A couple of days later, the tires on my dad's '52 Ford were slashed beyond repair.

This was the worst that happened to the family, but Warner was far from popular in school: "I certainly don't blame her [his mother] for my troubles as a kid, but because of the situation, I began to take some damn hard looks around me."[17]

Uncivil Rights

For those growing up in the South in the 1950s and 1960s, there was certainly much to observe. The landmark 1954 U.S. Supreme Court ruling, *Brown v. Board of Education of Topeka, Kansas*, which found racial segregation in public schools unconstitutional, sparked the beginning of civil unrest and upheaval in the South. Many white Southerners were outraged by *Brown*, which reversed the concept of "separate but equal" from the *Plessy v. Ferguson* decision of 1896. White segregationists, many of them business people, formed committees called Citizens' Councils, which were more popularly known as "white collar Klans." These councils grew in number and spread throughout the South. Rosa Parks' refusal to leave her third-row seat, reserved for whites only in a city bus in Montgomery, Alabama, and subsequent arrest, sparked not only a city-wide bus boycott, but the beginning of civil rights demonstrations for the next several years. Sit-ins at a Woolworths' lunch counter in Greensboro, North Carolina, followed by demonstrations in Durham, Raleigh, Winston-Salem, Nashville, and Charlotte produced 3,600 arrests.[18] The emergence of the eloquent Martin Luther King, Jr. and The Southern Christian Leadership Conference (SCLC) prompted young whites from the North to head South to work for civil rights. Their unwanted presence in Southern cities and towns often led to conflict, violence, and even murder in the early 1960s.[19]

The involvement of Northern white students in the fight for civil rights, however, began in the 1950s. Whites in the North held rallies and protests on university campuses and organized "youth marches for integration" in the late 1950s.[20] As Sara Evans points out, the events of the late 1950s and early 1960s had a profound effect on the nation, and especially the young who saw the civil rights struggle as a beacon of hope and change:

The sit-in movement and the freedom rides had an electrifying impact on Northern liberal culture. The romance and the daring of black youth gave progressives an unassailable cause. The good guys seemed so good—Martin Luther King made them sound even better—and the bad guys seemed so horrifying bad. Many of those affected were former participants in the "old left.". . . The children of Northern liberals and radicals, however, were most likely to join the new struggle with passionate commitment.[21]

In 1961, in solidarity with civil rights concerns, the National Student Christian Federation and the U.S. National Student Association became members of the Student Nonviolent Coordinating Committee (SNCC), which was composed of Southern black students. In 1964, hundreds of white students traveled South to work on voter registration and other projects, in what became known as Freedom Summer. More than 1,000 people, the vast majority of whom were white Northern students, arrived in the South to work in projects and express their youthful democratic idealism. Freedom Summer, however, turned dark with the kidnapping and murder of civil rights workers Michael Schwerner, James Chaney, and Andrew Goodman. It culminated with the assassination of civil rights leader Medger Evers.[22] Many white Southerners resented the "intrusion" of Northerners and sympathizers to the civil rights cause in the South. At times their wrath was directed most severely toward fellow whites whom they claimed were traitors to their own race.

Many of the Southern draft dodgers saw the daily battles for civil rights up close in their childhood neighborhoods. One of the observers of racial tension and violence was future draft dodger Albert Caldwell. While waiting for a bus with his father in Lynchburg, Virginia, the young Caldwell watched as an elderly black man attempted to board a city bus: "The man had his right foot on the first step, and the driver just pulled shut the door and dragged the old man with his leg caught for a block." As bad as this incident was, his father's reaction left the deepest impression: "My father just muttered: 'What's that old darkie trying to do—man's got a schedule to keep!' " The entire episode "scared the hell" out of Caldwell; his mother refused to discuss the issue. "Kids at school essentially laughed at me when I told that story. I remember looking around the room, you know, thinking that I knew these kids, and considered some to be friends, and that people were not concerned what had happened, and not only that, but that it was somehow remotely funny, was frightening. . . . It was a real learning experience for me. After that, I pretty much kept to myself—stayed low, and waited for my opportunity to leave." Caldwell knew early that the best way for him to get away from his home town was to get good grades and go to college. "The South wasn't home, it was beautiful, and there were some people that really cared, but it has something akin to a soul that was missing."[23]

David Ward was born and raised in Alabama, and even though his family lived in the region for decades, his mother's work for "several civil rights organizations" made the family "even more hated than Yankees and blacks." Ward recalls that he was targeted the most because he was perceived as "selling out" the white race: "I was seen as a traitor to my own kind, believe it or not. I was jumped in the schoolyard on more than one occasion. Being called a 'Yankee' was common, being spit on by a girl was not common but it happened. When even your school teachers hate you, or act like they do, it's pretty difficult." Ward remarks that he did not even know what civil rights were but ended up as a target in school. He believes he would have made a "fine recruit" in Vietnam as he "learned to fight in the third grade."[24]

There are similar accounts from other studies of draft dodgers from this period. Writer Allan Haig-Brown, for instance, also interviewed draft dodgers in Canada who related similar tales of racism in the South, and the effect of those experiences on their disconnection from their country. Draft evader John Shinnick, for example, grew up in East Texas, and was appalled by what he witnessed. Shinnick recalled the following instance to Haig-Brown:

There was a garage right next door to my mother's photography studio. When I was about twelve-years-old, I hung out there with all the mechanics and the people who would come in to have their cars fixed. The police brought their cars there, and I remember watching these officers and some other people bully a black guy one day. They put handcuffs on him, threw him into the back of a police car, and told him they were going to turn him over to the local Ku Klux Klan. This man was a human being who had been driven to tears because, as far as he knew, he was going to be castrated, or tarred and feathered, or lynched, and these men thought it was a big joke. The Klan had this sort of presence in the town and that presence is still there. It is one of the reasons I would never go back and live there.[25]

Visceral reactions to racism were not uncommon among the Southern expatriates. Carl McCrosky also remembers his aversion to the outward signs of racism in the South. McCrosky was from Ohio, but at age 8 he moved with his family to Aiken, South Carolina, where he lived until he left for college. He describes his parents as "conservative, Presbyterian-Republican kind of stock, but quickly became atheist-agnostic, and stayed sort of formally Republican up through at least the 1960 election. . . . They voted for 'Tricky Dicky,' which I will never let them forget." McCrosky recalls that soon after the election, his parents began "breaking the mold." They were both "very active in the American Civil Liberties Union [ACLU], and became radicalized and liberalized around the early 1960s." While McCrosky believes it was then that he became politically aware, what shaped his views the most was growing up in South Carolina:

It was a critical part of my life; very impoverished culturally and spiritually—it was a backwards region. I did not like it. They were still fighting the Civil War and I was a "Damned Yankee" because I was from the North, and I actually got into childhood fights over that, believe it or not. I always felt (and I think my parents gave me a part of this in a large part), but I always felt that I was an alien living in some other culture because I was from the outside, and that gave me a detachment from my own culture, and my own country, I think.

McCrosky was acutely aware of racism in Aiken, and throughout the South. He saw the Freedom Riders as the "clarion call. Finally something made sense." As a boy he was aware of the racial divisions in his community and he believes that awareness helped to shape not only his views about his home state, but about the country.

I remember going shopping with my parents to Augusta, Georgia, or any place like that to a shopping mall or restaurant, and we'd see the water fountains; you know: "White," "Colored," and from the very earliest time I could even read the signs I knew it was wrong, I knew it. And the people [the Freedom Riders] came along with incredible heroism and just started fighting the system, and that one, I was on board from Day 1. And that began to loosen my loyalties to society. Not only did I dislike the system, but here there were people fighting it—and they were right. And it probably made it easier to fight it on my own later.26

Family Life: 'I Was Never a Joiner'

While these accounts suggest specific regional factors for societal disaffection, stories of alienation from community and society are not confined geographically to the South. Draft dodgers from the east and west coasts and the Midwest have similar recollections. One common element seems to be disrupted or troubled home lives.27 Future draft dodger Jim Tarris, for example, grew up in Muncie, Indiana. His father worked for the county, and his mother operated a small laundry service out of the family home. His parents were "middle class, conservative, Methodist." His mother, who also did community and volunteer work, wanted to open a dry-cleaning business away from their house. She was never able to get the support from her husband as he "held the financial strings pretty tightly . . . and, after all, it was *his* money." Tarris's mother worked from 1942 to 1945 in the war industries in Detroit, and enjoyed her time there. She "hated" Muncie and longed to return to Michigan to be closer to her family. "She was an activist," Tarris recalls, "who could never get anything off the ground in town. People thought she was an oddball by campaigning for nuclear disarmament and Estes Kefauver." She had a "general unhappiness" with her life and encouraged her son to do exactly what he wanted with his. "She wanted me to go to college and get a good job and leave towns like

Muncie behind. She, I think, instilled this belief that one could not wait around and let life happen to you, that it was bull by the horns, and not get stuck in a rut in life, to mix metaphors, but that was the gist of it." Tarris wanted to be a physician, and knew that he "could be a doctor anywhere."[28]

Several of the expatriates' mothers were involved with the war effort before marriage. Those who were, tended to become more active in post-war public activities. The mother of evader Bill Warner, for example, worked for the war industries in 1942. She began by coordinating drives for war materials and then went to Atlanta in 1943 to work in a munitions factory. Warner recalls: "She would talk about her 'glory years' in the war endlessly when I was a kid. I think she thought it was her heyday and nothing she could do as a wife compared. That is why I think she went looking for causes such as rights for blacks and peace movements and the like."[29]

David Ward's mother also worked for the war effort in Montgomery, Alabama. According to her son, she had fond memories of her working days before marrying his father: "She had scrapbooks full of fuzzy black and white pictures of her and 'the girls.' She was sad, though; she couldn't find her own niche after. I'm not sure if she couldn't find a job, or my dad wouldn't allow it; I don't remember, but I think her restlessness led her to become so involved in causes like civil rights. I think it put her feet on the ground. It did not have the same beneficial effect on me, I'm afraid."[30] Martin Strychuck's mother worked in Chicago during the war and, according to her son, she was bitter over her job's abrupt termination at war's end: "My mom liked the responsibility, the pay, and I think the physical part of it. There were few options for her after she got married and had me and my sisters. She wanted something more—something important and special." Mrs. Strychuck began working for the Committee for Non-Violent Action (CNVA) when Strychuck was a boy to "cope with some of her unhappiness."[31]

Disrupted family life and a disconnection from community are common themes among the expatriates. Future draft dodger John Conway, for example, also had a somewhat unusual upbringing and felt separated and distanced from community life. Born at the end of the war in 1945, Conway was raised in the Milwaukee suburb of Wauwatosa. His father, who was a senior executive at the Koehring Crane Company in Milwaukee, died in 1957 when the boy was 12. His mother experienced severe psychological breakdowns and was often institutionalized as a result. The family, however, was not destitute as his father had left investments and the "huge" family home. He describes his upbringing as "conservative, middle class, Republican, and privileged." They were "typical middle-class Americans." Unlike many other expatriates, the young Conway was not aware of the social and political climate, and does not remember his parents' social-political views. But like others, he was not terribly interested in external activities as a child. Educated in the Catholic school system, he entered a Catholic seminary outside Milwaukee following high school. Three of his next four years were spent in the Order of the Priests, with one year "in total isolation" at a retreat that was situated in the middle of a cornfield in Iowa. For four years Conway was "sort of in another world . . . not especially tuned into the social and political happenings of the day." He described his young years as "totally isolated. . . . All I wanted to be [was] an educator." Conway tells how he was wrapped up in his own world since childhood and never developed "those strong nationalistic allegiances to America."[32]

Michael Gillgannon was born in Kansas in 1947. His father was in the military and Gillgannon traveled with him when he was young. He was influenced by current events on television and especially the civil rights marches of the Reverend Martin Luther King, Jr. Gillgannon recalls his parents as "ultra-liberal," which helped him to be quite independent growing up. Like many of the other expatriates, he had no particular allegiances in his youth and no allegiances to the country that would prevent him from pulling up stakes and leaving for Canada. Gillgannon maintains that from childhood on he "was never a joiner" and was an unlikely candidate to accept conscription into the U.S. military. But as with all the future draft dodgers who were raised in the shadow of the bomb, he did join with others in his memory of the Cuban Missile Crisis.[33]

COLD WAR DAYS: 'I DIDN'T WANT TO BE A COG IN ANYONE'S WHEEL'

Long before the dark days of October 1962, the Cold War, with the ever-present threat of nuclear confrontation, troubled some Americans. Such concerns grew during the 1950s and coincided with the reemergence of peace and disarmament groups. The peace movement, which was on life support after several years of the Cold War, received a welcome boost from Martin Luther King, Jr. King began to take on a pacifist tone and instructed his congregations: "War is not the answer. . . . Communism will never be defeated by atomic bombs or nuclear weapons. . . . Our greatest defense against communism is to take offensive action in behalf of justice and righteousness."[34] King's words gained converts by the mid-1950s, and the public appeals for peace, reason and disarmament became national news, which helped to recharge the peace movement.[35] While not great in numbers, ordinary citizens, many of them women, became involved in peace activities. The Women's International League for Peace and Freedom (WILPF) and the War Resisters League (WRL) eventually regained their prewar strength and size. The WRL supported and organized the burning of draft cards in the 1950s, and joined with other groups in establishing a central committee for conscientious objectors. The WRL was also involved in launching *Liberation* magazine, which was intended to serve as a forum for social issues from civil rights to disarmament. Out of this grew the Committee for Non-Violent Action (CNVA) and the National Committee for Sane Nuclear Policy (SANE), founded in 1957.[36]

These activities did play a role in the home lives of several future draft evaders. Interestingly, two-thirds of the expatriates interviewed for this book had one or both parents involved in some sort of public activity or activist organization ranging from the ACLU to SANE. They also subscribed to magazines, such as *Liberation*, which represented much of the new interest in pacifism and disarmament. The first editorial in *Liberation* (March 1956) warned of the "decline of independent radicalism" and "the silence of prophetic and rebellious voices."[37] A poll of *Liberation* subscribers in 1959 revealed that its readership was composed of mostly middle-class intellectuals, with two-thirds holding college degrees. Many had socialist leanings with memberships in the WRL, the National Association for the Advancement of Colored People (NAACP), CORE, and SANE. They also read other left-leaning periodicals such as *The Catholic Worker*, *Nation* and *Peacemaker*.[38] These various groups reflected much of the tension, frustration, and fear over the Cold War and the prospect of nuclear war. It was a fear that is fairly common in the expatriate narratives. Their early exposure to the problems and dangers in American society, from civil rights to Cold War politics, had a profound effect, not only on how they perceived the world, but how they felt about their country, its direction and its future in the age of the nuclear bomb and nuclear terror.

Fallout

The expatriates were raised in the midst of social strife and with a heightened awareness of local and global problems. They were the first generation to grow up with regular air-raid drills at school, and to fear atomic bombs falling from the sky. One such person was future draft dodger Jonathan Burke. Burke grew up in Jersey City, New Jersey, and lived in one of the first high-rise apartments in his area. Born in 1947, he was 10 when the Soviets launched the first satellite into space. Some of his fears began when he overheard classmates at school discussing how the Russians were targeting big cities, such as Los Angeles, Chicago, Washington, D.C., and New York. Burke could see part of the New York skyline from his window; he looked to the night skies expecting to see Soviet planes approaching to deliver their nuclear payloads. He recalls his bleak view as a child: "I know it seems strange now, in retrospect, but those were real fears that I had for a few years when I was young. That knowledge that all could end—and there were times that I was positive about it, was something that I'm sure that shaped me somewhat. I remember looking to the future and wondering how much I was going to really see. I never thought I would see my 13th birthday. I wanted to be a teenager so bad."[39]

Another evader with similar memories is Manchester, New Hampshire, native Merrill Condel. He remembers in 1958 at age 8 sneaking outside at bedtime to sit in his tree house, so he would be safe from the bombs that might hit his house in the middle of the night. "I know that that didn't make much sense, but I was pretty much . . . terrified as a kid of all the shit that was happening. . . . I know it had an effect on me later. I would read about it, watch TV programs and movies about nuclear war—it may be silly from our standpoint today, now, but who knew? No one did, that we would be free of it for the next three decades, without a nuclear exchange. No one knew then, and they would be lying if they were to suggest otherwise."[40]

Others clearly remember the air-raid drills in school. Brian Linton recalls that "the level of tension in grade school was tremendous . . . so when those damned air-raid drills went off it was . . . like I always thought it was the real thing. It didn't help any that my parents were continuously speaking of it."[41] Nick Theason recalls the routines children learned to "protect" themselves from a potential nuclear blast: "Even as a 9-year-old, it was all so stupid . . . so damn silly. We all saw the reels of the bombs in Japan and the desert . . . so we knew that rolling under a desk at school was hopeless. It all seemed rather hopeless, then."[42] Expatriate Ron Needer also had a similar bleak view as a child: "I can't recall many days between say [ages] 9 and 15, when I didn't think it would all come to an end. And part of me, as a kid anyway, wondered if it would be such a bad thing." Needer equated this feeling with other events: "I saw it all on the same level as the time when I saw a black woman get shoved by white teenagers in front of a car at Lucky's Store. Both things terrified me; both were wrong. It was a fucked up, stupid society, Cold War against communists, and a war against some of our own people at home. It was a joyless time."[43]

Carroll Obline, like his father, believed when he was a boy that the United States should have launched a preemptive strike on the Soviet Union. "I know that's how I felt. . . . Part of it was boyish malice, but most of it was fear—daily dosages of impending doom."[44]

Sociologist Todd Gitlin made similar observations on the effects of nuclear terror on childhood in his examination of the Sixties generation:

Whatever the national pride in the blasts that pulverized Bikini and Eniwetok atolls, whatever the Atomic Energy Commission's bland assurances, the Bomb actually disrupted our daily lives. We grew up taking cover in school drills—the first American generation compelled from infancy to fear not only war but the end of days. Every so often, out of the blue, a teacher would pause in the middle of class and call out, "Take cover!" We knew, then, to scramble under our miniature desks and to stay there, cramped, heads folded under our arms, until the teacher called out,

"All clear!" Sometimes the whole school was taken out into the halls, away from the windows, and instructed to crouch down, heads to the walls, our eyes scrunched closed, until further notice. Sometimes the air raid sirens went off out in the wider world, and whole cities were told to stay indoors. Who knew what to believe? Under the desks and crouched in the hallways, terrors were ignited, existentialists were made. Whether or not we believed that hiding under a school desk or in a hallway was really going to protect us from the furies of an atomic blast, we could never quite take for granted that the world we had been born into was destined to endure.[45]

It is easy to overstate this fear of nuclear war as a widespread form of childhood terror during the height of the Cold War, but it is clear that it did have a profound effect on some, and for those for whom it did seem to be a probability, their views on life and the future were irrecoverably altered. Michael Rossman addresses the same point in an article in *Commonweal*, writing that "though there may be many of my generation who can't remember waking up with those nightmares, there's enough who can so that they're probably our most common property. But nobody ever said what that meant. What it did to us, to learn as children to imagine the death of the world . . . . At some deep and irrevocable level, I submit, we imagine . . . absolute annihilation. . . . It's all over . . . gone, done, that's it."[46]

Few could escape the reminders of potential atomic disaster. If destruction did not happen quickly in a direct blast, Americans were told, it could come silently and slowly as radioactive fallout. While there was not widespread fear, some Americans worried about their air, their water, and milk for infants, as well as for "growing children." Cancer, birth defects, and genetic abnormalities were widespread concerns. Some worried that the Atomic Energy Commission (AEC) was "withholding . . . essential information" on the dangers of fallout and atomic testing.[47] These fears were reinforced by science fiction and Hollywood.[48] Groups, such as SANE, believed it was their duty to answer these concerns. Formed as a committee to stop Hydrogen bomb tests, SANE aimed to bring the realities of the thermonuclear age to the public's attention. SANE's first move was to advertise in *The New York Times*. The ad was entitled: "We Are Facing A Danger Unlike Any Danger That Has Ever Existed."[49] The group intended to drive home the point that there were enough nuclear weapons on the planet to "put an end to life on earth." SANE and CNVA hammered away at the atomic-testing issue, and some members even sailed into test areas in the South Pacific to disrupt nuclear experiments.[50] *Liberation* magazine believed it had its finger on the pulse of American society. The publication suggested that there was a "sense of frustration and discouragement with the arms' race, and with American foreign policy." The magazine argued that there [was] a feeling that something [was] missing in it, that there [was] no hope in it."51

While the majority of Americans were not preoccupied with such issues, several of the future draft dodgers were wrapped up in the various twists and turns of the Cold War era in which they spent their formative years. This awareness of an uncertain future remained with them as they matured, and added to a belief that there was little time to waste; it added an urgency to their desire for success. For these middle-class baby boomers, opportunities for the "good life" were real. They realized early in life that college was the ticket. In the backs of their minds, they felt that they needed to be successful, self-reliant, and to make something of themselves before it was too late. This was combined with a concern that their country was heading hopelessly in the wrong direction. This belief was shared also by some of their parents, a belief which they occasionally passed on to their children. The expatriates' early impressions and experiences seem to have added to their sense of urgency to live life and, interestingly, contributed to their disinclination to waste valuable time in anti-war protests and the counterculture in later years.

Portland, Oregon, native and draft dodger Timothy Unger embodied this attitude. Unger's father was a career navy man who saw action in the Second World War. His mother worked in the war industries in Los Angeles, but lost her job in 1945. She was college educated but was unable to find work to her liking. Unger remembers: "She was always restless . . . involved in groups, activists, peace groups—things I think to give her life some meaning." Unger's mother was gone frequently when he was young, leaving him to care for his younger brother. His father was usually absent for months at a time. As a youngster, Unger was perplexed at his mother's actions, "especially when she was arrested for some stunt in California." There was a considerable amount of tension and friction in the family home with an activist mother and a career navy man as a father. Mrs. Unger told her boys that the U.S. government would "eat them up and spit them out if they weren't careful . . . and didn't stand up for [themselves]. She thought she had lost one husband to the country and "was skeptical about the nation's future." His mother, according to Unger, wanted to change the nation's conscience, and involved herself with groups to effect social change. But while Unger sympathized with her, even as a child he believed that the country could not be reformed. Like other dodgers, Unger simply wanted to get a good education, a good career and avoid some of the "disruptions and disappointments" his parents and their generation endured. "I think that there was a lot of wasted time in my parents' generation. They had all this potential and prosperity staring them in the face, yet they were unhappy. I did not want to waste my time in life. It is something I just knew from very young."52

Expatriate Brandon Hockwald also wanted to take a different road than his parents did, even if it meant leaving the United States to accomplish what he wanted in life. "My parents were pretty liberal and radical for the time. By the time I was 10 in 1959, they instilled in me a kind of awareness that I think matured me, but scared me at the same time." His parents were high school teachers in Denver, Colorado. Hockwald became disenchanted with American society at a young age. He felt the country was heading in a dangerous direction with the Cold War. "I was determined not to become a cog in anyone's wheel. I wanted to take my own path. While I'm sure I sympathized with the civil rights movement in my early teens—and the Cuban Missile Crisis, and all that—I really wanted nothing to do with it." He does not recall having any allegiances to the country in any fashion beyond age 14. "It was just that way always since I was a kid. That sense of belonging to the States on any level just evaporated as I grew older if it was ever there at all."[53]

Michael Shannon also recalls his sense of disconnection from the political and social interests of his parents. Born and raised just outside Boston, his father was a physician and his mother was a clothing and interior designer. Shannon's father was a lifelong Democrat who voted for Johnson in 1964 but never cast a presidential ballot again after 1968. Shannon's father was upset both with the nature of the Democratic convention that year and with the demonstrations against it outside the convention hall. He could not, however, bring himself to vote for Richard Nixon. Shannon grew up in an upper-class, suburban environment, "where there were absolutely no black people. It was a very insulated environment. Our neighborhood was quiet; there was no crime, no poverty—my future looked planned." Both of Shannon's parents were involved in "various disarmament groups." His mother was the most active, "holding small meetings and get-togethers in [their] house." Shannon recalls: "I remember thinking as a kid that I didn't get it. Probably around the fifth or sixth grade, when I didn't want to hear anymore about world troubles. It was a strange dualism. On one hand, I lived in this privileged, insulated environment, yet I seemed to be, you know, inundated with causes. I cared, yet I didn't care." He remembers feeling that the country was about to come apart at the seams and he hoped to still have some of the opportunities his parents had before the world situation worsened. "I think, in a way, I knew too much as a kid. I wasn't excited about flag waving and all that, and I grew up wanting to have my kick at the can before it was too late. In retrospect that seems utterly foolish, but when you are younger, your motivations and the way you view the world and yourself can be quite narrow."[54]

Draft dodger Brian Anderson also cannot remember, even as a child, having an affinity with his country of birth. Anderson was raised in a small town in Pennsylvania, where patriotism and nationalism were "breakfast foods." Whether it was during "The Pledge of Allegiance" or singing "America the Beautiful," the young Anderson found he could not escape those "mainstream American truisms," which he disliked intensely. Anderson's parents immigrated to the United States from Sweden after the Second World War, and were uncomfortable with strident American patriotism: "My parents only seemed to notice what was ,wrong with the American outlook on the world. They seemed disillusioned with Cold War rhetoric." His father had come to the United States to go to medical school at Johns Hopkins University. Anderson's parents impressed upon him and his brother that the country was a great place for personal opportunities, but not to be influenced by the rhetoric. Anderson remembers growing up quite detached: "Many of the kids I went to school with were in troops and Boy Scouts, but I never joined in." Anderson was quite aware of what was going on in the world and, like many others, was planning to get the most out of life from an early age and take advantage of his position and intellect. "I had this, like, one track mind, very driven as a boy, you know, get the most, best out of life; I was raised that way—the country told you to be that way . . . our teachers taught us that way with books that told us we were in the very best country in the world. And we could do what we wanted in life."[55]

Draft evader Martin Strychuck's early experiences also helped him focus on his future while he was still in childhood. He spent his primary years in Joliet, Illinois, and is an only child. His mother had worked in the war industries during the Second World War and began working for a local chapter of CNVA when he was 10. She was often busy with committee activities and left him in the care of babysitters: "I remember being upset by that. I was a jealous kid. My father was ambivalent, so she always gave me a daily description of what she was doing, and the perils of the planet. All I wanted to do was go to university and leave it all behind. I knew that before I was 13." Strychuck is quick to point out that while he believes that his mother's efforts and those of others had merit, he did not want to worry about those sorts of issues. Rather, he felt that he had to mature quickly and plan for his future.

There was a sense that the future was going to evaporate—disappear before I got a chance to experience it for myself. I don't know if it was the Cold War, or social unrest, or what it was, but blind allegiance or chanting the Pledge of Allegiance in school was not going to do it. The people I grew up around in our community, the school, the neighborhood, I thought, were just brainwashed and they could not see reality for what it was. I wanted to move ahead and I had little in common with them. I, as an individual, was going to make my future. That's how I felt, and I'm not going to apologize for it now."[56]

What can one make of these various accounts? Their experiences may differ because of geography, but the outcomes were similar. Whether raised in the Midwest, small Southern towns, large New England cities, or coastal towns, a picture of disconnection and alienation from community is clear. It does not seem to matter if they were transplanted Northerners, children of Southern liberals, or raised by activist parents, the circumstances of their early lives put them at odds with their communities and these experiences became the origins of their disaffection. These future expatriates had failed to assimilate into American society. The question of why this happened is as important as how this disconnection from society shaped their later decisions on the Vietnam War. While the draft dodgers don't state directly that the reason they avoided military service (and fled to Canada) was in part a condition of their formative years, their testimonies reveal this to be the case.

Because of their early experiences, they were not joiners in their teen years, but grew to be independent, self-reliant, and resourceful young men— ironically, everything their country had taught them to be. In coming years they sought validation for their sense of alienation and their emerging thoughts about individualism and liberty, and found it in early American literature and thought. Interestingly, they were American children who could not wrap themselves in the flag, but began to immerse themselves in the ideals the flag represents. They were also raised with a sense of urgency in a generation which grew up in the shadow of the bomb. It was an atmosphere that contributed to their belief that to hesitate in life meant risking all. They emerged from childhood and became young men who wished only to focus on their futures, to make their own choices, unmolested by the forces around them, including the demands of state. It was how they learned to live as children.

3

Adolescent Philosophers:
From Teens to Draftees

[T]he disaffected middle class young are at hand, suffering a strange new kind of "immiseration" that comes of being stranded between a permissive childhood and an obnoxiously conformist adulthood, experimenting desperately with new ways of growing up self-respectfully into a world they despise, calling for help. So the radical adults bid to become gurus to the alienated young or perhaps the young draft them into service.[1]

From the testimonies and actions of those who permanently left for Canada, it is clear they embodied early in life the essence of American individualism in their refusal to blithely conform to state demands. A desire to chart their course and remain true to themselves was evident in adolescence as several of these draft dodgers, as teens, actively sought alternatives to their experiences as children. While some chose avenues away from mainstream culture, the majority planned in earnest for futures far away from their childhood communities. In either case, their actions reveal young adults who, while disaffected from the country, knew what they could achieve for themselves in American society, and had firm future plans. They were individualists who intended to move beyond the boundaries of their formative years and strike out on their own to reap the benefits of higher education and a prosperous economy. While several became interested in early Beat and counterculture figures, such as Jack Kerouac and Allen Ginsberg, the majority did not become radicalized, nor did they join others in activist causes. Rather, as teens, these expatriates tapped into alternative literature and ideas for validation of their social alienation and as testaments to their individualism. They looked also to some of the more influential American writers, thinkers, and philosophers for support for their emerging world view. For most, it was a way to commiserate and deal with their experiences while affirming that it was the society in which they were raised that was off-track, and not themselves. Their tastes and interests connected them early in life to a heritage of American core beliefs: namely the right of individual action in defiance of state demands.

They also came of age during John Kennedy's New Frontier, a time when there were increased calls for public service and lofty reminders that with the privilege of citizenship comes obligation to country. In the shadow of the Cold War and its handmaiden, Vietnam, these expatriates as adolescents found their nation's stance and demands in contradiction to the country's ideals, as was the case for many young men of draft age in the 1960s. They were also children during the birth of the information age; they had more access to information than at anytime in the republic's history. They received international news coverage from newspapers, magazines, movies, radio programs, and, most important of all, television. They were a generation more exposed to images and information from around the world than any other in human history. Television brought them some of the more craven and violent images of the day, from the battles for civil rights in the South to television coverage of the assassination and funeral of JFK. As teens they watched news coverage of the beginnings of protest against American involvement in Southeast Asia, and saw the first coffins of other young Americans arrive at Andrews Air Force Base. They were well informed as children, worldly even—and their early impressions contributed to their views about America, and their place in it. These themes, in the period from their late teens to the eve of the arrival of their draft notices, are the focus of the pages that follow. The circumstances of the expatriates' late adolescence and early adulthood are examined through their tastes in music, literature and television. Examined also are their views on society and politics, as well as their family relationships as they prepared to leave home for college. The narratives of these expatriates further illustrate that their disaffection with the United States did not inhibit their allegiance to steadfast American principles and ideology—an ideology that contributed to their future draft evasion.

THE NEW FRONTIER

Let the word go forth from this time and place. Let every nation know, whether it wishes us well or ill, that we shall pay any price, bear any burden, meet any hardship, support any friend, oppose any foe, to assure the survival and success of liberty. And so my fellow Americans: ask not what your country can do for you— ask what you can do for your country.[2]

With those now famous words uttered during his presidential inaugural address on January 20, 1961, new President John F. Kennedy called a generation of young Americans to duty, perhaps not foreseeing, or conceivably, seeing all too well, the challenges that lay ahead. While there was considerable optimism and acceptance for Kennedy's call for public service, not all were eager to jump on the New Frontier bandwagon. The sparkle and promise of the youthful president's vision was tempered by civil unrest in the South and a growing entanglement in Southeast Asia. Even Kennedy's own words that snowy day in Washington, D.C. shadowed his brash optimism. The "torch" had indeed "been passed to a new generation of Americans" who were well aware of "the hard and bitter peace" won by the previous generation. While many were undoubtedly moved by his rhetoric of "bearing any burden" and working diligently for the good of the nation, just as many were unmoved by the young president's brinkmanship during the Bay of Pigs and the Cuban Missile Crisis, nor captivated by his message of public service. Many of those who would later avoid the draft for Vietnam saw their future choices only through the lens of their own community experiences, and intended instead to focus on their education and career. As they stood at the dawn of a new decade and set off on their own for university or to compete in the booming workforce, the call to public service and to "bear any burden" fell on deaf ears.

The majority of these future draft dodgers felt that they had no obligation to the state and that the only obligation that they did have was to themselves. They held that the hallmark of a strong society was individualism, a creed that was taught to them by American society since they were old enough to walk. This feeling applied especially to their thoughts on military service in Southeast Asia. Draft dodger Aston Davis as a teen believed in social and civic responsibility, but not what was being asked in the early 1960s. Davis summed up his thoughts this way:

I don't want to be misunderstood. I believe in social responsibility, the responsibility to look out after your family, friends and neighbors, and upholding basic laws, but what I'm against, and have always been against, is when your social or civic responsibility becomes extended to the point when the state comes reaching to your door and insisting that you must comply with directives—that they can plan your life for you or, if need be, take it. This idea, the one I think is the most pernicious, is the idea that Kennedy was speaking about in his Inaugural, that I think crosses the line between performing good works of public service, and this demand for a form of state servitude, that one owes something to the state by [the] mere fact of being born in that country. I think what you owe is to obey the laws, treat people like you wish to be treated yourself, and help others when you are able. This did not extend to the war or anything else connected to war, and I believed that all when I was still an adolescent.[3]

Draft dodger Bill Warner, as a teenager, likewise did not swoon to Kennedy's call to arms or public service, but was sympathetic to the president's efforts to support black Americans in their struggles for civil rights. He remembers that what he witnessed in the South as a child helped to shape his own views about standing up for what one believes. Warner looked to the example of civil rights instead as the one to follow in his life, and not "play the good, obedient role just because you were told to." Growing up in the South during the civil rights demonstrations, Warner witnessed heroic actions by black Americans. He credits these experiences with helping to shape his early views on life and personal autonomy. "I grew to believe that there were times that breaking the law and following your own belief systems was the right way to act. I grew up believing that one should never let anyone, any individual, any government, or any law dictate your life. Everything that I read and everything that I saw around me as a teenager confirmed that."[4]

Draft evader Curtis Erickson also remembers feeling dubious about what was being asked of him when he was an adolescent. "I thought this at the time, that there seemed to be a fever about doing things for America, and to be involved with countless civic activities, to wrap yourself in the flag, wear it on your sleeve, this communion if you will about America, and much of that leached into the heroic war films from the Second World War, and tried to leach into public duty with Vietnam. There was also this unquestioning thing about it mixed in, like we were not supposed to challenge it, but I think something like that is quite un-American." Erickson said that the mood in the country in the early 1960s did not fit with his thinking: "I thought that I was the best one to make my plans, and I would be the one who decided how I would serve my country, and it would be my decision, when, and if, I did it; it would not be: 'here are your choices, young man. Take it or leave it.' "[5]

Dodger Brian Linton loved Kennedy's enthusiasm, but disliked what he believes was the uncompromising, blanket approach to national duty. "I don't think there is a one-size-fits-all type of nationalism—that's a bad thing. It's not democracy any longer when you can't, with vigor, with confidence, or with silence or indifference, object or reject what your country demands of you, or holds up to be patriotic, or not patriotic."[6]

The issue that draft dodgers, such as Warner, centered on was the state demanding that individuals make personal sacrifices. Draft evader Dale Friesen likewise was suspicious of the motives of the government and Kennedy's call to duty. He and others remember that one of the problems associated with Kennedy's first year in office was the idea that one had to "support [one's] country and government at any cost." Friesen felt that this always meant service in the military, and in locales, such as Korea, Laos, or Vietnam.

I knew that he [Kennedy] was a navy man—a military man. He had served in the forces in WWII and paid a price, lost men, and believed in public duty—he in his position as the son of a millionaire, if he had wanted, would have never got himself into harm's way unless he had wanted to. He believed in that, much like Eisenhower, who was a general in the Second World War, and mark my words—if Kennedy would not have been assassinated, I would have, and the rest of us, would still have been drafted into Vietnam—nothing much would have changed—Kennedy was a hawk. And I was suspicious as a kid—I wondered what was going on. You could sense it, in a way, that we were going to be sent into a Korea-type operation, where there were terrible losses, and for what? And then it was Vietnam, and our turn. Something about it all, and the draft building up, just was not right.[7]

Another factor that contributed to their suspicions of public pronouncements, policy and demands for their service was the actual assassination of the president. Their thoughts and impressions concerning his death contributed to a growing mistrust about their government and the nature of their society. Kennedy's assassination on November 22, 1963, jarred the nation as few events had before. It has been said that America lost not only its innocence that day, but its youth. Controversy still surrounds not only the circumstances of Kennedy's death, but his plans in Southeast Asia. The president's own conflicting statements on Vietnam in the months preceding his death do little to clear up this mystery. While his plans for staying the course or pulling out of Vietnam had little to do with the decisions of the draft dodgers to head north, his assassination did have an effect on how they viewed their country in the years prior to receiving their draft notices. For some, Kennedy's untimely death contributed to an increased suspicion and mistrust of government and of their nation's direction.[8]

Dodgers, such as Carl McCrosky, recall that the assassination of Kennedy represented more than the loss of a political leader, as he equated it with all the things that were wrong with America in those years. McCrosky said that with events, such as the assassination, America often behaved "like a mad dog, ripping the guts out of itself." Aston Davis remembers Kennedy's assassination as a "black hole" in his childhood "that nothing could really fill." Davis said he was not traumatized by the experience, but was "disturbed" by what it signified about his country. "Nothing was the same after that—nothing was permanent—you could not rely on anything, or anybody, except yourself, because it was like we were just waiting for the next shoe to fall—and believe me it did with Vietnam." Martin Strychuck recalls that the assassination was the end of an era and the beginning of a worse one. "I have always said that the Sixties began on the day he was shot. I'm not saying that there would not have been a war—I'll leave that to Oliver Stone, but that it seems that's when things turned ugly at home—with other assassinations, and [President Lyndon] Johnson and [Secretary of

Defense Robert] McNamara and the war—everything fell apart. Whatever we had going for ourselves, began to crumble from that point forward. . . . Something like that really makes you stand up and take a look around at—you know—what the hell is going on." Draft evader Ron Needer remembers that his mom was terrified and dismayed by the news of Kennedy's death. "I felt so sorry for her—she was such a political-file, and such a Democrat—she hated the Republicans, and thought they were behind the murder—nothing I ever thought—but the point is, is that this tragedy really made many of us who grew up in that time, in that generation, much more aware of the depths of our country's problems. And I never once thought that it was the work of one man—it really troubled me—lots of things troubled me—when was it all going to stop?" Interestingly, these events made these adolescents more independent; they looked inward for answers. Strychuck says, "All of this makes one very independent minded as a teen—you don't trust, and you look out for number one—you don't put a lot of faith in institutions."[9]

For others, one of the reasons that the assassination had such an effect on them was the manner in which they learned of events. Draft dodgers like Michael Shannon are able to recall vividly the Kennedy assassination as if it happened recently. He says that the reason the event is so imprinted on his memory is that he watched it, along with his parents, on television.

THE TELEVISION GENERATION

Perhaps the greatest single invention of the information age is television. Since its inception TV has revolutionized not only the way America views itself, but the world. Never before could images of local, regional, and world events be sent to any point on the globe in an instant. It not only made the world smaller, but it made events appear more personal and immediate. While television sets were uncommon in American homes in the 1940s—there were only around 7,000 primitive sets, all black and white in 1946—by the middle of 1950s, most Americans had one in their living room. By 1960, 9 out of 10 American homes had a set. By the end of the Eisenhower administration, fifty million high quality sets beamed words and images and constituted a multibillion dollar industry. TV changed the way Americans interacted and saw the world.

Television became the focal point for a family's entertainment, supplanting time previously spent on other activities, such as going to movies, playing, visiting, reading, or even listening to radio programs. For some it even replaced sitting around the dinner table. Families, instead, gathered in the living room, and ate their dinners in silence, rather than in conversation. In less than a decade, television transformed the patterns of social life. The medium changed not only the way some adults viewed the world, but had a tremendous impact on the perceptions of children.[10]

While the majority of the expatriates interviewed for this study say that television was not central to their childhood, most recall it playing an above average role in forming early impressions of society. This was especially true in helping to shape their attitudes concerning the actions and role of their government in international affairs, the social strife on the streets of America in the fight for civil rights, and later, the growing protests against the Vietnam War.

Draft dodgers such as David Ward says that television was like a window to the world outside his home community, and helped give him a different perspective on life. "My parents bought one of the first TVs on our block—at least I think it was one of the first—and people would just drop in on us, even at supper time. It made me realize what a big world there was out there, that people felt different about things, that there was a plurality of views on every conceivable issue. And I remember thinking that our own American view was only one of them, and not necessarily the right one."

Ward recalls watching documentaries about the Second World War and the Soviet Union, and turning into the evening news, which often featured stories concerning civil rights. "All these things were just burning issues then, and TV made it so real and vivid, it was really incredible. As I got a little older, about 12 or 13, something like that, I never the missed [The CBS Evening News with Walter] Cronkite, and all of this stuff made me very politically aware and very much a kid who would sit alone and think about these things and what they meant."

Ward says that at the time, when he looked to the future, he was trying to discover a way to avoid some of the issues that were troubling the country. "I wanted to look beyond what was happening then to the country in better days. I had this idea that in some ways the world was not going to get better—let me put that another way: I was skeptical that things were going to improve anytime soon, and I remember liking those nice, family scenes from some of the shows like *Leave it to Beaver* and *The Honeymooners*. That to me, as laughable as it seems now, was what I wanted—people to be happy, getting along, no world troubles. I yearned for what I didn't think was going to come my way, but I hoped for it, and God, the beginnings of the war, I was young, very scared, and wanted to get away from that anyway I could. . . . I just wanted a future free of what I saw." Ward admits that it is ironic that he was so attracted to watching and learning about the things that he feared, such as troubling issues on the evening news. "I could not stop myself from plopping down in front of the set and taking it all in."[11]

Draft dodger Michael Shannon feels that while exposure to TV by itself does not make a person act in a particular way, he does believe that the access to information afforded by television in his early years had an effect on his perceptions of the future.

I thought, and I would ask my parents this: what is happening in the world, why are we killing each other, why are police dogs ripping the clothes off of innocent black people on the street? Why are we testing nuclear weapons? Why, why, why was always the thing going through my head. My parents came to this country to get ahead in life, and that seemed like a great thing, and I was seriously wondering if I was going to get that same opportunity. I thought, sort of wrongheaded, that my parents' generation were the lucky ones—they had the peace and prosperity, and we had the social strife and Cold War—but that of course is wrong. They had the Depression, the Second World War *and* the Cold War, and as adults they were experiencing the same things I was. But as a kid you don't see it that way—you just think that, *damn*, I'm going to get screwed![12]

Albert Caldwell says that to him television meant separation and isolation from his family and community. "I think TV was, and to a certain degree still is . . . about escape, dividing yourself off from conversations, interactions with others, and it closets you off with your own thoughts—this can be a good thing, and it can be a bad thing. I think that in some ways the box helped me through some rough times. I also liked television, and still do, but I think that the interesting thing about TV is that while it was a solitary occupation, it also was a tremendous provider of information and resources—much like the computer is today—but with much greater impact, because there was nothing like it before. In this way it was much different than radio as it was something where you had to keep most of your attention on it."

Caldwell says that television added to his means for gathering information. Along with books, magazines and radio, it provided greater access to information about the world and his choices as an adolescent than his parents had. "We definitely had more options, and could visualize more options than our parents, before we were set in our ways. I think that the previous generation had more of a 'settle for your lot in life, accept what is handed to you, and not question authority.' That was *not* our generation, and I think that is an important part of what TV offered us."[13]

Draft evader Merrill Condel agrees with these observations, adding that it was very difficult for those inclined to accept the status quo on any issue. "It was not in many of us to blindly accept the world as some would have it appear. Duty to country, without question was gone—it had evaporated—we knew too much, heard too much, and saw too much—not only in our own neighborhoods, but in everybody else's neighborhood through television. The reasons to say 'no, I don't agree with what you say, government,' came through each night on TV. I don't care if it was civil rights, the National Guard going into Selma, Alabama, or protests against our involvement in

Vietnam, it showed us that there were definite differences of opinion and it was all right to disagree, and make our own decisions about life."

Condel adds that his parents' generation grew up with less information about the world, and because of that, they were less inclined to turn down public service or calls to duty in uniform. He says that because his generation had more information and because there were significant, divisive issues taking place in the country, citizens were less likely to accept the government's demands as they had in other times in American history. "There [have] been other instances I know in the past when Americans, en masse, said no to their country. They did during the Civil War on both sides, and they did in the War of 1812. There [were] some in the First World War, and to a much lesser extent in the Second. But I think if there were to have been even greater dissemination of information about, let's say, the Civil War, the draft riots would have been far greater." Condel believes that the extra factor faced by Vietnam draft dodgers was that there was also concerted social unrest. "I think we had both things when I was growing up . . . untenable political, social and international conditions, at the same time that this generation was coming of age and was being called upon to bite the bullet, so to speak. We were being given information like never before about choice, and different perspectives on issues, and TV played a definite role in this."[14]

Dodger Nick Theason said that television armed his generation to combat state demands as it brought all the problems of the world into their homes. "TV increased our vocabulary of the world as it was . . . I mean my generation knew more of what was going on in the world than, I think, ever before. And what did this do? you ask. Well, it made us, I think, a little more cynical, suspicious, and leery of public boasts and pronouncements, and a little more cognizant of what we should do and how we fit, or didn't fit into society's plans or direction." Theason and other draft dodgers say that while television made them more cynical, they don't view that as negative. "I don't think that cynicism is necessarily a bad thing. I think that there are healthy doses of cynicism, but what I think is that it does make you more inward looking, more individualistic, especially when you develop this as a kid, and especially as an adolescent. I don't think any of this is particularly novel or earth-shattering, but those types of feelings, attitudes, if you will, were affected by our sources of information. TV played a big part of how we saw our place in the world, because it gave us so much of our visual information—very compelling when you are young."[15]

Dodger Brandon Hockwald remembers TV in the early 1960s as a window into a less-than-friendly, unstable outside world. "I think that if television showed my generation anything it is that there were a lot of screwed up people out there; there were killings in the South, our president gets blown away while the cameras roll. And we take all of this in—all on

TV—all these images that we are helpless to manipulate, yet it sometimes feels that it is happening to us." Hockwald suggests that his reactions to this negative stimuli contributed to his disconnection and disassociation from American society, and he sympathizes with people who had alternative views on the nature of society. "I used to write songs about this type of thing when I was 15 or 16, and good for me my parents always supported that attitude in me, that searching attitude—trying to make sense of it all, and so much was already bombarded at us from the TV screen, and not all of it was very good as images of America. It was war, killing and death—I wanted none of it."[16]

Ron Needer said that TV was akin to shock therapy, and most likely contributed to shaping his views. "We watched tragedy unfold. . . . I'm not saying that's the reason I ended up in Canada, but hell, these things do make you look differently at life, and what one's choices are. Watching Kennedy's untimely death and funeral on TV said to me one major thing: life was short—don't waste it."[17]

Draft dodger Michael Fischer said that his personal views of the world, life and America were in reaction to what was taking place around him in his adolescence. Because of this he knew early on that he was interested in discovering alternative points of view about society and his country of birth. As a teen Fischer began to "disengage from the country's plans" for him in earnest after the inaugural address by President Kennedy in 1961:

I was already in the frame of mind to reject everything that Kennedy was talking about, but his speech, as I vividly recall, made me nauseous. Especially that line: "Ask not what your country can do for you, but what you can do for your country, yada, yada, yada." This was the kind of thing that really bothered me. I would ask the question: Why was I required to do anything that I didn't want to do? No country gives you any guarantees. Anyway, that was my attitude as I got ready to leave home for college, and it was nice to know that others were not getting bogged down in the rah-rah attitude that Kennedy and his band of yo-yos were pontificating.[18]

Fischer, like most of these young men, began looking at alternative forms of literature and works of history, trying to find validation for their emerging views and attitudes about the world. They believed that they had the right to get ahead in life, and that meant getting a good education and taking care of themselves. It was an ideology that they formed early in life.

'A MAN OF LETTERS WAS A MAN OF INDEPENDENCE'

In Jack Kerouac's *On The Road,* the novel's protagonist meets groups of disaffected young men and women with whom he identifies on his journey across America.[19] These individuals, whom Kerouac refers to as the "beats," signified a segment of young Americans seeking alternatives to predominant modes of thought during the late 1950s and early 1960s. It is interesting to note that much of this sort of literature was not readily available to those who may have been disaffected during the Second World War or the Korean War. The majority of the expatriates were teens in the first years following the publication of *On The Road,* and several found themselves identifying with the book's quest for community. By most accounts, while growing up, these future draft dodgers were voracious readers, something that helped shape their attitudes about both their country and life.

Draft evader Albert Caldwell was 17 in 1963 when he sought literature outside the mainstream: "I had always read voraciously since I was little; my mother encouraged it and I knew from an early age that I was going to go to college, so I read a great deal. It was also a way of escaping. Around the time Kennedy was shot I began to read Bill Burroughs and Ginsberg, and, of course, *On The Road.* I liked where he was coming from. My world seemed to make a bit more sense after Cassady." Caldwell recalls that literature written at the time he was coming of age forced many of the people that he grew up around to look inward and have deeper thoughts about themselves and their place in the world. It also helped to shape their attitudes about the society in which they were raised and made them consider carefully their choices for the future. "Reading and thinking deeply about what I read was a huge part of my young life—it really wasn't taking part in sports, or little league, or scouts, and I wasn't into youth and teen clubs later on, but I was into ideas, and being my own person, no matter what stood in my way, and no matter what people may say about me. I think that for the most part that kind of attitude has to begin when you are young. I think it is a very hard thing to learn later once you have already learned how to bow to the will or convention of others."[20]

Other dodgers, such as Martin Strychuck, shared these literary tastes, as well as the thought and ideas behind them. Strychuck began his appreciation for the written word while reading Ernest Hemingway as a young teen, and later the poetry of Ezra Pound, T. S. Eliot, and Allen Ginsberg. These authors and poets provided him with something that appealed to his personality and interest in alternative ways of looking at society. "Lights began to go off in my head, and I realized that there were others who had a rough time as well as me. I buried myself in all the cool writers like Greg Corso, Lucien Carr, Lawrence Ferlingetti, and so on. It made such a difference. I discovered then that I was right about how I felt about things, and the people that I was raised around were screwed up; the entire society was." Strychuck latched on to these writers and believed that they had something to say about the individual and society that spoke directly to him. "Reading and thinking and examining these new ideas were really visceral, and key to my early development and attitudes. I wasn't interested in following specific examples of what these characters did or did not do, but there is a certain specific ideology that I think just spoke to me, and I don't think that made me very mainstream or likely to follow the flow, as it were, as I headed into my late teens and early twenties. I took a divergent path, as early as then."[21]

While several draft dodgers felt that the literature they read helped them form alternative views as adolescents, they also are quick to point out that reading influential works by contemporary writers and thinkers helped them cope with the circumstances of their youth. Dodger Brian Linton recalls that literature kept him "grounded" for the last few years before he left his parents' home for university: "If it wasn't for books I would have gone crazy before I left home. I never had many friends growing up, because of my family situation, so staying home and reading people like Kerouac and Goodman and Mandell showed me that I wasn't alone in thinking the country was messed up, and it gave me something to focus on. I began to take stock of my life and not make the kind of mistakes that others made. I was determined to be happy and do what I wanted with my life."[22]

Carroll Obline believes that his life was much like a Kerouac book: "It's funny but I was like that character in *On The Road*. I felt that I might float around my entire life for a while and never find anything or any place to hang my hat. I never seemed to fit in anywhere until I started to read. It was something that I could do on my own, and draw my own conclusions from what I was reading." Obline decided that he needed to listen to his conscience and not let anyone tell him he was wrong: "You grow up hearing that you're always wrong and that you're from the wrong place, and the scary thing is, is that you begin to believe it." Throughout his teens, Obline read everything he could, which helped him mature. "I grew up a great deal. I knew from 18 on that what anyone else told me to do, or what not to do, was probably wrong."[23]

It is interesting to see that what these young men found in the literature of the time was a sense of validation for non-cooperation with the system. As they read they examined texts which supported their emerging world views, and sought more examples that taught similar lessons. David Ward remembers vividly the first time he read *One Flew Over the Cuckoo's Nest* by Ken Kesey: "The book blew by mind. A couple of people that I chummed with had also read it and we were all thunderstruck, as I recall." Ward identified with the protagonist, R. P. McMurphy, a trouble-making patient in an otherwise orderly run insane asylum. Ward recalls: "I felt like that guy. Everybody thought there was something wrong with me when I was a kid, but they were the problem. And that evil nurse that McMurphy was trying to pull the fast ones on, was like the establishment in the States. She represented, for me, the sanctimonious community I was raised in."[24]

The expatriates realized early in life that education was key. While they identified with the beat generation writers, they were not ones to blithely follow examples but latched onto particular elements in this writing which supported and conformed to their emerging ethos. Jonathan Burke, for example, remembers a Kerouac quotation that "a man of letters was a man of independence," and took the statement to heart: "I began to think about my future earnestly from 14 on. I wanted to get out of Tulsa as soon as possible, and I knew that if I really was going to have some control over my life, in regards to what I did and where I lived, I needed to get a good education. The lack of control that I felt growing up, I think, really contributed to that drive to get ahead and let nothing get in my way."[25]

Burke's account mirrors those of several other expatriates. The majority of the Canadian-bound draft evaders began to focus on their careers early. They were in part motivated by a sense that they lacked control over events in their lives as children, and that they needed to anchor themselves in a time of political and social upheaval. It appears that the literature in which they immersed themselves provided reassurance and a sense of direction and purpose. This is not to say that this material alone shaped their views, but that their identification with it helped validate their sense of alienation and their belief that they needed to take care of themselves and ensure their futures. Draft evader Jim Tarris, much like Burke, began to consider seriously his future from a young age and says that the material he read played a role in the development of his attitudes. In Tarris's case, his mother was instrumental in the formation of his early outlook on life, and for helping him set priorities. "My mother was a big influence on me. Since I was small she was after me to get my butt out of Indiana and make something of myself. Things, of course, were never good for her at home, and her sense of powerlessness, I think, really made me want to be sure that I was the one calling the shots in my life and no one else." Tarris also credits his mother for introducing him to alternative writings before he left home: "She had *Naked Lunch* by William Burroughs and a lot of other interesting books that I don't think many others were reading that I went to high school with." The book that captivated him the most, however, was *On The Road*: "When I first read the book, It was as if I had discovered a new language. I identified with the feelings of the characters, if not their actions, and that was the most important thing. It was one of the few books that I packed with me when I left home." Tarris believes that it was at that moment when things changed for him: "I really began to drop out of what society had planned for me and focused on my own dreams of the future. I had my own ethos."[26]

What explains part of the fascination and attraction to works such as *On the Road* among expatriates is that the material provided them with a certain confidence about individual action and personal autonomy that was encouraged only selectively by society when they were children. They craved the examples of "doing one's own thing" and taking one's own path in life, not from societal and community examples, but in what they read. Aston Davis also believes he and others latched on to the sense of alienation and disaffection present in the early counterculture and alternative writings as it provided both an important example for self-expression and the confidence to break with the past and begin planning for life at an early age: "Discovering Ginsberg, Kerouac, and even Ken Kesey, allowed me to come to terms with some of the problems of childhood. Actually, far from being some renegade looking to dodge the draft down the road, I really had my shit together. When you grow up on the defensive like I did, you want to ensure that it doesn't follow you throughout your life. I knew exactly what I wanted. I wasn't one of the ones who was trying to 'find myself.' "[27]

As their emerging ideologies took form, the expatriates began to examine and identify with some seminal historical writings and thoughts concerning what it means to be American. Some believed that it was their birthright to resist what they considered to be the state's unnecessary and tyrannical intrusions on their individual liberty. As young Americans versed in the early history of their country, they felt that they could not reconcile the idea that they could be drafted against their will in a republic that was founded on refusing the demands of government. Evoking the words of Thomas Paine and Thomas Jefferson, several of these future draft dodgers found validation for their early adult views on refusing duty to the government in the American past.

CORE AMERICANS: 'YOU CAN TAKE THE BOY OUT OF THE COUNTRY BUT YOU CAN'T TAKE THE COUNTRY OUT OF THE BOY'

Brian Linton is one of several draft dodgers who proudly says that many of the writers who interested him as a teen spoke of the great American traditions of individuality and freedom. He, like many draft evaders, was moved by his initial exposure in high school to the works of Emerson and Thoreau: "It was amazing stuff, the wealth of ideas and ways of looking at the world and your country and your place in it. I loved the idea—that Jeffersonian ideal of inalienable rights—and what would happen to those ideals if those rights were denied or infringed upon."[28] Many expatriates state that their early interests in the writings of eighteenth and nineteenth century American philosophers helped not only to shape their views, but supported their ideas for later personal action. Dodger David Ward, for one, remembers his attraction to these ideas with his initial exposure in the 11th grade: "It made an impression on me, there is no doubt. Thomas Paine, Jefferson, Locke, Horace Mann, they all had a real resounding ring and I locked into that early on; I learned that it was honorable to be a non-conformist in the way one thought and acted, and maybe being alone with the way one thought was not such a bad thing."29

Thus was born the conviction among expatriates that their country's founding and most important principles allowed them to think the way they did, and act upon those thoughts and beliefs when they were later confronted with the draft. Several expatriates trace their philosophy to influential American writers and philosophers, who they claim justified their beliefs about duty and country. Evader Nick Theason remembers that when he completed high school, the Vietnam War was already underway, and even though he planned to attend college, he worried about the draft. The increasing protest against the war and some of the principles upon which the war was based made him think he was justified to refuse enlistment. "There were a few of us who spoke about that; one of my friend's older brothers, who was at the University of Minnesota, told me to read [Alexis de] Tocqueville, that I would find some precedent for thinking that it may not be wrong to refuse an order or directive from your government. I'm not saying that it was that alone that dissuaded me from accepting enlistment, but I really believed those things—those ideas that one had a right to refuse [and] to take one's own path. It seems to me that that is one of the hallmarks of liberty in a truly free state, and because of that, the very idea of conscription was anathema."30 Theason is not alone in suggesting that he looked for historical antecedents for validation of his desire to evade the draft. Draft evader Merrill Condel also remembers reading Tocqueville and finding his words applicable to his own life: "Tocqueville warned about an invasion against personal rights by the government, an invasion from the top enforcing or creating a community or social pressure to force public opinion to one degree. I thought that that was happening in the war and in the draft, and that I had a right on those grounds to refuse, even if that sounds pompous today."31

Michael Shannon agrees, suggesting that the very nature of American ideology, in what children were taught in primary and secondary education, reinforced the power of individual action and autonomy in the face of government intervention. "I was attracted to it, and bought it hook, line, and sinker. I read Margaret Fuller, and loved Thomas Jefferson, and sensed, even then, that the country was going wrong and that I wanted nothing to do with it. The war was anti-American, anti-freedom of choice, and Jefferson, had he been alive, would have said it was wrong."32 Shannon, like several others, claim loudly that it was more than simply the Vietnam War that they were against, but the whole thrust of American leadership in the Cold War, and the idea that the citizens could be marshaled at will to fight for particular ideological concerns. Shannon believed the country had lost its way and had strayed from its initial philosophy of avoiding foreign entanglements. "One only had to look to history to find support for what I think many of us thought. Many Americans thought we had no business in Korea, and little in the First World War. World War II was different as we were attacked, and I think that is very different, but Vietnam and the entire Cold War ideology was ill conceived, and wrong from an American perspective."[33]

Michael Fischer, and others, are quick to point out, however, that they did not use the ideology of the Founding Fathers and other political philosophers as excuses for their refusal to conform, but believed that it was their right of birth, and that they had a sense of duty and obligation to the very ideals of America to resist what they believed was wrong. "It does seem ironic, I know, that me and others could turn our backs on the States and still spout the American jargon of individual rights, but all that stuck, it was all so instilled in us when we were young, all of us, and so we really believed that we had these rights as Americans, even if we became disgusted with the country."[34]

Carroll Obline agrees, adding that "it's the old saying that you can take the boy out of the country, but you can't take the country out of the boy. In this case we are talking about the actual country, but the metaphor works. We were still Americans who happened to be at odds with our society. The situations—the circumstances of growing up and what was going on in foreign policy—converged and pushed ones like me out of the country. It forced us to choose. The nation as it stood was not worth staying in, so we took our good old American individualism, the stuff we were taught as kids, packed it up and trooped across the border."[35]

Music

If the type of literature these future draft dodgers were reading and contemplating diverged somewhat from others their age, it should not be surprising that their tastes in music differed as well. While the majority enjoyed rock 'n' roll music, for example, their overall choices suggest young men trying to distinguish themselves from mainstream trends. Michael Fischer, for one, did not listen to country music growing up because it reminded him of all "the bad, backwards, and close-mined rednecks that [he] saw when [he] was younger." Fischer, however, like a number of others, was not captivated by rock 'n' roll either: "Everyone was listening to it, and I never thought it was the greatest thing. All I ever listened to was classical music."[36] Brian Anderson also eschewed rock. He listened to jazz, as "it was something that I discovered on my own and *that* made it much more attractive than pop music."[37] Carroll Obline remembers liking rock music, especially Buddy Holly, but preferred blues and jazz: "I think I was different than everyone else. Even in music I seemed out of step with what was going on. I liked Billie Holiday and Ella Fitzgerald, instead of Chuck Berry; the Beatles never particularly appealed to me."[38] Even some draft dodgers born after 1950, who were teens in the mid-1960s, were ambivalent about pop music and unmoved by early protest songs and music. Martin Beech recalls: "When I heard Joan Baez tell everyone that music could be used as a vehicle to end the war, I shook my head. I didn't believe that Bob Dylan was going to have any effect on ending the war in Vietnam. I was always too much of a realist for that."[39] Ron Needer was also disinterested in popular music: "I wanted to find out where all the good engineering schools were and could not be bothered by the frivolous and pointless messages in pop music. Even the '60s music, I thought, was pointless and commercially driven. I much preferred music, such as classical and baroque, that had no cultural relationship to what was going on in my life. I was a hard-head, and probably still am."[40]

Curtis Erickson also believes he was too much of a "realist" to be attracted to popular music: "I sort of shut myself off from that whole scene. I didn't go to school dances, as I thought I was above all that nonsense, and closeted myself with science journals at home, or was stargazing and mapping the constellations. What was going on with music wasn't even a consideration." Erickson, like most expatriates, began focusing early on his professional career and was not moved by cultural trends.[41] Others, however, believe that rock music made it okay to have divergent opinions, and make one's own way in the world. Brandon Hockwald said that the music in the late 1950s and 1960s pushed the limits of what young people could do and say, and worked in conjunction with other counterculture trends. "I think that popular music raises the bar on what a person, especially a young person, can get away with, or at least think about, and that was true in my case to a certain extent." Others say that rather than rock music being a force in their lives, it simply was a reflection of the loosening of society, and the diverging of opinion. Draft dodger Jonathan Burke says: "Music of the Sixties shadowed what was going on in the world and in politics, it did not lead to movements, but followed and commented on what was going on. . . . I think that persons such as myself were too driven to be swayed by anything going on in pop culture. I liked music, it did not change my life, but it did represent much of what was going on at that time."[42]

Dodger Brian Linton recalls that as a teen he shunned much of the popular music and television programs that most of his contemporaries followed: "I really liked to read much more, especially poetry and classic literature, and I was quite interested in Ginsberg and Kerouac, and they were not that well-known then, certainly not nearly as popular as today." Linton states that he "was not at all in-tune with too much other than moving away from home and beginning university."[43]

COLLEGE BOUND

The numbers of young Americans who enrolled in colleges and universities skyrocketed between 1940 and 1960.[44] While college enrollments eventually began to attract greater numbers of women and minorities, the majority of the post-war rise came from the sons of the ever-growing middle class. All the draft dodgers interviewed for this study were either in university or had plans to attend when they were drafted, a fact consistent with findings in other studies. For the future expatriates, however, not only were they a college-bound and a highly motivated group, but they were also determined individuals who doggedly persisted along their chosen paths. When the day of their high school graduations arrived, 80 percent of those in this sample were accepted to college, with 60 percent enjoying some type of scholarship. And, as David Surrey found, they and their parents were educated far beyond national averages. They were inclined to let nothing get in their way of achieving success and have vivid recollections of leaving home; for most, that day was greeted almost as an escape.[45]

Draft evader Nick Theason, for example, recalls: "Leaving home for me meant that I could finally make my own choices on my life and live where I wanted. It's the time when you start over. It wasn't really a sad day at all. I really can't remember it being bittersweet with thoughts of returning home for a visit soon."[46] Merrill Condel had similar recollections: "As I recall, there wasn't this great wave of emotion, but a nodding certainty that this day had to come, and the sooner the better. I could not wait to leave."[47] Dale Friesen could not sleep for the last week before he left the South for Indiana: "It was the great escape. I was finally on my own with the past behind me. I knew that I could finally do what I wanted, and nothing—nothing was going to stop me."[48]

While such reactions from young men should not be surprising, what does stand out is how many did not care if they ever returned to their childhood communities. David Ward, for example, speaks of the alienation and disconnection that the majority of the expatriates felt when they were about to leave their parents' home and childhood communities: "I never, even as a small child, felt a part of what was around me, the community, the town, the school; even my parents were on a different wave from me, and from each other. I thought the South was backwards and racist, and I could not stand it anymore. College was going to be the great escape, but then the Vietnam War began to appear on the horizon."[49]

Carroll Obline, like Ward, also did not feel any sentimental attachment to his place of birth: "I really did not have any sense of home, and what home was. It was always me and Mom against the world. My father and mother had parted ways after the war and no one else seemed to want us where we moved to. So leaving 'home' with any thoughts of returning was out of the question. There were no attachments there and, as it turned out, there wasn't much of an attachment to the country either."[50] Dale Friesen remembers that he hated stating on his university applications that he was from Macon, Georgia, because he never felt that it was his home as his family was from the North: "I always had a problem, as I recall, with who I was, where I was from, and where I belonged. It felt strange putting my home address as Macon because I felt like writing: 'It's just where I happen to have been raised, and really, they don't even want us here.'" Friesen could not wait to leave and "didn't care if [he] ever returned."[51] Bill Warner sums up much of the expatriate attitude, stating:

You have to understand that the very idea of home and country, I believe, was erased from people like me as we were growing up. We never had those positive experiences, those patriotic experiences which brought us into the greater community. I was raised with loving parents with a good standard of living, but we were definitely the unwanted "Yankees" in our own community. My mistake was the naive idea that all of this feeling would go away once I left home, but by the time I graduated from high school, the entire country was beginning to fall apart at the seams. All I wanted to do at that point was to get an education, get a good job and have a family. That was my frame of mind as I entered campus life, far away from home.[52]

As teens these future expatriates tended not to be joiners. They were not enthralled by Kennedy's call for duty to country, and became independent, thoughtful, and introspective. Tending to withdraw from the more mainstream movements, they tapped into alternative writings, thought, and music. Some began to identify with the sense of alienation and disaffection of the Beats and found solace and like-minded individuals whose writings validated their estrangement from American society. As a group, however, they were highly focused on their future prospects and seemed inclined to let nothing prevent them from reaching their goals in life. These middle- and upper middle-class young men were already on the road to success with college education and bright futures awaiting them in the healthy economy of the 1960s.

Despite disaffection with the United States, however, these expatriates were raised in a society that taught them that all dreams were possible. They were indoctrinated early with the core American philosophies and ideals of freedom, individuality, personal honor, liberty, the pursuit of happiness, and the rejection of state tyranny. It proved to be an education that shaped not only their attitudes for decisions on the draft, but the balance of their lives. It is ironic that the society from which they had learned so much failed to be one they could identify with, let alone fight and die for. They looked at the approaching Vietnam War with abject horror; it signified all that had gone wrong with their country and was linked to the experiences they had had since childhood—experiences that had left them disconnected and unlikely to be interested in military duty, especially not in Vietnam. They also had greater access to information about their choices—and all that they wanted to avoid in their country—through books, magazines, radio, and, most of all, television. The expatriates' testimonies reveal that for many reasons, and in many different ways, they had not assimilated into the greater American community. While loners generally, they were also highly educated, well-heeled, and driven to get the most out of life, while feeling little loyalty to the demands of the state. They arrived on university campuses in the mid-1960s and witnessed the beginnings of massive protests against their country's involvement in Vietnam and the direction of the nation. The government's growing need for young men found its way to their doors, calling them to serve their country through Selective Service. Draft boards from across the nation sent notices to thousands of men who refused to answer that call. No one knew that some young Americans had stopped answering years before.

4

Selective Service and Vietnam: Deferments, Loopholes, and Class Privilege

It was clear that any man with an ounce of brains, money, or education could beat the system.[1]

The draft for the Vietnam War was rife with inequities. While it is true that the majority of the military personnel who served in Vietnam were white males, those from less privileged backgrounds and racial minorities served in Vietnam in numbers highly disproportionate to their percentage in the general population. The latter were also the front-line soldiers, serving mostly in combat positions. White middle-class and upper middle-class young men who were unlucky enough to get drafted more often than not served out their terms in safer, rearguard, and administrative, non-combat duties. The Selective Service deck was stacked in their favor. Where this advantage was really telling, however, was in the ability of the more privileged classes to avoid ever being inducted. For this group of potential draftees, there were numerous methods to avoid military service without resorting to drastic means, such as going underground or fleeing the country. More education and greater affluence meant more connections and greater access to information on university campuses concerning the numerous methods to avoid conscription, including educational and occupational deferments. The vast majority of the expatriates in Canada came from this group—the least likely to be sent to Vietnam.

In examining the mechanics of the draft, it becomes clear that the expatriates had several ways to avoid it, other than to leave for Canada. As we will see, had they desired to do so, these options would have kept them both out of the military and in the United States.[2]

THE QUAGMIRE BEGINS

When Lyndon Johnson assumed the office of President of the United States following the assassination of John Kennedy in 1963, American involvement in Southeast Asia was costing taxpayers a whopping $400 million annually. Over 12,000 U.S. military advisors were stationed in Vietnam, and dozens had already lost their lives in skirmishes with the Viet Cong in the four previous years. Despite this, the nation was not yet concerned or preoccupied with their military's deepening commitment. A poll at the time revealed that two-thirds of Americans paid "little or no attention" to the war. The alarms were not ringing on Capitol Hill either. In the summer of 1964, Congress passed the Gulf of Tonkin Resolution with only two dissenting votes. The passage gave President Johnson what his aides called "the functional equivalent of a declaration of war."[3] On March 8, 1965, following the lobbying of General William Westmoreland and the recommendation of the Joint Chiefs of Staff, Johnson sent in the 9th Marine Expeditionary Brigade to protect the air base at Danang. The marine deployment constituted the first U.S. ground forces in Vietnam—the last of which would not leave until nearly 11 years later in 1975.[4] The deployment of Marines was clearly the most significant decision to date of American military involvement, yet it was mostly ignored in the press and Congress, as the president had managed to have it appear as a "short-term expedient." Johnson, however, instructed Westmoreland to "assume no limitation on funds, equipment, or personnel." The general saw no quick end to the war and requested large combat deployments. Westmoreland informed the president that "we are in for the long pull. . . . I see no likelihood of achieving a quick, favorable end to the war." On the afternoon of July 28, 1965, the president went on national TV taking his case for action to the people. Johnson said: "I have asked the commanding General, General Westmoreland, what he needs to meet this mounting aggression. He has told me. And we will meet his needs. We cannot be defeated by force of arms. We will stand in Vietnam."[5] By the height of the war in 1967, more than 500,000 American soldiers were in Southeast Asia.

While the majority of Americans supported their military's involvement in 1964 and 1965, opposition to the growing American presence intensified. On September 30, 1964, the first of thousands of protests against the U.S role in Vietnam took place at the University of California at Berkeley. By the time Johnson deployed the Marines in the spring of 1965, student protests were taking place across the country. Students were well aware that Johnson's promise to Westmoreland to provide all the "funds, equipment, or personnel" meant them. Because of the unpopularity of the war among many men of draft age and because of the way the Pentagon and Westmoreland planned to conduct it, through attrition, there was a great burden on

Selective Service to conscript ever increasing numbers of men into the armed services. By the fall of 1965, student protests against the undeclared war against North Vietnam became widespread.

"BE ALL YOU CAN BE—BE A DRAFT DODGER"

Avoiding the draft in the 1960s was not isolated to a few thousand men. Over 60 percent of the 27 million draft-eligible males found successful methods not only to lessen their chances of combat but of serving in the military altogether. According to a survey conducted at the University of Notre Dame, up to 50 percent of servicemen took steps themselves to secure better and safer non-combat positions.[6] Thousands, however, wanted more than a safer military life, they wanted to avoid military service altogether. War meant personal hardships; loss of income; delays in one's education; leaving wives, girlfriends, and family behind; and the prospect of losing one's life. For white, educated, middle-class young men in the affluent 1960s, there was little to be gained by entering military service in Vietnam. It was this group of potential draftees that had the best access to information on how to elude conscription and were often the most vocal and active in their efforts to avoid the draft.

An interesting segment of the protesters were those who feared that serving in uniform in Vietnam would not only threaten their life, but "mess up" their career and education plans. Much of their opposition was not just against the war, but how the lost time would negatively affect their plans. In October 1965 students from across the country voiced their opposition to the draft as an intrusion into their lives and a disruption of their futures. One student remarked: "I would view service in the army as a waste of two years, at a time when I have a great deal of planning to do, a great need to straighten out my career." Another student added: "I don't think I'd particularly enjoy the sort of life that military service would require. . . . [C]ertainly there would be better ways to spend two or three years."[7] Another simply stated, "I've got better things to do than get shot at by a bunch of Vietcongs."[8] Richard Kapp, a draft dodger from Illinois who went to Canada, described himself as the son of a "lower-class racist," and refused to be inducted because he believed he had better choices: "What's in it for me? I don't want to die. I've got a money hang-up, a lot of livin' to do." Another draft dodger simply stated, "Why should I get my ass shot off for nothing."[9] Another student from the University of Michigan said that he would not accept a draft notice for Vietnam as it would cost him $16,000, and he had already paid $10,000 for college. According to Baskir and Strauss, such attitudes applied to millions of young men who had exemptions and deferments.[10] Many young Americans did not feel they had any obligation to serve the country in uniform, especially when they had better opportunities facing them in the prosperous economy of the 1960s. Most were dismissed as ungrateful and selfish. A Chicago draft board official commented on the situation this way: "I would say that 99 out of 100 do not want to go into the military service today. They feel they're not obligated to this country in any respect—they want to take and do not want to give anymore."11

For those inclined to avoid military service and carry on with their lives in the United States, there was no lack of support and information on college campuses by the middle of the 1960s. Student groups were created solely for the task of instructing men on how to avoid conscription. Most of these individuals and organizations did their advising in the open, without fear of retribution, making information on draft avoidance easily accessible to most university students and those with access to television. One student boasted of his plans for instructing young draftees in front of cameras for the *CBS Evening News*: "If you don't want to serve, there are any number of valid reasons, then there are ways to get out. . . . We're putting together a booklet that's going to run down everything that we've been able to find out about how you can get out of serving. . . . This book will talk about the standard things that have been done over and over—such as the feigning madness, the homosexuality, the bureaucratic ways of getting out, the conscientious-objector ways."12 Soon after, *The ABCs of Draft Dodging* was published by students at Berkeley, with headings that included: "Be a C.O.; Have a demonstration [which meant freaking out at the physical]; Refuse to sign; Be gay; Note from doctor; Jail record; Play psycho; Arrive drunk; Arrive high; Be an undesirable; Be a troublemaker [and] Bed-wetting."13

Organizations were bold in their efforts to assist and inform young men on how to circumvent the draft process. Universities, such as Wisconsin, hired full-time draft counselors to help students learn ways to keep their deferments. Even more conservative institutions, such as Harvard and Yale, saw professors working on their students' behalf. At Harvard, Dean Fred Glimp (following an appeal by 4,190 undergraduate students) sent a telegram to President Johnson asking "for de-escalation and negotiation with Vietnam." The telegram was signed by 54 percent of the Harvard faculty, prompting professor Edwin O. Reischauer to state, "I think it's remarkable that 54 percent of the Harvard faculty signed any statement. You couldn't get more than 80 percent of them on a statement to vote for motherhood."14 In April 1968, the *Christian Century's* editorial called for community draft counseling services. The column argued that "there are thousands of poor boys—white, Negro, Spanish-speaking, school dropouts—who have nowhere to turn for help in their case. . . . A young man facing possible death in Vietnam has only his wits to rely on." The editorial called on churches, high school teachers, university professors, pacifists, peace groups, as well as the greater community to act as counselors and instruct young men on how to avoid the draft.[15] Draft counselors, by most accounts, were plentiful—and successful in their efforts. David Caplan was one of hundreds of attorneys who specialized in draft avoidance across the country. Caplan belonged to a fraternity of attorneys who counseled potential draft dodgers for nominal fees, while charging blacks and poor whites "absolutely nothing." He remarked: "The first thing to realize is that anyone can get out . . . without doing anything illegal or extralegal. We are able to keep 99 percent of the people who walk in here out of the draft."[16]

It became clear that with determination one could find methods to avoid service without going underground or to prison. Would-be draft evaders could find information about avoidance techniques on university campuses, coffee houses and even classrooms. It became common knowledge that one could safely do so, and this was certainly the case for the expatriates who went to Canada. Ohio University history professor Jeffery Herf, once a member of Students for a Democratic Society (SDS) at the University of Wisconsin, Madison, comments on the situation this way: "Any man with an ounce of brains, money, or education could beat the system."[17] As the Notre Dame Survey suggests, the vast majority of men who dodged the draft were not protesting publicly or fleeing the country, but instead quietly used loopholes in the system, deferments or faked medical and psychological symptoms to disqualify themselves from military duty.

Avoidance, rather than outright evasion, was the safest and the most practical way of staying out of the draft. Several of the "ways and means" of avoiding conscription, such as pretending one was homosexual, actually worked quite well. For example, Maryland's director of Selective Service, Brigadier General Henry C. Stanwood, admitted the difficulty of assessing who was gay and who was faking: "As for the attempts to flunk the qualification test by feigning homosexuality or that sort of thing, this is harder to assess. We do not administer these tests; the Army does that at two examination stations used by Maryland inductees. But we would know immediately if the percentage flunking the test were to rise, and it hasn't."[18] Feigning homosexuality, however, was not uncommon. One official remarked that "the number of homosexuals seems to be growing."[19] Numerous men avoided service this way simply because it was impossible to determine who was actually gay. Sheri Gershon Gottlieb discovered several men who evaded induction by claiming they were homosexual. Among them was Hollywood actor Chevy Chase. A military psychiatrist asked Chase: "Do you like girls?" He replied that he did. He was asked if he liked boys, and he again replied affirmative. The psychiatrist then asked him "Which do you like better?" "Boys," Chase said.[20] Young men, such as Chase, were dismissed from consideration for having a "moral defect."[21]

Other methods of avoidance included deliberately scoring low on the IQ and other military tests in order to frustrate government workers and slow the military bureaucracy. One slightly puzzled and weary draft board employee stated: "I don't see how some of these college boys can make such low scores on their tests."22 In Texas, officials tried to explain why so many Texans were failing the IQ tests. The state director of Selective Service in Austin, Colonel Morris Schwartz, stated that "boys are more patriotically inclined in this part of the country. They have got their feet on the ground. Our main difference is that we're dumber than we are unhealthy. Our rejections for failing to meet mental standards are 2 to 1 over those for physical reasons."23

The most prevalent method to disqualify oneself was to fake medical and psychological symptoms. According to figures uncovered in the Notre Dame Survey, more than 1,000,000 men evaded service by feigning medical problems. Some faked drug problems by poking their arms with pins, while others actually injected heroin to make their symptoms appear more believable. Some draftees who suffered from allergies or asthma deliberately aggravated their ailments before their physical exams. Others went as far as to break bones, while one 19-year-old put a 22 caliber bullet in his foot.24 One evader explained that he failed the medical exam by ingesting "two handfuls of the contents of the Hoover vacuum cleaner." The man suffered from allergies, and his breathing became extremely labored in the physician's office. He had given himself a "terrible asthma attack."25 Another rubbed solvent on his feet and wore heavy wool socks all night with solvent on them in order to claim he was allergic to army-issue wool socks. He developed blisters so severe he could barely walk and was found unfit for the military.26 Max Ghiz pretended he could not read the eye chart, commenting to the examiner: "What eye chart?"27 Some men flunked their hearing tests, while one claimed he "doctored medical records . . . used many pens, and backdated remarks in the charts."28

Nearly one quarter of all who gained deferments and exemptions were turned away because of psychiatric problems. Students at some universities studied psychology texts to better able themselves to fake symptoms of mental illness; others stayed awake 48 to 72 hours prior to their medical exams so they would mildly hallucinate or appear listless and weak.29 Some went to great theatrical lengths to force disqualification. One man said that at the testing station he took a couple of hits of acid, and then would "just sit in the corner and cry."30 Another man, "who ceased bathing two weeks prior" to his exam, wrote on his evaluation sheet that his occupation was "wizard."31 One man described that he began "bleating on the floor, rolled up in a fetal position, and inside I'm thinking, 'Jesus, did I go too far?' "32 One man recalled sitting there "dripping blood onto the wooden bench, apparently sawing away at myself with a pocket knife." The next day he was classified as a "permanent 4-F."33 Others simply received assistance from sympathetic psychiatrists and psychologists, who wrote letters to draft boards on their behalf.[34] Others thought that persuading a psychiatrist at an induction center that one was mentally ill was going about it the hard way. Men were rejected for any manner of minor reasons, including hypersensitivity to bee stings, severe ingrown toenails, or too many or too obscene tattoos. Stiff arms, flat feet, or the loss of a finger or a trick knee could also disqualify one's induction. The most famous of the "trick knees" was that of New York Jets quarterback Joe Namath. Colonel Robert A. Bier, chief medical officer for the national Selective Service System, said that anyone who may later prove to be a hazard to himself or other soldiers could be turned down. According to Bier, the general rule was that "if in doubt, reject."[35]

Another method of evading the draft, or at least to avoid combat roles, was to become a conscientious objector. In March 1965, the U.S. Supreme Court declared that confirmed pacifists were conscientious objectors (CO), regardless of religious background.[36] Draftees could be classified 1-AO (a CO available for non-combat military service), 1-O (available for civilian work that would contribute to national health, safety, or interest), or 1-W (one who is currently, or has already completed, his civilian contribution). Taking the CO route still meant service to the country as the ones granted status were required to do some sort of rear-guard or public service role. Almost all of the 170,000 COs were required to perform two years in menial, low-paying positions—jobs which were always a considerable distance from their homes. Some worked as hospital orderlies and others as conservation officers in wilderness camps. For those who wished to avoid government service and carry on with their own lives, the CO route would still seem to be a major imposition.[37]

One method of lessening the chance of a combat role was to become a member of the National Guard or the reserves. Throughout the Vietnam era, the guard was known as one of the best ways to avoid going overseas. The majority of guardsmen were from affluent backgrounds, were better educated, and a greater percentage of them were white. Joining the guard to avoid combat became so well-known that for a time in 1968, under the pressure of Senator Richard Russell, about 15,000 guardsmen were sent to Vietnam. But this was short-lived. A million men served in either the reserves or the guard during the Vietnam era, and that brief period in 1968 was the only occasion when they were sent abroad. The National Guard and reservists continued to be a haven for draft evaders. One 1966 pentagon study found that 71 percent of guardsmen were motivated to join by draft considerations. By 1970, 90 percent of reservists and guardsmen were believed to be draft-motivated.[38]

Some men also used methods to slow or frustrate the Selective Service draft boards to avoid induction. This was especially true for informed and educated potential draftees who understood the workings of government bureaucracies. Potential 1-As learned that one effective tactic of stalling the process was to send in repeated changes of address, as it took the government months to process the information and determine where to send proper documentation. Some made the effort to change draft boards numerous times to slow the bureaucracy, until their draft eligibility expired.[39] The nature of draft boards themselves further complicated the various deferments and classifications. In the early 1960s there were more than 4,000 draft boards, staffed mostly by lower level civil service clerks, and policies on granting deferments varied from board to board. Even the policy of individual boards was in a constant state of flux. The system, in the estimation of one member, was "like an accordion. Sometimes you stretch it out and get generous with deferments, and then other times you squeeze it up tight." Sometimes it was simply luck—based on the mood of the local draft board, or how determined one was to resist induction.[40]

By far the most common method of avoiding the draft was educational deferments. University students, and high school students up to the age of 20, were exempt. While university graduate students were exempt until January 1968, when most deferments were ended, the system varied in its application. Local boards used their own discretion for both graduates and undergraduates. If a draftee came in and pleaded his case with a parent, teacher, or employer, they reduced their chance of induction with a sympathetic board. If the draft board considered a draftee a troublemaker, deferments could be withdrawn. Some students had their on-campus conduct scrutinized to determine if they were protesters and troublemakers. In Michigan, for example, draft officials began to investigate students arrested in sit-ins at the Ann Arbor draft board headquarters. Colonel Arthur Holmes, director of the Michigan Selective Service, stated that if it was found that the students in any way impeded the draft, their draft status would be changed from a 2-S (student deferment) to a 1-A without hesitation.[41] Other draft boards as early as 1965 began to insist that university students enroll in at least 15 credit hours to keep their deferments.[42] Keeping up one's grade point average was also important in staying out of the draft. Grades in universities were often referred to as "A, B, C, D, and Nam." Even Bs and Cs could affect one's draft classification. According to Baskir and Strauss, however, any graduating student or working man with connections could avoid the draft by having his employer lobby the local draft board to classify the young man as "essential" to the business. The draft boards' "rule of thumb" allowed business to designate certain employees as "indispensable." In such cases, special 2-As and 2-Cs were granted.[43]

One of the most effective, but perhaps least known, methods of evasion was simply failing to register for the draft at age 18. It was virtually impossible to correct this problem because it was a violation of U.S. law for anyone to cross-reference registrations with Social Security and Internal

Revenue files.[44]   Whatever the means employed, it is clear that for those with connections, education, or determination to avoid conscription, the draft system could be circumvented. Curtis Tarr, adjunct senior research fellow at the National Defense University, stated: "bewilderment comes, even yet, from trying to understand how the old system worked as well as it did."[45] Republican Congressman Alvin Konski from Wisconsin simply stated at the time: "If you are I-A you are a nobody. . . . You happened to get caught because you didn't know any better. If you are not 1-A, you have status."[46]

CLASS AND RACE

While there has never been equity among those who have served in the front lines of America's wars, it was not until Vietnam that the inequity became so apparent. Not only was there inequality in the percentage of minorities and under-class men who served in combat, but there were also inequities across the entire spectrum of conscripts. During the Vietnam era, having status was key for any young man who wished to avoid the draft. Even though many sympathetic health care professionals went out of their way to hand less-advantaged men (who were more likely to be drafted and see combat) deferments, it was the white middle class that was the most successful in taking advantage of anti-draft programs and induction loopholes. Even at help centers at predominately black colleges the vast majority of those who sought assistance were white, educated, and middle-class.[47] It was common knowledge that for white middle-class college students, there was "ample information—and widespread agreement: the idiosyncrasies of the draft boards and the ease with which white middle-class youth are avoiding the draft have created one of the most inequitable institutions in the country."[48]

Cast in this light, it is interesting to recall that the vast majority of expatriates in Canada came from white, middle- to upper middle-class homes. Most were college educated or were about to enter or graduate from university, and thus were clearly in the best position to avoid the draft and remain in America.[49] Perhaps most striking is that this group of men also had the smallest chance to actually see combat in Vietnam, had they accepted induction. The Notre Dame Survey determined that middle- to high-income college graduates comprised only 7 to 9 percent of combat troops in Vietnam, and at least one-half of this number were actually volunteers who requested combat placements.[50] Essentially, young men in college or with university education had little or no chance of carrying a rifle through a rice patty. In his book, *The New Exiles*, Roger Neville Williams effectively points out this reality:

In 1969, for example, out of 283,000 men drafted, only 28,500 had attended college. Even Stewart Alsop . . . could correctly point out that "the radical young, especially in the prestigious Eastern Ivy League colleges, talk as though they were a lost generation, condemned by the system and hauled away to Vietnam and killed or wounded—this has been the theme of many a youthful valedictorian. But it is nonsense."[51]

Not surprisingly, very few sons of Congressmen saw the front lines in Vietnam. As of 1970, out of the 234 sons of Congressmen who were of draft age, 118 received deferments, only 49 wore a military uniform, and none of these served in Vietnam. Twenty eight served in support positions; none was killed or went missing, and only one, the son of Congressman Clarence Long, received a leg wound.[52] It was these sorts of imbalances that eventually led more conservative columnists, such as Stewart Alsop, to conclude:

Under the system, the clever sons of prosperous parents managed to avoid the draft entirely, or if they were very unlucky, they were actively encouraged by the system to escape into safe, non-combat jobs. Meanwhile, the sons of blue-collar workers or small farmers or blacks, were drafted into the infantry, and went stolidly off to fight, and too often to die, in Vietnam. The abominable system was so devised that by 1970 almost all the front-line "grunts" were draftees, while the regulars had cushy rear-echelon jobs.[53]

By the late 1960s and early 1970s, middle-class men had become so adept at manipulating deferments that weary draft officials realized that the real problem was not evasion but avoidance. The issue of concern for the draft boards was that they were not equipped or trained for the strategies employed by those who were determined to use any means to avoid conscription.[54]

Black Americans, in contrast, had one of the more distinct disadvantages with conscription. With fewer secured employment and education deferments, they had limited options to the draft. Without connections, higher education and job skills, going to Canada, for many, was not a realistic alternative. As a result, they comprised a much smaller percentage of draft evaders in Canada. When blacks did go to Canada, however, they went often not as draft dodgers but as deserters from the military.[55] In 1969, Black draft dodger E. J. Fletcher, himself a product of the black middle class, gained some insightful impressions of the black resistance community, and the differences in class and race between deserters and draft dodgers. Fletcher found that draft evaders tended to be from middle-class backgrounds while deserters were from a poorer class both economically and educationally. Fletcher said that it was not uncommon to encounter a black deserter with little more than a 10th grade education. Fletcher recalls meeting many more black deserters from the military than draft dodgers. He explained that one of the reasons he felt there were not more black draft dodgers in Canada was that for young black men growing up in the United States, although the military was "just as racist" as the rest of American society, it provided an opportunity to have a job, receive training, and receive "three squares a day with no hang-ups." Fletcher maintained that the military provided opportunities for blacks that were not attainable in the rest of society, and that wasn't the case for middle-class whites. "Thirty percent of the army in Vietnam is black. Also I think of the alternatives, what's open to you, is much more available to whites, especially white middle-class college kids who've been through the whole Vietnam peacenik trip, the same trip that I went through more or less. Black kids don't have the same access to information."[56]

This fact and the realization that disproportionate numbers of young blacks were being sent off to fight in Vietnam were two of the most contentious issues facing the black leadership in the 1960s. Julian Bond, a black legislator from the state of Georgia, joined other leaders and spoke out publicly against drafting black men into the Vietnam War. Other leaders in the black community, such as Malcolm X, Adam Clayton Powell, comedian Dick Gregory and boxer Muhammad Ali spoke out against further black participation in the war. In fact, the black movement converged with the anti-war movement and many black civil rights workers took up the cause against conscription. In the summer of 1965, the Mississippi Freedom Democratic Party began to issue leaflets against black participation in the war, viewing the draft in racial terms. The party saw the U.S. government as an imperialist state that was using its war powers to oppress and conquer other people of color around the world. One of the leaflets read: "No one has the right to ask us to risk our lives and kill other Colored People in Santo Domingo and Vietnam, so that White America can get richer. We will be looked upon as traitors by all colored People of the world if the Negro people continue to fight and die without a cause." The Nation of Islam also entered the fray, stressing that black Americans were a colonized people, and thus had more in common with Third-World revolutionaries, such as those in North Vietnam, than they did with white America. Even celebrities, such as heavyweight boxing champion Muhammad Ali, openly opposed the war, claiming that he was exempt from the draft because he was a minister in the Nation of Islam. In June 1966, the Student Nonviolent Coordinating Committee (SNCC) adopted a formal position paper against the Vietnam War. It stated:

We believe the United States government has been deceptive in claims of concern for the freedom of the Vietnamese people, just as the government has been deceptive in claiming concern for the freedom of the colored people in such other countries as the Dominican Republic, the Congo, South Africa, Rhodesia and the United States itself.[57]

For the first few years of the war, the most conspicuously silent person concerning the war and black participation was Reverend Martin Luther King, Jr. King had maintained a more moderate position on American military involvement in Southeast Asia, and was caught between the vocal SNCC and the Black Panthers, who denounced the war as racial imperialism, and the more moderate NAACP and the Urban League, which were still in the throes of the civil rights movement. All that changed in 1967 as King made one of the more eloquent anti-war statements of the decade. Delivered in a sermon from the pulpit at Manhattan's Riverside Church to an audience of 3,000, King said that America was

faced with the cruel irony of watching Negro and white boys on TV screens as they kill and die together for a nation that has been unable to seat them together in the same schools. . . . Somehow this madness must cease. I speak as a child of God and brother to the suffering poor of Vietnam and the poor of America who are paying the double price of smashed hopes at home and death and corruption in Vietnam. . . . The initiative to stop must be ours.[58]

Despite the growing number of voices telling them not to cooperate with the war-effort, young blacks not only continued to accept conscription, but they also continued to volunteer. Why? African Americans, as draft dodger E. J. Fletcher pointed out, had fewer opportunities than their white counterparts, and many needed to take whatever they could. Unlike middle-class whites, blacks in the 1950s and 1960s were fighting for civil rights. They were struggling for inclusion into mainstream society. While gaining entrance into the military itself was not a civil rights issue, blacks desired equal access, participation and acceptance into the mainstream American community.[59] Military service was clearly one of the better methods of achieving this, and for some, it was a way of making a living and a chance to begin a career. It was also one of the few areas in American public life that was desegregated. While there were integrated units in the Korean War, Vietnam was the first war that troops were fully integrated. For most black Americans, the prospect of leaving for Canada with university degrees and bright futures in tow was unthinkable. While arguably just as alienated and disconnected from American society as white expatriates, the majority of black Americans did not have the means to sojourn north to compete with Canadians for employment. Blacks accepted their draft notices in large numbers despite the fact that much of the black leadership was highly vocal in its efforts to dissuade them from enlisting.[60]

Like black Americans, disadvantaged whites and minorities also had fewer options to military service. With lower incomes and less education, they had fewer viable and realistic opportunities for success in American society. Their horizons and expectations were different. Their families also lacked the incomes for trips overseas or to Canada when they were children, and thus, they knew little about their options outside the United States. Military service was one of the better opportunities to leave their small towns, farms and urban areas, and begin careers with some sort of future. They, like black Americans, also had fewer marketable and transferable skills, which would have made temporary or permanent relocation to Canada difficult.

The result was general inequalities throughout most combat battalions. This point was illustrated clearly by General S.L.A. Marshall: "In the average rifle company, the strength was 50 percent composed of Negroes, Southwestern Mexicans, Puerto Ricans, Guananians, Nisei, and so on. But a real cross-section of American youth? Almost never."[61] It was this injustice based on race and class that was so troubling for so many families who saw their sons and brothers go off to the front lines to fight and, too often, to die. Their frustration was magnified not only by the loss of a family member, but the knowledge that the price their family was paying was not shared by the wealthy. In Robert Coles' *The Middle Americans*, a firefighter tells of his feelings about losing his son in Vietnam.

I'm bitter. You bet your goddamn dollar I'm bitter. It's people like us who give up our sons for the country. The business people, they run the country and make money from it. The college types, the professors, they go to Washington and tell the government what to do. . . . Their sons don't end up in the swamps over there, in Vietnam. No sir. They're deferred, because they're in school, or they get sent to safe places. Or they get out with all those letters they have from their doctors. Ralph told me. He told me what went on at his physical. He said most of the kids were from average homes; and the few rich kids there were, they all had big-deal letters saying they weren't eligible. Let's face it: if you have a lot of money, or if you have the right connections, you don't end up on a firing line in the jungle over there, not unless you want to. . . . I hate those peace demonstrators. . . . What bothers me about the peace crowd is that you can tell from their attitude, the way they look and what they say, that they don't really love this country. Some of them almost seem glad to have a chance to criticize us. . . . Let them leave if they don't like it here. My son didn't die so they can look filthy and talk filthy and insult everything we believe in and everybody in the country—me and my wife and people here on the street, and on the next street, and all over. . . . The world hears those demonstrators making their noise. The world doesn't hear me, and it doesn't hear a single person I know.[62]

The expatriates, as sons of the white middle- and upper middle class, clearly had choices and alternatives to military service. Despite their litany of options, they, by and large, passed up the deferments open to them and moved to Canada. Their actions, combined with their testimonies, reveal that their decisions had less to do with the draft—and the unlikely prospect of military service in Vietnam—than it did with their feelings and attitudes about the United States. Most did not pursue CO or non-combat positions, nor did they become protesters against the draft, as they felt no obligation to stay and try to change the system. This contrasts sharply with those who protested vigorously against the war. That the expatriates passed up on the many options open to them to avoid the draft says much about deeper motivations for their choice to leave for Canada. In their actions and attitudes, they contrasted sharply with the thousands in their class who used loopholes, connections, and deferments to avoid the draft. They differed also with the anti-war crowd who burned draft cards and filled jails as the battles raged on the streets of America. When the draft boards called them to serve their country, these conscripts cast a permanent eye north.

5

Northward Bound: Dodging the Deferments, Evading the Country

We the undersigned men of draft age wish to announce that we refuse to be drafted into the United States Armed Forces. By withholding our participation we are saying 'no' to the continuing barbarism of the Vietnam War. We are responsible for our actions. We openly say 'no' to conscripted military service. *Our refusal to participate in the madness of the Vietnam War in no way implies a renunciation of our country. Our act of refusal is in fact an act of loyalty because it aims at redeeming rather than smothering human potentiality here in the United States and around the world.* We are taking this stand both to assert our personal integrity and self-respect and to try to stem the kind of assumptions and policies exemplified by the Vietnam War. We are urging all young men of draft age who can conscientiously do so, to assume responsibility for their lives and to join us in this stand.[1]

In April 1967, 127 members of the Wisconsin Draft Resistance Union signed the above "We Won't Go" declaration, stating their clear refusal to fight in the Vietnam War. This sort of action was not restricted to the University of Wisconsin. College campuses across the United States saw similar acts of student protest as public resistance against conscription occurred with greater frequency as the decade progressed. Thousands of young men and women organized sit-ins, marches and rallies; published articles; passed out fliers; and spoke publicly, not only against the war, but the country's direction. As seen in the previous chapter, young men of draft age educated themselves on the "ways and means" of avoiding induction, and organizations were created solely to help educate potential draft evaders on methods of beating the draft. Like the students who signed the Wisconsin declaration, the majority of those who publicly protested wanted more than just to avoid military service; they were actively demonstrating for a change in direction and ideology on the part of the government. They made it clear that they cared about American society. Several of these groups, including Students for a Democratic Society (SDS), joined forces with members of the black civil rights movement to work to change society at the grassroots level. By the mid-1960s, the war became the focal point for most of the decade's reform movements. The key section of the Wisconsin pronouncement was that the signers' stated refusal to fight in Vietnam did not mean a rejection of their country. If anything, the statement declared their concern for the country's future and demonstrated their willingness to be activists to reform the nation rather than renounce it.

The term draft dodger seems to be straightforward and easily defined. But the phrase became universally tagged on anyone who avoided military service. There are, however, clear distinctions among resisters. Dodgers who protested the draft yet remained committed to reforming the country, along with others who simply shunned military service and quietly avoided induction by using loopholes, exemptions, and deferments within the draft system, have fundamental differences with those who left the country permanently. A comparison of the expatriates in Canada with state-side draft evaders further illustrates that for the Canadian-bound dodgers, more than the Vietnam War motivated their actions.

When faced with conscription, the expatriates made little or no effort to explore alternatives readily open to them to avoid the military and remain in the United States. Most simply left the country on the arrival of their first draft notice. This is despite the fact that as a group, they were in the best position of all draftees to avoid military service. While they believed the war to be morally reprehensible, their experiences since childhood led them to pass up deferments and loopholes in the draft system afforded by their class.

EVASION

Draft evader Ron Needer was 19 in the summer of 1965 when he received his draft letter. He was in his second year of university and was surprised at the news. He thought he was safe for an additional two years and took his induction badly: "I went to my room and practically screamed at my roommate—well, not practically, I did scream at him to get the fuck out and leave me alone. He was with his girlfriend, and was pretty pissed at me. I was shaking and upset, and thought it was hopeless, and I remember that there was no way in hell that I was going to fight for Uncle Sam." Needer's grades were not as good "as they could have been, and I guess they thought I would make good cannon fodder." Needer wanted to complete business school and find a job. It never occurred to him to look for a loophole to avoid induction: "I really had had enough. I grew up in a community that we were not welcome in, and I finally got out of the South and into college and they wanted me to go into the military to fight. No, it wasn't a gut wrenching move to pack my bags and leave the country. Most of my credits were transferable to Canada, so I went. Leaving my family was difficult, but not the United States." For a short time he considered applying as a conscientious objector, but was uncomfortable with complying in any manner with the government, especially when it involved the Vietnam War. "It was not something that I felt was particularly appetizing. The war, and I'm not just saying this in retrospect, but the war was reprehensible to me then. 'What the heck were we doing [in Vietnam]' was my thought. I thought that our country was an embarrassment on so many levels, and the war was just another bad pull to the right, and I really don't think that was the right way, or the way that our Founding Fathers had imagined we would go—fighting a war halfway around the world. Where is that in the American Constitution? It was not a difficult decision to pack up and go. I just left." Needer's reaction is typical of a number of the expatriates.[2]

Draft dodger Michael Fischer was ill most of his senior year with mononucleosis, and his grades suffered. A few weeks into his second quarter he was notified that he was to take his physical examination by the military. Even though he had lost weight and "looked like hell," Fischer did not challenge his notice: "I didn't think it was worth struggling over. I just concluded that the way the system worked that I would have gotten screwed over anyway and they would have had me on the first plane to Vietnam. I knew I wasn't going from Day 1, and I'm not much of an actor." Instead of being frightened about the prospect of fleeing to Canada, draft dodgers like Fischer were actually excited by the opportunity to have a fresh start. "I can't remember being terribly captivated by public service, and really wanted to get ahead like my father; and not being at all patriotic I felt no obligation to sacrifice my time to the government."[3]

Following high school, draft evader Aston Davis decided to work with his father and uncles in Texas to finance his way to Europe, but then he was drafted. Davis had saved little money, and thoughts about fleeing to Europe were short-lived. He refused the help of his parents (who supported him in his decision to leave) and decided to strike out on his own. Since he felt Europe was too expensive, he emptied his bank account and left for Canada. Several of his acquaintances were drafted and had complied out of a sense of duty. Davis saw it differently: "I could never see the reason why anyone had to be forced by the government to fight in the military and give up your life for some hare-brained war on the other side of the world. I did not grow up with that sense of red-blooded patriotism that so many others were so eager to buy into in Texas, and the thought of protesting like a barking dog turned my stomach." Davis did not think it was worth trying to beat the system as he "believed that you don't beat the system in those situations, the system beats you." He, like many others, had no intention of "groveling" before the draft board. "It was really no problem as I was not pining to stay in the country anyway."

Davis exhibits a common feeling of disconnection that the expatriates had about the country. They thought the transition of moving to Canada would not be a major burden. "I never really felt, you know, connected to anything much there and thought I could be just as happy anywhere else and even go to university when I was ready, not because of the draft, and that's what I did." Davis admits that he knew "a little" about Canada before his problems with the draft, and began to do some research to learn if it would be a place he could call home. "It was difficult to find out anything much about Canada living in the States—they don't teach you anything about Canada in school. Universities rarely offer courses on Canadian history, and nothing was ever said about Canada or Canadians on television. This was a time before the Internet, so getting quick information on my possible destination was difficult." Davis learned what he could from the library, and spoke to some acquaintances who had vacationed in the Rocky Mountains in Alberta, and decided that he could make it his home. Davis was in Canada less than two weeks after receiving his draft notice.[4]

Several of the draft dodgers were resigned to the fact that they could not avoid induction, and even if they were successful and remained in America, the nation would eventually demand of them other service they were unable to give. Carroll Obline, for example, believed that his draft notice represented all that was wrong with the country and that trouble was going to follow him throughout his life. "I shook my head when I got the notice. It was just like when I was a kid, and things were out of my hands." Obline had recently graduated from college and had begun work at a graphics firm when he received the news. "I thought I was away from the worst of it, you know, growing up in the South, up to here with militarism and the gung-ho mentality, and people who either didn't want you around, or wanted you to conform to some strict ethos. I never wanted any of it." Obline did not have any thoughts of accepting his draft notice and failed to show up for his medical exam. He, like others, had paid little attention to the war and the protests against it in college and felt no reason to begin. "I really wanted to be just left alone without anyone telling me what to do and that I was wrong. I had enough of that when I was a kid." Obline did not try to find ways to circumvent the draft board, and although he was aware of campus groups which counseled potential draft evaders, he was unmoved: "I was very sympathetic to the cause, people were right, and it was right for them to dust it up in the streets, but it was not the thing I felt passionate about even though it affected me in a direct way. I didn't see the point of struggling to avoid the draft; the system was confusing and the deck was stacked against me, and even if I had beaten the draft, somehow they would have gotten me another way." Obline did not consider an alternative service in the National Guard, or as a CO, as he believed that "the country had never done anything much for me. I honestly can not remember a time when I felt the tugs of patriotism and nationalism, which, without question, set me apart from the people I was raised around."[5]

Brian Linton was beginning his first year of graduate school in 1969 when he was called in by his local draft board. Most deferments for grad school had been phased out, and Linton did not attempt to find other methods to gain deferments or protest his induction. He, like several expatriates, knew from the first moment he received the news that he would leave the country: "There was never a doubt of what I was going to do. I was no protester and was not all starry-eyed about changing the country like a bunch of people seemed to be. I knew what I wanted to do and that was to continue on in graduate school and not get myself killed for a country that I never felt any allegiance to, as bad and ungrateful as that may sound. No one else was in my shoes, and I looked out for myself." Linton was not aware of the loopholes to avoid conscription and stay in the country and was not terribly interested in discovering them: "I knew what I wanted. I knew from reading that I could resume my life quite well in Canada, without the problem of losing my draft protection again even if I had wrangled out of it once. Three years was a long time in which to get drafted and I was only twenty-three. [Twenty-six was the maximum age for draft eligibility.] And besides I wasn't too keen on America in those days." Linton recalls that some people he knew were activists, but he was not one of them: "They had great hopes, but I think history has proven them to be in vain."[6]

Draft evader Carl McCrosky had a 2-S draft protection at the University of Kentucky as an undergraduate, but when he moved to Ann Arbor to begin graduate studies, he lost his draft protection. Soon after his arrival, he was called to Detroit for his medical exam. He was number 69 in the new draft lottery. "It was preordained that I was going to be drafted." He did not consider himself to be a "left-winger" but a moderate. He briefly considered going underground, but the radical route did not appeal to him.[7] When his draft board realized that he might be a problem, they offered him a CO exemption for religious reasons and tried to enlist the help of his father. McCrosky refused. "I was an atheist to my core, and appalled by the offer." He felt caught in the middle; he could stay and cooperate with the system or take the radical approach and disappear underground. But neither appealed to him as he wished to complete graduate school and pursue his career. He described his predicament with the draft as "a watermelon seed being squeezed out between two fingers. There was a radical course and there was the cooperating with the system course, and both of those just appalled me, and so I got squeezed out of the country—'bing.' I felt I had no choice in the matter to remain consistent with my own beliefs and political and moral beliefs, [and] there was nothing that I could do which involved staying in the country. So the decision to go to Canada was in a sense preordained. There was nothing rational in it. I had to."

McCrosky's refusal to cooperate with his draft board and gain a deferment was typical of the majority of the expatriate narratives. Their feelings of personal conscience and autonomy made them refuse to accept legal means to avoid military service, which, at times, was a rare occurrence in their home communities. McCrosky knew that there were few draft dodgers from Southern states, such as South Carolina. "That is the kind of culture that I came from—very militaristic, and devoted to the system and there is no questioning it. And the conflict between that and what I am, to me, is one of the defining characteristics of my life." This feeling of cultural and political alienation seems to be a key element in several dodger testimonies, and says much about McCrosky's decision to avoid service and go to Canada. Some members of McCrosky's family were less than pleased with his decision to head north and avoid military duty. His uncle, who was a colonel in the army, and his uncle's wife were particularly distressed with their nephew's actions. "They were career army people, [and] of course [were] appalled—the wife more than the husband by my decision." His father's sister was also "shocked" by what he did. One of the more interesting aspects of his family's reaction, however, came in the form of a letter from a "radical" uncle in Boston. "He wrote condemning me for what I did, saying that I should have gone into the army to subvert it from within." After McCrosky had been in Canada for awhile, his parents began to accept and agree with their son's position and became a "rock" of support for him.[8]

The majority of these expatriates, like McCrosky, refused to become conscientious objectors. It was indicative of their refusal to appear, even passively or indirectly, to be aiding the war effort, or to be forced into public service. As a result they neglected to utilize some well-known ways to avoid the war—namely to become a member of the reserves or the National Guard. Some dodgers, such as John Conway, were willing to do alternative, nonmilitary public service, but were declined. Conway, prior to the draft, split time between a Catholic monastery and completing a degree at Marquette following high school. He recalls that he was "sort of in another world over those four years, not especially tuned in to the social and political happenings of the day." Conway was never involved in any protest movements, but knew that when he left the Order in 1967 that he would lose his draft protection and did it anyway because "[he] had plans for [his] life." Conway was drafted within months of leaving the monastery: "The war just fell in my lap . . . and I had other things to do in my life. . . . I wanted to be an educator." Conway entered graduate school to restore his deferment protection, but, in 1968, deferments for most graduate students ended. Unlike many of the other expatriates, he made several trips to his local draft board in a vain attempt to gain some sort of deferment. But, in step with other expatriates, challenging the system through public protest or going underground, did not sit well with him: "I was from a straight middle-class background. I wanted a career and I wanted to pursue my own interests in psychology." Conway opted for Canada quite quickly with no thoughts of going back home. He remembers having "not much nationalism as I left so quickly. There wasn't a great wrenching away from America. I didn't have those strong nationalistic allegiances to America."[9]

Brandon Hockwald, on leaving high school, "traveled across the country, playing guitars and writing what· [he] hoped [would] be the great American novel." Hockwald wanted to grow and learn something about himself and others, and experience life on the road, before returning to university to study English and creative writing. But a draft notice sent to his parents' home in Denver in 1966 changed his plans and the course of his life: "I remember calling home from a pay-phone in Sante Fe, New Mexico, to find out how the family was, and Mom told me I had a notice from the Selective Service or something, so I asked her to open it and read it to me. When I found out, I almost died. My mother was upset. Both her and Dad were dead set against the war from Kennedy on." Hockwald had planned not to return to school for two years, and had no intention of changing his plans for the purpose of gaining a deferment. So with little more thought, he returned home and, with the financial support of his parents, made his way across the border into British Columbia. As with other draft dodgers, borders held little significance: "I didn't have a patriotic bone in my body. I think I was raised that way. I remember not thinking much about student protests against the war, even when the war was affecting me. All those people who were out protesting against the war, I didn't really get it. I was just so wrapped up in my own plans that the country and the college demonstrators who were trying to fix it meant little to me, as bad as that may seem today."[10]

Baskir and Strauss observed that "about one third of all exiled draft-resisters refused to accept deferments and exemptions for which they apparently qualified."[11] One of the reasons they cite is that these men did not make the effort to find accurate information to avoid service. One draft dodger who went north to Winnipeg, Manitoba, did so because his self-admitted paranoia made it impossible for him to examine his options. Another young man said that the process left him bitter and disillusioned so he neglected to investigate his options.[12] Roger Neville Williams found similar examples from draft dodgers he encountered in the late 1960s and early 1970s while doing research in Canada. The vast majority of the expatriates interviewed for this book expressed little desire to remain in the United States, and their primary concern was carrying on with their lives and careers that were at times well underway.[13]

Draft dodger Timothy Unger graduated with a degree in electrical engineering and was beginning his career when he received his 1-A (available for military duty) classification. His employer offered to help him with the draft board, but Unger declined: "I didn't want to bother anyone else with my problems and really didn't think it was worth the hassle. I thought that the way the country operated, I would get caught sooner or later. I was in great shape, and I wasn't about to pretend that I was gay for a draft board. I also did not want to pretend to be mentally incompetent as that would not have looked good for future job prospects had that gotten out." Like Hockwald, Unger wanted to focus on his career and had no intention to fight in the army "with a rifle in my hand or sitting behind a desk in the military. . . . I didn't believe in official public service, especially to the government or to the military, and was not won over by any patriotic rhetoric and never was since I was a kid. Fighting for 'my' country and giving up a portion, or all, of my future, seemed crazy. I simply was not going to do it; I didn't care enough to try to find ways to beat my classification. It was a signal to me that it was time to leave the country." Unger made his arrangements to leave quickly with the active support of his mother, but not his father, the career navy man: "My father and I [sigh] came to blows on the night before I left. . . . Mom had stepped in between us, and I accidentally hit her on the back of the head. It was—it was a terrible scene. I should have just left, but I was a kid and had to explain to my Dad why he was wrong and I was right and how the country was full of shit, and all that, and he was furious."[14]

Albert Caldwell's family was also angry and incredulous with his intention to dodge the draft: "My father said that I was a shame to the family and should be arrested for treason. Mom was equally upset as her Dad and my uncle had both served in the navy. The only support I got from her is when the old man actually picked up the phone to call the police on me, and I still think to this day that he was serious." Caldwell's mother gave him the money to finance his trip to Canada. "I took a year off from school because that was what I wanted to do. I knew I was tempting fate, but I really didn't care. I learned how to take care of myself growing up as a 'Yankee' in Lynchburg, Virginia." Most of his possessions were at his parents' home, so after receiving his draft notice, he returned to his father's hostile greeting. "I wasn't surprised at it. Things were not great growing up there and leaving and going far away seemed best. I did not have the heart to go underground or to become a clown to fool some draft committee. I wanted to move ahead with life. I made a good choice." Caldwell explains that his choices were motivated by more than just the Vietnam War. "I had been at odds with

American society and life since I was a kid, and obviously my family relationship was strained at the best of times. I decided it was best to start over somewhere else, and I had no plans to return."15

RADICALS OR CONSERVATIVES?

The expatriates stood in stark contrast to the draft dodgers who remained in the United States and protested against the draft. While the expatriates did not protest on the streets, burn draft cards, or even contemplate it, young men across the United States were highly demonstrative in their opposition not only to the draft, but U.S. foreign policy. While thousands of young men left for Canada, many others stayed at home and participated in public rallies and protests against the war. "We Won't Go" type pronouncements became commonplace on university campuses by 1966. The events were highly visible outings designed to attract public and media attention. One of the more memorable of these events took place in December 1966 when 175 students from Cornell University set their draft cards ablaze. Martin Jezer, editor at the time of *Win* magazine, participated in the event. While Jezer believed the student actions were in the great American tradition of standing up to tyranny, he makes it clear that the acts did not constitute a renunciation of the country:

To destroy one's draft card is to place one's conscience before the dictates of one's government. [It] is the highest tradition of human conduct. This country was not created by men subservient to law and government. It was created and made and made great by civil disobedients like Quakers who refused to compromise their religion to suit the Puritan theocracy . . . by [the] Sons of Liberty who burned stamps to protest the Stamp Act and who dumped tea in Boston harbor . . . by black Americans who refused to ride in the back of the bus; and by the more than one hundred young Americans already in prison for refusing to acquiesce in the misguided actions of their government. So when people tell me that I have no respect for law and order and that I do not love my country, I reply: "Jefferson, Tom Paine, Garrison, Thoreau, A. J. Muste, The Freedom Riders, these are my countrymen whom I love; with them I take my stand."16

As Jezer points out, hundreds of draft evaders, on principle, went to prison rather than report to their draft boards. As early as 1966, the Justice Department reported that 827 draft violators had been sent to federal prisons.17 These men maintained that their actions were not renunciations of their country, but rather, actions which were motivated by a desire to change and redeem the nation's future.

Protest to the war took on many forms during the decade. Activists blocked supply trains and troop trains, lay in front of military vehicles, and staged protests and sit-ins outside recruiting offices and military institutions across the country. Many were arrested for civil disobedience. But, tragically, some demonstrators against U.S. policy in Southeast Asia made the ultimate statement. Far from simply burning draft cards, some individuals in Saigon and in the United States burned themselves alive in protest. Among them were Quakers, such as 32-year-old Norman Morrison. Morrison drenched himself in gasoline and set himself ablaze outside the Pentagon under the window of Defense Secretary Robert McNamara. Less than a week later, Roger La Porte set himself on fire outside the United Nations in New York, and in Detroit an 82-year-old woman named Alice Hertz immolated herself in protest against the war.[18]

Some expatriates claim that their decisions to leave for Canada were also, in part, acts of protests against the war. They suggest that by going to Canada, they did their part in ending American involvement in Southeast Asia. Their overall behavior, however, suggests they were uninterested in reforming their country. Most of these expatriates knew that when they left the United States, they had no intention of returning, despite the war's outcome. Indeed, many American anti-war activists at the time maintained that the draft dodgers who fled to Canada were not doing their part to end the conflict. Anti-war activists, such as Joan Baez and Stokely Carmichael, were outspoken in their criticism of the dodgers who fled to Canada. In 1967, for example, Carmichael told a crowd of Canadian anti-war students in Toronto that: "Those cats can't kick the bastards in Washington from here. They oughta come on back and go to jail with me, if racist McNamara has the guts to draft me."[19] Even Students for a Democratic Society (SDS) found the dodgers' actions suspect, and not radical acts that aided the anti-war movement. In *The New Exiles*, published in 1970, Roger Neville Williams, himself a deserter, wrote that "for a short time SDS groups considered going to Canada a radical act," although they recommended that it would be better to remain in the country and harass draft boards "for as long as one could, and then if possible, going underground." SDS president Tom Hayden was also concerned that the draft dodgers who went to Canada were not necessarily having much of an effect on resistance to the war. Hayden hoped that the dodgers would come home and enter the protest movement. But, as Williams pointed out, such a development was unlikely as at least one-half of the evaders he met in Canada had no intention of returning. "Tactically, this may be sound, but [Hayden's] thinking does not recognize the exiles, perhaps half of the total, who have no intention of ever returning to the U.S. and who are not even thinking about it yet."[20]

Several expatriates also doubt that their moves to Canada were motivated primarily by a desire to stop the war, or that those actions had any effect on the course of the war. Nick Theason, for instance, remarks: "I never thought of us, the ones who left the country, [as having] any impact at all on U.S. policy in regards to Vietnam. We really weren't protesters as we left the country and took our voices and opposition with us. What we did by leaving the country was to in fact silence our voices in regard to the war." Curt Erickson agrees: "[L]eaving the country, vowing never to return, as far as I'm concerned, was not an act of protest in trying to reform the country. We were saying 'sayonara.' I think it's easy in retrospect to look back and say that 'we did our part to end U.S. imperialism' and all that, but in reality we were doing it for ourselves and no one else."[21]

The most vocal and radical of the exile community in Canada were not draft dodgers but deserters from the military. Deserters were much more organized and committed to speak out against American foreign policy in Southeast Asia, and worked to gain amnesty for themselves back in the United States. These deserters were also bent on embarrassing the government and the military by protesting against their country on foreign soil. There were more than 500,000 desertions between 1966 and 1973. The majority of those who served in the armed forces in Vietnam were from the working class a large percentage of the deserters were also from lower socioeconomic classes. In contrast to the draft evaders, this group protested loudly against the war in Canada. Some deserter groups even offered up their own manifestos against the draft while in exile. The following is an excerpt from the "Deserters' Manifesto" from the American Deserters Committee in Montreal in 1968. It exemplifies the political consciousness of these military deserters:

We American deserters living in Montreal, in opposition to the U.S. imperialist aggression in Vietnam, have banded together to form the American Deserters Committee. We deserters and associates view ourselves as an integral part of the world-wide movement for fundamental social change. We express support and solidarity with the National Liberation Front of South Vietnam and the black liberation struggle at home. We are prepared to fight side-by-side with anyone who wants to bring fundamental social change to the U.S.

Our aim is to help U.S. deserters and draft resisters gain a more political outlook toward their own actions—to show them that desertion and draft resistance are in fact political moves. Forced to live our lives as political exiles, we view ourselves as victims of the same oppression as the Vietnamese and the American people, not only the minority groups, but also the broad masses of American people who are becoming more aware of the need for change. We will work to develop the political consciousness of American deserters and to form a well-educated and determined group which will have a clear understanding of U.S. internal and international polices, especially those which affect Canada and Quebec.

We express solidarity with our fellow servicemen who are still in the military, and as yet are unable to resist in the same way—DESERT. We recognize U.S. imperialism as the greatest threat to the progress of freedom and self-determination for all people, and view desertion as the most effective way to resist.[22]

While some draft evaders were involved with similar types of political activities, the majority tended not to be involved with the anti-war movement once they arrived in Canada, and did not consider themselves to be living in exile. Dodger Carroll Obline echoes the sentiments of Curt Erickson and Nick Theason concerning a disinterest in protest. "I didn't care about the war in any great sense. I wanted it to end of course, and I didn't want anyone to die there, but I thought the country was a hopeless place, and never for a moment did I consider that my actions in leaving the country, in any way, affected the outcome or the policies of the government. How could a few thousand men leaving the country affect the foreign policy of a superpower with 250 million people? I have never understood that illusion."[23]

A CLIMATE OF SUPPORT

The expatriates looked on their decisions as highly personal choices, not connected directly to any group or united effort. The interesting aspect of this is that when these future expatriates were attending university, campus protests and the growing mood in the country against the war provided some with the additional support they needed to dodge the draft, and the country. Draft dodger Dale Friesen believes that the liberal atmosphere at the University of Illinois provided him with the opportunity to be much more adventurous in his actions: "My experience with observing the campus protests, even though I was not involved, seemed to steel me for the decision that I made when I was drafted. It may have been a lot different had it been 1956, instead of 1966." Friesen was a transplanted Northerner who grew up in the South and believed that university life allowed him to trust his instincts. It was a climate quite different from his home community: "I was forever watching my step and what I said in public, because it always seemed to get me in trouble as a kid. There was a shell, or a ceiling, on my personal freedoms and opinions that I always wanted to break free of." University changed that for Friesen. "There was this intensity—an energy in the air—a feeling that one could do or say anything and have it validated. It was truly a remarkable time."[24] Dodger Timothy Unger agreed that there was an "anything goes" atmosphere on campus: "Being disenfranchised from America was not viewed as a bad thing. I didn't have to hide my feeling of disconnection and unhappiness with the country. It was in fact, encouraged and validated at every turn."[25] Alan Kidd, although alienated from the country and having plans to leave permanently for Canada, nevertheless was captivated by campus protests and what they represented. He admits that the atmosphere of social and political protest aided his move north: "It made it much easier for me to go ahead with my decision to avoid the draft and leave the country."[26]   Most, however, were not captivated enough by the protest movements to consider joining them. These future expatriates concluded that it was not worth joining the throngs of students on the streets, as they did not believe the country could or would change its direction. And more important, they did not care enough about the United States to be moved to fighting for its redemption—a constant theme throughout the expatriate narratives.

Jim Tarris was at Stanford studying medicine while the protests against the war were taking place, and, while sympathetic to the cause, he thought that the prospect of student protests ending the conflict was unrealistic: "I sincerely believed that it was a no-win situation. I thought that the protesters were wasting their time and their futures trying to effect some change on the direction of America. I believed that then, and I believe that now."27 Merrill Condel holds a similar view: "I had friends who were gung-ho into the whole rebellion thing, but without direction and combined with some starry-eyed, somewhat naive, belief that they were going to change the world. I knew what I wanted in life, and I wasn't about to waste my time fighting for the country or for the end of the draft. In a strange sense I was much more conservative than many of my contemporaries, but much less patriotic."28 Brian Anderson also maintained that he lacked the patriotism and the will to protest to change the country: "I really was not raised with a sense of duty to country and flag and never really had those patriotic pulls at my heartstrings, which made me not terribly interested in righting a country gone wrong. It was not my responsibility. My sole responsibility was to take care of, or to ensure, my future without the interruption of a foolish war."29 Roger Neville Williams explains that as the war progressed, the nature of it had a dramatic and permanent effect on how many young Americans began to feel about their country of birth. He wrote that his country's policies in Southeast Asia became associated with the entirety of what was going wrong with America. "These events caused a lot more young men to leave the country for they either didn't care about America any longer or they cared too much."30

PERMANENTLY NORTH

Perhaps the most revealing aspect of the expatriates' recollections—one which demonstrates that their actions were not motivated by protest—is their admission that they knew their decision to move to Canada was permanent. Even the few expatriates who believe that their actions were in part a protest against the war vowed that they would never return to America to live, regardless of the war's outcome. Ron Needer, like all these expatriates, knew from the first moment that his decision was final: "It would seem like it should have been one of the hardest decisions in the world for anyone to make, yet it was actually—the decision part—was quite easy."31 Carroll Obline did not remember having any reservations about the decision: "As I said before, other than my mother, there was little to keep me in the country. Leaving for Canada and escaping—and I don't use that word lightly—was my only real option. I never thought of myself as a real American, whatever that is."[32] David Ward remembers that "it was a no-looking-back move. It wasn't the fact that I could get arrested if I went back, because I had no intention to return. It was bye-bye America and all the crap that I saw growing up. You have to remember, I was still only a kid, and that was how I saw it."[33] Albert Caldwell says that "it was my disgust with all that was going on in the country, the racism, the militarism. That was the thing. And when the war came around, and they started looking for me . . . well, it made my decision pretty easy."[34] Interviews conducted by Baskir and Strauss reveal many of the same attitudes. Dodger Chris Parker, for example, stated, "When I left, I had to set my mind to the fact that this was a permanent change in my life."[35] A survey done in 1968 in Toronto, where the majority of the draft dodgers first congregated, also support these findings. The study found that the men were not pining to return home as "most of the draft dodgers [in Toronto] have turned against their country completely. They make statements like 'They ought to tear down the Statue of Liberty because it doesn't mean anything anymore.' "[36]

It should be made clear that the expatriates did not view Canada as a "promised land" but rather as a convenient place where they could pursue their interests while leaving behind their problems with the United States. Dodger Brian Linton remarks that "I didn't view Canada as some shining beacon of liberty or anything; I would have gone anywhere where I could work. The real thing was that it wasn't America. . . . It wasn't the place that didn't want me when I was a kid, yet wanted me to die for the country."[37] Several draft dodgers, in fact, knew little about the country that was about to become their new home. Carl McCrosky made a trip to Canada after receiving his draft notice to see if "it was actually a civilized country. I really didn't know. I thought maybe people lived in igloos; I was an American then [laughs]."[38] For many draft evaders Canada was simply a place where they could carry on with their lives. Aston Davis recalls that "Canada had everything that an American draft dodger would want. The customs and the language, the cars were the same, but without all the baggage that we had to carry around with us. The country [Canada] was both an escape hatch and a place where we could resume our lives with a minimum of fuss."[39]

An Open Border

During the late 1960s and early 1970s, Canada indeed appeared to be a hospitable place for draft dodgers and deserters of all types. Because Canada had no draft of its own, draft dodging was not a crime, and as a result, no extradition procedures were carried out.[40] Immigration officials, from most accounts, were not harsh on fugitives from the draft. This was especially true for white middle- and upper middle-class young men with a university education. For those so inclined, physically crossing the border was not difficult. Draft dodgers could apply for and receive landed immigrant status, which entitled them to apply for citizenship after five years, and most did. Many draftees who looked to Canada as an option understood that the Canadian government at the time was quite sympathetic to their plight. As Carl McCrosky and several others recalled, then Canadian Prime Minister Pierre Trudeau openly welcomed draft dodgers. The controversial Canadian leader stated that Canada should act as a "refuge from militarism." Positive remarks about the former Canadian prime minister are common in expatriate accounts, and contributed to the desire of some to become Canadians. One draft dodger told Roger Neville Williams: "Trudeau is such an incredible diplomat. He rolls with the punches. Couldn't have a better guy. . . . I think he is really good. Canadians don't know what they've got. Canadians really don't have a clue about how good they've got it. I'll take citizenship out as soon as I can—two more years."[41]

There were other reasons that caused Canadian immigration officials to cast a benevolent eye on the young American males crossing their border. Canada generally welcomed draft evaders with open arms because these new immigrants brought with them skills and education, and were not likely to become a burden on social agencies. Williams points out that "by early 1967 it was apparent that the American war resisters were the best educated category of immigrants in a country which needed skilled manpower according to the Department of Manpower and Immigration."[42] Draft dodgers, however, comprised only a fraction of the northern migration of Americans since the end of the Second World War. This fact is well articulated in James Dickerson's book, *North to Canada*. Along with a half-dozen draft evaders, Dickerson also interviewed women who emigrated north, ostensibly, due to their opposition to the war, U.S. foreign policy, and the country in general. What is striking is the number of Americans who sojourned north during the Vietnam era who were not affected by the draft. These numbers easily dwarf the estimates of actual draft evaders. The unstated conclusion that arises from Dickerson's research is that Americans, including draft dodgers, were leaving America for much more expansive and complicated reasons than their reaction to the Vietnam War.

Similar findings were put forth by Robert Gilmour and Robert Lamb in 1975. The authors wrote that many draft dodgers "left for Canada not because they were evading the draft but because they were 'fed up' with America." They add that, "In fact, a breakdown by age and sex of those who qualified as 'landed,' or permanent immigrants to Canada at the height of the war resistance, showed that draft age men alone did not account for the increasing numbers."[43] As with draft dodgers, the war was only the catalyst for disaffection for thousands of Americans who emigrated north during the Vietnam era—a finding which further supports a pattern of alienation for young Americans in the decades following the Second World War. While the subtitle to James Dickerson's *North to Canada* is *Men and Women against the Vietnam War*, the author's respondents speak as much, or more, about problems with American life and attitude, than they do about the Vietnam War. These former U.S. citizens appear much more as men and women against America.[44]

In the end, the expatriates were much more than "refugees from militarism." They had completely turned their backs on their country of birth. As a result, they met the arrival of their draft notices with derision. Draft evader David Ward, like others, thought it was quite ironic that while growing up in the United States he was treated like a "traitor to his own kind" in his community because his mother worked in the civil rights movement in Alabama, and was a "traitor" once again when he refused to be inducted to fight for the United States in Vietnam: "It seemed like I was always on the wrong end of every issue, and there was nothing that I could do to please the country. Believe me I did not grow up loving the United States of America. So when the draft notice came along, I just laughed." Ward was home from college visiting his parents for the summer when he received his draft notice. "My father was worried that evading the draft would follow me for the rest of my life in the States, and he didn't want me to go [to Canada] for that reason alone." But Ward explained that he had no intention of serving in the military in any capacity and did not want to do the "two step" around the local draft board: "I wanted to have a career and to do my own thing, and I sure didn't feel obligated to the country. I never felt that kind of loyalty or patriotism. I can't say exactly what it was that made me that way, but I felt that way when I was a kid. I did not feel like I belonged to American society. I grew up thinking, in fact, that it was all wrong."[45]

Draft dodger Larry Allison also believed that it was the country that was wrong, not him. He refused induction on principle: "[I] never intended to weasel out of the draft. Going to Canada was the only moral option available to me. I was not willing to go to jail, because the country was wrong; I wasn't. I thought civil disobedience would be futile and harmful to my life. I saw bumper stickers saying 'America, love it or leave it,' I just chose the second option." Allison's words echo among the majority of the draft evaders interviewed for this book. They, like Allison, believe that when they planned to avoid the draft and leave the country, it wasn't merely a maneuver around the draft but a permanent change in their lives. Allison's refrain was a common one: "Once I moved to Canada, I no longer regarded myself as evading the draft. I was immigrating. I had broken my ties with the United States." Allison concluded that instead of the decision being a dramatic and uprooting step, the opposite was true: "It's remarkable how unremarkable it was."[46]

Perhaps one of the most interesting, and surprising, aspects of the expatriates' testimonies is that they often appear more conservative than radical, which is not the "textbook" description of draft evaders. They showed little interest in protest and were, from most accounts, not connected to the counterculture. In this way they stand in contrast to the thousands of draft dodgers who protested on the streets of America, found numerous methods to beat the draft, and went to prison if all else failed. While some speak of their actions as activism, the sum of their lives and decisions suggest they were young men who wished to avoid confrontation and trouble.

Leaving for Canada was not as disruptive as it may have appeared; buoyed by their education, skills, and class privilege, the move allowed them to continue with their plans without the disruption of war or the conflict of fighting for a country from which they felt estranged. It was the quickest and easiest way for them to restore the status quo in their personal lives. It also explains why privileged whites, even though they were in the best position of any to avoid the draft, nonetheless comprised the largest percentage of draft dodgers in Canada. Their disaffection from America also goes a considerable distance in revealing why the expatriates never returned to the United States following the 1977 amnesty by President Jimmy Carter.

Draft dodger Bill Warner summed up the feelings of many expatriates on why they evaded the draft and stayed in Canada by borrowing the words of philosopher Thomas Paine. In an echo of Paine's words concerning the colonialists' separation from Britain, Warner said simply, "'Tis time to part."

6

"Boys Without a Country":
Exiles or Émigrés?

[A] frustrating sadness settles upon you after talking to a dozen or more of
these young men. Saddest are those who have come here with a half-
digested kind of New Left idealism, attracted by the hip glamour of being
political refugees from the United States militaristic dictatorship or
whatever. . . . Many evaders unquestionably are cowards pure and simple,
hiding behind protestations of idealism, afraid either to go to war or to take
the consequences of their refusal.[1]

In 1967, Toronto *Globe and Mail* reporter Oliver Clausen wrote an
article for *The New York Times Magazine* about American draft dodgers
living in Canada. Throughout the piece, Clausen was harshly critical of
the new arrivals. He described one young draft dodger from Texas as
someone "who looks and sounds just like a boy many a citizen of Wichita
Falls, Tex., would love to give a good spanking to."[2] Clausen appeared
determined to portray evaders to an American audience as unfortunate boys
making tragic mistakes. He wrote that they would soon come to the
"realization that this is something other than a youthful-rebellion lark, like
wearing long hair or a beard. It means loss of country and home." These
dodgers, in Clausen's view, were "boys without a country."[3]

Despite his caustic remarks and obvious distaste for this group of
young Americans, the article ended up informing more potential draft
evaders about the Canada option than dissuading them from using it.[4] More
important, the majority of his examples betrayed the mournful image of lost
young men. Clausen was unable to deny this fact and had to admit that a
"composite portrait" was difficult to assess. He added that the draft dodgers
included "sincere, apolitical pacifists as well as young men who started on

business careers and refuse to interrupt them for service in the army since they intend to become Canadian citizens anyway." The last, and most "conspicuous" group, he argued, were the ones who simply "hate America."[5] The picture of sad young exiles fails to emerge in the article. If anything, the opposite is true. One young man from Detroit told Clausen that it was not "that I particularly believe in . . . revolutionary ideas. It's that every time I've crossed the Detroit river to Windsor, I've had this feeling that I'd escaped from a police state, like over the Berlin wall."[6] Draft dodger Mark Satin agreed, claiming: "I've cut all bridges with it [the United States]. I don't care if I ever go back. My old man wouldn't either. You don't know what s.o.b's they are in Wichita Falls."[7] Satin, as with many of the draft evaders interviewed for this book, was a transplanted Northerner in the American South. He had grown up in Muirhead, Minnesota, and hated his new home in Texas where his family had moved. Satin referred to his former hometown as "a bigoted hole."[8] Despite the tone of the article, Clausen admitted, "most draft dodgers are unquestionably quite sincere in wanting to remain [in Canada] as Canadians."[9] He was not alone in reaching this conclusion. Several American journalists who ventured north during the war discovered similar sentiments, although they seemed reluctant to portray the men they met as anything other than pitiful exiles. The struggle over what journalists expected, and what they encountered, is evident in much of what was written at the time. It appears that some American—and Canadian journalists—could not fathom the idea that, not only were draft dodgers not living in misery, but they had no intention of returning south. Their testimonies and actions reveal that fleeing the draft and moving to Canada were not the acts of youthful indiscretion, but reasoned choices that enabled them to carry on with their lives without feeling obliged to serve the state in uniform. In Canada, as we will see, they seldom fit the mold of typical draft dodgers. They were not generally connected to the exile or anti-war groups north of the border. Rather, their behavior in concentrating on their lives was the same as it was in the United States. Their testimonies and actions reveal that these Canadian-based draft dodgers were not exiles—they were new émigrés to Canada.

ARRIVAL

The expatriates' transition from America to Canada did not lead to significant upheaval in their lives. Not only did these American draft dodgers not behave or live as exiles, they did not feel like exiles. Within weeks of crossing the border, they vanished into regular middle-class jobs and lives. Draft dodger Nick Theason, for example, remembers that the adjustment period was no different than moving to another region or city in the United States:

I think the biggest part of it was like one feels when they move or start a new job, or move away from people you know, like friends and family. I don't recall culture shock, per se, there was a little of a strange feeling, 'what did I just do?' but it really was not a dramatic change; I came, I got a job, I stayed. . . . I don't mean to be glib, but it wasn't a hard thing to do, other than to find the grocery store, and try to find substitutes for some of my favorite brands of foods that they didn't have. . . . Some people who discover that I'm a draft dodger today are amazed that I don't miss my country and that I could live up here all these years without wanting to return to where I had come from, but in many of the good ways, Canada is not all that different than America, just less of that attitude, the bravado, the arrogance, and the militarized culture. Canada is very much unlike the States in that respect.

Theason didn't feel the need to contact support groups or seek out fellow Americans. "I just felt that my new Canadian friends were much like the people that I did like when I was kid. The people I met in school and work in Canada were my kind of people; sitting in an exile hostel, talking about a revolution that was not going to happen, didn't really appeal to me. Yes, there were a lot of things about America that were not right and it would have been nice to change them, but I was a realist and living in exile was not how I saw myself."[10]

David Ward said that upon arrival in Canada he felt that he would need the support of others like him. He felt uncertain about the wisdom of his move as he tried to become accustomed to his decision to leave his country. "The first three or four nights in Canada I could not eat or sleep; I cried at night until my face hurt from the strain and the sting of the tears. I was by myself, lost, bewildered, and all of my confidence that I had left with disappeared with missing my girlfriend at the time, being so far from family, and second-guessing myself." Those early thoughts of dread and regret, however, left him after a few days, and he began to feel good again about his decision.

I pulled myself together, looked around at where I was, and why I came here, and realized that I had made the right decision. It was hard, very difficult getting mail from home, you know some of the family [were] not impressed by what I had done. Some thought that I had ruined my life and, for a while there, I started to believe them. Not so much about what was happening with my thoughts about Canada, but how people can affect the way you think about your decisions for a time, especially if there is more than one person saying the same thing. And believe you me, I had some family that would have killed me faster than the Vietcong. But I knew enough, had enough self-awareness that I knew that I had done the right thing. . . . That feeling has not changed 25 years later.[11]

A study of draft dodgers by Dana Spitzer and John Cooney in 1969 for *Trans-Action* magazine also supports the contention that there were few second thoughts amongst the expatriates. The authors concluded that "very few deserters or draft dodgers in either Canada or Sweden felt remorse at the prospect of not being able to return home," and were thus not compelled to seek out the exile community.[12]

Most draft dodgers felt like immigrants, rather than runaways. They looked for ways to assimilate into Canadian life, rather than to seek out other Americans who were more interested in protesting the war back home. Draft evader Dale Friesen was aware of the exile groups in Edmonton and Vancouver where he lived for his first three years in Canada. He was not, however, interested in them as he did not consider himself an exile but an immigrant.

I didn't move to Canada away from the war and a country I felt little allegiance to, to then become involved in an activist lifestyle. If I had wanted that, I would have stayed at home and took on my draft board and whomever, straight on—head on, but I was not wired that way in those days. Canada was going to become my home. I was certainly sympathetic with what was taking place on college campuses across America. You could not escape them. They were on the news each and every night in Canada, as well, and they had my heart. It was tough to see people who really cared about the country, shouting and marching and having sit-ins, all to little avail. I respected that, but I really was not involved, and I really didn't think that I was wrong to walk away. That was my choice, my prerogative, but as I saw it, America was not redeemable. Maybe this is foolishness, to write off any country, but it was the way I saw it from my admittedly little, small perspective as a 19-year-old. There was a process for me over time, I think as I matured, and that was what it comes down to. I lost faith in America; she did not exile me.[13]

Expatriate Aston Davis felt much sympathy for the exile community, with whom he was casually acquainted during his first years in Canada. It did not translate, however, to a desire to belong. "It really was no different here. I didn't want to become part of the protest crowd anymore here than I did south of the border. I had friends, people that I hung around with, that were inclined, and I even went to a few rallies, but it just seemed a little out of touch. Although this seems rather cynical, and I don't mean it to be, but I thought it was a waste of time." Davis, like the majority of the draft evaders, was a loner and came to Canada for his own reasons. He did not feel he needed to belong to a group for support:

It wasn't like we were exiled in Siberia, and we needed contact and moral support from our own kind; they were very individual decisions. And Canada did not seem much like a foreign country where one was in exile. Most things were similar enough, food, cars, females (laughs), customs, sayings, even apartments and architecture. It was not this foreign country where after being there for awhile, one had to go out looking for the 'American club' where people spoke your native tongue. In fact, it was difficult to escape American culture as it was on the radio with music, on TV in every conceivable form. It was also in newspapers and magazines, in food items, and everything else in the stores, was American, or associated with America, the car I drove as well. We have a lot in common with people here. The ways of thinking to some respect, and you had something in common with others. It was not foreign; Canada was not like that at all.

What little contact Davis has had with other dodgers in the past decades has only reinforced his assertion that their choices were highly individual ones. He explains:

I've had some contact with other dodgers over the years, and many feel the same way I did, meaning that we wanted to avoid the war, mainly because we felt that we owed nothing to the country in that sense. The war was wrong, America was going in the wrong direction, we had no real allegiances to America and nationalism, and Canada was a good, sound option. And I, like others, had options, and there was no way I was going to sacrifice it for some imperialist war. We were in good shape and probably because of that we did not depend on each other all that much for support. It really wasn't all that much of an ordeal, even though it may seem that way in retrospect.[14]

Their new lives, for the most part, were not fraught with struggle, but contained many positive experiences as jobs were plentiful for those with a college education. Interviewees in books, such as Dickerson's *North to Canada*, reflect similar attitudes. Draft evader Andrew Collins, a member of the upper middle class from Memphis, Tennessee, moved to Canada after being drafted and landed a job soon after he crossed the border. He realized that Canada was a sympathetic country with a good economy and a place where he could easily fit in and resume his life. Collins remarked that he "was a mainstream kind of guy and adjusted quickly to life in Canada."[15] Dickerson's research supports the view that the majority of the expatriates did not see themselves as exiles. Speaking of Collins as an example, he concludes, "Like most of the war resisters, he did not seek out the company of other Americans, preferring to make a new life for himself among the people of his new country."[16]

MEDIA STEREOTYPES

There remains, however, a persistent myth that draft dodgers are still on the run from the law, and hide as fugitives from justice. While some of this is ignorance of the past, it can be explained in part by the initial impression constructed by the media when draft dodgers were leaving for Canada. As stated earlier, the idea that draft dodgers were living happy, middle-class lives in Canada without regret, has never fit the persistent stereotype. It was a picture that was, in part, created and reinforced for an American audience in mainstream press accounts. While the aforementioned journalist Oliver

Clausen discovered that most draft dodgers he met planned to remain in Canada and did not consider themselves exiles, he still portrayed expatriates as spoiled children ready to run home to their parents' homes at the first opportunity. Clausen was not alone. Several journalists who sojourned north to cover Canadian-based draft dodgers were also surprised when they failed to find throngs of sorrowful young men pining to return. This resulted in some contradictory journalism as they tried to give their readers—and their editors—something they expected, and perhaps *wanted* to hear. What they discovered, however, was when expatriates found employment, "the adjustment is relatively painless."[17]

Such a message was a tough sell as mainstream journalists were inclined to portray draft dodgers as either "boys" who made big mistakes, or cowards and "hippies"—members of the "great unwashed." *Newsweek* columnist Stewart Alsop, for example, characterized all draft dodgers in Canada as similar to those connected to the activist exile communities in cities, such as Toronto. Alsop told his readers, "exiles" have "lots of hair, granny glasses, unwashed feet, poor-boy costumes for the boys, either micro-minis or sweet-little-girl costumes for the girls." In other columns, Alsop admitted that there were two classes of exiles: the draft dodgers and the deserters, but he did not make great distinctions in their overall behavior or motivation for going to Canada. Sad exiles seem to be the way he felt they would end up once they matured. Alsop wrote: "One wonders what will happen to these young men as, inevitably, the war, the reason for their self exile, ends, and even more inevitably, they cease to be young."[18] But those to which Alsop alludes comprised only a few of the draft evaders who came to Canada. The enduring image of men hanging out in lonely hostels waiting for rescue and repatriation was far from the case. Indeed, Robert Gardner, the coordinator of the Canadian Council of Churches' ministry to U.S. draft-age immigrants in Canada at the time, remarked: "Everything written and broadcast in the U.S. has been done so from the perspective that dodgers are poor, sad, lonely exiles. This is nonsense. . . . Many have made new and successful lives for themselves." Gardner's observations of the émigrés led him to conclude that the largest group consisted of "privileged young men from an educated class. They are reflective and politically aware. They arrived here with monetary resources and with plans because they had made their decisions carefully." Gardner observed that even men with fewer skills and education, adapted easily and were faring well in their new country. "Many of them are no longer exiles. They've become new Canadians."[19]

Indeed, as Roger Neville Williams observed, many expatriates were unaware that organizations existed to help them in their flight from America. Most draft dodgers had a good idea before they made the trip across the border what it would be like, and had already made plans for college and employment before their departures. Some expatriates had gone on "scouting missions" to Canada before crossing the border permanently. Because of this, there were no throngs of displaced young Americans on the streets of Canadian cities. Williams went on to say that meeting draft dodgers who were employed and comfortably settled into Canada was not uncommon. He said that many of them "had never heard of the local exile organizations."[20] Draft dodger Merrill Condel, for example, arrived in Toronto in the winter of 1969. He recalls that the last thing he wanted to do was to become involved in an exile community longing to rejoin America at the first opportunity. "It was really a strange time. I realized of course that I was in another country, but it wasn't this foreign place that one needed to congregate with a bunch of other Americans for identity. I knew what I wanted, really, and what I needed to do. The offices that were counseling newly arrived draft dodgers were helpful, I'm sure, to a lot of the guys at the time, but I didn't really need them. So I surely wasn't going to seek out exile groups, which ostensibly formed to protest against the war and ensure their safe return to the United States." As a result, Condel explains, he was not very aware of the exile community, nor the places they frequented, and like other draft dodgers, soon settled into mainstream Canadian life. "It was a much easier transition to make than one would think. I think that I could have made that transition in any other European country, even Sweden, Norway, Great Britain, but Canada was just closer, easier, more open to us, and we spoke the same language. It was not dramatic, other than the winters." As Baskir and Strauss point out, for college educated draft dodgers, going to Canada "was like checking into a hotel."[21]

These expatriates clearly do not fit the stereotypical draft dodger mold. Eventually, American correspondents traveling to Canada during the late 1960s and early 1970s reluctantly agreed with this view. The draft dodgers they met had considered the ramifications of their actions, and intended to remain in Canada. *Time* writer Henry Muller was first among the journalists who correctly perceived the type of draft dodger living in Canada. Muller wrote: "There is a stereotype of the draft evader or deserter in Canada. He is shaggy, has no job, lurks in 'hideouts,' fears the Mounties and yearns for homemade bread back in Iowa. Certainly the type exists, but one must also count the law students, bank employees, doctors, surveyors, social workers, university teachers and accountants."[22] But it was a myth that once begun, was hard to eliminate. In a limited sense the stereotype did exist. The self-styled exile communities were, however, purposefully the most visible, engaging in demonstrations against the war. They stood in sharp contrast to the expatriates, who resumed their education and careers and settled into mainstream life. Some expatriates were somewhat shocked when they did encounter their more radical brethren in the "exile" community. In *North to Canada*, draft evader Patrick Grady recounts his surprise when he found the "textbook" example of what draft dodgers were thought to be like in

Canada: "I remember going in there [the Toronto Anti-Draft Program at the University of Toronto campus] and it was a textbook example of what people think draft dodgers are—these guys sitting around with long beards, dressed like hippies. One of them was reading Chairman Mao's little red book. I thought, 'oh, my God!' "23 Grady, who worked at the Bank of Canada at the time, was typical of many expatriates who found themselves distant from the small exile community.24 Baskir and Strauss reached a similar conclusion, finding that few expatriates were connected to—or looked for assistance from—the resistance community. "Not many exiles asked for help. A good many were scattered across Canada, did not subscribe to *Amex*, and were not part of a formal or informal grapevine."25

Canadian Activists Cry Foul

The expatriates in Canada did not fit the expectations of the media, nor did they always fit those of the Canadian anti-war and counterculture movement. They tended not to be the committed leftists and activist radicals many Canadians and Americans thought they would be, or *should* be. The behavior of the new American émigrés not only surprised but angered many Canadian anti-war activists. The radical young in Canada expected that all draft dodgers were like-minded and ready to join them in the fight to stop the war and alter America's "imperialist policies" in Southeast Asia. Dodger Timothy Unger is typical of the draft evaders who failed to meet the expectations of northern activists. Unger recalls his estrangement from the Canadian anti-draft scene when he crossed the border to resume his life. "I lived in Montreal for the first three months of my new life in Canada, and it was just after the FLQ crisis.26 Some of the people—a sort of little clique I was hanging around with at the time—were very politically active and aware, which was very much unlike the people I grew up with." Unger's new friends were all Canadian, and involved in Quebec provincial politics, and some were FLQ (Front de Liberation du Quebec) sympathizers. "They were not only active in the Canadian scene but were vehemently anti-American and against the Vietnam War even more so than I was. The main reason I was accepted, I think, is that I was a draft dodger so I had passed some standard." His new colleagues were nonplussed, nonetheless, because Unger was essentially unaware of local exile groups, was detached from the anti-war movement and had little interest in contacting them. "It actually led to a falling out of sorts because I was eventually seen as someone who did not share their attitudes. I remember feeling out of touch as I didn't come to Canada to just to return south, and I was quite content to keep working. I was about to be transferred to London [Ontario] with my job and that was good because my French was lousy at best and it was really, in many ways, the best time of my life. The last thing I wanted to do was to bring myself down looking for a political war to win; I had just avoided a real war in Southeast Asia."[27]

The testimony of draft dodger Patrick Grady makes it clear that there was a prevailing assumption in Canada at the time that draft dodgers must be radicals and counterculture participants. But as he pointed out to Dickerson in *North to Canada*, such was not always the case:

In the old days, there was a misconception that the people who came to Canada were all student radicals, left-wing types—very few were, though some were. I knew some students in SDS [Students for a Democratic Society] at the University of Toronto, but most were just ordinary people. Most were opposed to the war, but some, I guess, just didn't want to go into the army. I don't necessarily think high moral principle guided everyone's decision.[28]

Such attitudes did not sit well in many activist circles in Canada at the time. Canadian activists did not want to see young Americans fleeing the Vietnam War who were not ready to join them in the cause they took so seriously, nor live up to the romanticized vision of draft dodgers as courageous fighters of imperialism. Canadian writer and journalist Myrna Kostash observed that, "contrary to some Canadian fantasies, the draft resister turned out to be not an ultra-militant, superlunary being but a deeply offended middle-class moralist just like them." In her semi-autobiographical account of the Sixties generation in Canada, Kostash found that many young Americans coming to Canada at the time were perceived rightly or wrongly as "middle-class shits who didn't give a goddamn about Vietnam or anything else except to carry on in Canada where they'd left off in America, in a career and lifestyle into which they vanished unremarked."[29]

Given the political climate of the 1960s, it is easy to sympathize with the young Canadian radicals' point of view. What they expected to find in draft evaders were soulmates; what they found often were young men who wanted to continue with their lives unobstructed by the ebb and flow of the political and social landscape. That these draft dodgers were not heavily involved in anti-war groups should not come as a surprise. While growing up in the United States these individuals were not joiners and their behavior north of the border remained consistent as they made their transformation to Canadian life.[30] Most draft dodgers have blended so well into Canadian society that native-born Canadians cannot easily identify them. Allan Haig-Brown, in reference to one draft dodger he interviewed, offered the following as an example: "In so many ways then, John is typical of the many Americans who came to Canada during the Vietnam War. They have fitted themselves into the stream of Canadian society so completely that their compelling and courageous stories can elude even a native-born individual, like myself."[31] The more radical of the American exile community, composed largely of deserters, were not impressed. Articles in *AMEX-Canada* began to demonstrate a strain of resentment against the middle class draft dodgers who were not inclined to be radicals but who wanted to settle into Canadian life as best they could. The magazine began to complain that too many draft dodgers "have carved their little niche in the Canadian middle class. They wish to stay invisible and resent the visibility of field jacket and combat boot clad deserters trying to survive in the street."[32] Few dodgers, however, report having any conflict with the more radical of the exile community, including deserters. They were often more surprised, as Patrick Grady was, when they encountered this crowd, as they seldom frequented the coffee houses and other establishments that attracted those involved in the anti-war movement. The expatriates found that Canada was their best option, as they were able to resume their lives with little difficulty. As draft dodger Jim Tarris pointed out, crossing the border was the best way to continue with his chosen course in life:

It really was the path of least resistance, and the best way for me to live my life. I had other options, but Canada seemed like the best one under the circumstances, and as I look back over the past 25 years, there are few days that I would trade back in this country; I'm not saying that it is a paradise, and the U.S. is a sewer, far from it. What I'm trying to get across is that Canada was the *best* of my choices, how I saw them when I got my draft notice, and that has not changed.[33]

Clearly most expatriates have never considered themselves exiles, but émigrés to Canada. The transformation to Canada was not a difficult one as they were able to resume their education and careers with little disruption. They claimed at the time, and still do today, that it was *their* decision to leave. They settled easily into mainstream Canadian life and lived their lives the way they wished, without forced service in the military and what that meant to them as Americans. They demonstrate with word and action that their decisions were not inconsistent with the ideals on which their country of origin was created. They made their decisions to leave the United States as *Americans*; decisions they have never had cause to regret.

7

Traitors or Quintessential Americans? Reflections from Across the Border

> We are a rebellious nation. Our whole history is treason; our blood was attainted before we were born; our creeds are infidelity to the mother church; our construction, treason to our fatherland. What of that? Though all the governors in the world bid us commit treason against man, and set the example, let us never submit.[1]

To suggest that Canadian-based Vietnam draft dodgers were in some way true-blooded Americans may seem blasphemous to some. The American past, however, is laden with those who refused to conform to the dictates of state. Since the beginning of the American Revolution when Patriots threw off the yoke of British authority, individualism—the freedom of person, speech, thought, and conscience—has been the ideal Americans have aspired to, and honored. It is, however, difficult for some to accept that those who refused to serve the United States in uniform can be considered quintessential Americans. Perhaps it is even more difficult to accept because the war was a disaster on many levels, and blame was spread widely. Following the war, Harry G. Summers, Jr., a colonel and an instructor at the Army War College remarked to a North Vietnamese officer that "you never defeated us on the battlefield." His former adversary simply replied, "That maybe so, but it is also irrelevant."[2] Vietnam produced few heroes.

Consequently, many Americans would like to forget about Vietnam and the toll it took on the country. For thousands of draft dodgers who went to Canada, they could not have picked a more apt place to be forgotten. Since these men made their move north in the 1960s and early 1970s, they have, essentially, vanished from American consciousness. This is explainable partly because for many Americans, Canada is an enigma.[3] It is viewed often as a cold, barren place that produces hockey players, trees, bacon and beer. Canada has been regarded by some as little more than the attic of the United States—a place of storage, a place to forget, a place insulated from memory. Moreover, Americans do not wish to remember draft dodgers. These men bring to mind an embarrassing episode in the nation's recent past. They are often perceived as traitors to their country and, as a result, unworthy of memory.

Are they, however, traitors to core American beliefs and ideals? Nearly 25 years have passed since the granting of full amnesty by President Carter, and thousands of expatriates remain in their adoptive country. The draft dodgers are now middle-aged men and it is from this vantage point that they recount their choice to move north. The pages that follow look at their views on America today, which are, in part, shaped by watching the developments in their country of birth from across the border over the past three decades. We see men whose decisions were shaped not only by the draft, their feelings about the country, and the benefits of a prosperous economy, but their allegiance to central tenets in American ideology, which shaped both attitude and action. Although it may appear that they have repudiated their past, bringing dishonor to themselves and their nation, they have in fact remained, in essence, quintessential American men, in what they stand for, and what they stand against.

ACROSS THE 49TH

By all accounts, life has been good for the expatriates in Canada. They appear to live prosperous, rewarding and happy lives. Upon arrival in Canada, the vast majority continued to pursue undergraduate or graduate degrees, and later found employment suitable to their liking. The rest were gainfully employed within weeks of crossing the border. Today, they live in comfortable homes on tree-lined streets, enjoying the fruits of their labors. Among their ranks are physicians, lawyers, writers, psychologists, university professors, scientists and business owners. As a group, they are considerably more successful than the many deserters one encounters when looking for individuals who avoided the draft. Many deserters from the U.S. military seem less settled in both careers and relationships; they are not as connected, educated, or successful as the draft dodgers. While there are, of course, exceptions to this, the draft evaders, unlike the deserters, appear to have had a firmer grasp of what they wanted in life and were able to make long-range plans and stick to the goals they made for themselves. Deserters, for the most part, came from less advantaged socioeconomic backgrounds. Their numbers were composed primarily of the working class and under class, a fact that left them with fewer options on either side of the border. Their class also left them less prepared to make some important decisions and choices in their young lives. They had limited horizons and thus were more susceptible to accept conscription and more inclined to go along with their peers. This point was made quite clearly by John McDermott in an article in *Viet Report* in 1967. McDermott wrote:

An upper middle-class boy is nurtured by his family and school experience to think himself capable of dealing with the decisive components of his life. A privileged boy gains sufficient confidence in himself, in his soul place and in his judgment of events so that he comes to assume a competence to control his own destiny. . . . By contrast the fundamental experiences of lower class and blue collar boys are proverbially authoritarian. Their school experiences emphasize the value of "staying in line" and out of trouble. The likelihood of early marriage, uncertain job prospects, the great certainty of being drafted and the pressure of like-situated friends all combine to teach them the same lesson.[4]

In contrast, the draft dodgers, are among the most educated and affluent immigrants Canada has ever received. Works by Allan Haig-Brown and James Dickerson highlight the talents of these prosperous draft dodgers.[5] Through their efforts, these men have made significant contributions to the Canadian economy and society while "proving that the American Dream was alive and well—if only in Canada."[6] These talented men also served to reverse the trend which some feared was a "brain drain" of skilled Canadians relocating south of the border during the 1960s. The expatriates have undoubtedly made numerous contributions to the country, and life there has been good for them as well. The evidence comes from meeting and talking with them, either by telephone or in their homes. They speak openly about their positive feelings about their "new" country, and any sense of regret is practically nonexistent. Their feelings concerning the United States, however, have changed little with the passage of time.

Brian Anderson presently lives and works in London, Ontario, and runs two small businesses. He has no regrets about his life over the last 31 years: "Sometimes it really seems like another life, such a long time ago, and at other times, it was only yesterday. But I have no regrets. There are always some things you would like to do over, but not the move here. It was the right thing for me then, and it remains so."[7] Timothy Unger agrees: "I did the best thing for myself over the long-run. It seems, in retrospect, that it must have been an unconsidered act of a rebellious youth who didn't know what he wanted in life, but it was just the opposite." Unger, a graphics designer and small business owner, claims not to second guess his move: "Life has treated me well. I should be thankful for all the advantages I had in my life. The only real regret that I have was being so young and not knowing how to handle my father better. I was never able to set things right with him before he died. Perhaps it was not meant to be."[8] David Ward still cannot believe what he did when he was younger: "I guess you change; I don't mean grow up so much, but you lose your nerve and are not so adventurous. I'm glad I did what I did because my whole life is here, but it seems like another life now. I was always headstrong, and I knew the country wasn't what I needed, and the war was wrong. I certainly have no regrets, but I'm a much more conservative guy these days."9

Carroll Obline also believes that his choice to move north was correct. "Canada has been good for me. I can't say that I ever had a moment's regret, other than it was impossible to see my mother until 1978, when I returned for a visit." Obline's feelings toward the United States have not softened with time: "I don't think the country has changed much; if anything it has gotten a bit worse."10 Alan Kidd agrees: "While I was angry for being drafted and its disruption in my life, I'm glad that it happened, because of the way things have gone up here, with my life, for me, I have never regretted it. I was absolutely certain that I was doing the right thing, and never really questioned my decision before or since. I always thought that under the circumstances that it was the right thing for me."11

Michael Fischer believes that it was somehow "destined" that he should live his life across the border from America: "I've always been at odds with things or nations which have too much power, and as the last 25 years have played themselves out, it turns out that I was right after all." Fischer believes that the country has the same problems today as it did then: "The more I look at the country, the more that I'm glad that I did what I did. Time has proved to me that I was right and the problems I left behind were much more than being a spoiled child who refused to serve his country."12 Brian Linton agrees: "So many people suggest that we were cowards, and we're the results of permissive parents and society, but the past decades of American history, I believe, have vindicated us. We have all witnessed the disastrous results of the Vietnam War, Watergate, Iran-Contra, and even more racial division than when I was growing up. We left a country that was the problem; it wasn't us."13

Bill Warner also feels justified when looking back at the events of the past few decades: "I never liked being equated with the excesses of the 1960s. I didn't like it at all being associated with people bummed out on drugs and having no direction. It seemed for the longest time that anyone involved with any dissension in the 1960s were somehow cowards or not up to the same mettle as previous generations. And while many people still don't understand who we were, at least the past decades have proved that it was the country, and the people that ran it, were the ones who were wrong."14

Curtis Erickson also believes that events in the United States have served to support and validate his feelings as a young man: "There was often this insinuation in the U.S. media that we were weak, transient drug takers, who cowardly sneaked across the border to avoid serving our country, but practically no one feels that way any longer. Look at the results of the war, the Pentagon Papers, Watergate, the bombings of Hanoi and Nixon's little illegal adventure into Cambodia. I realize that I have the benefit of hindsight, but we sensed that it was wrong, the nation was wrong, and we needed to look out for ourselves, and I, for one, am glad we did."[15] Draft evaders interviewed by James Dickerson hold similar views about the United States as a country—views which have not changed with time. Dodger Oliver Drerup, for example, said that "Somewhere between the Bay of Pigs and the start of the war in Vietnam, America lost its way and still hasn't found its way back.[16]

Despite these feelings, there are many conflicting thoughts among these draft evaders regarding their feelings about the country and the nation's ideals. Carl McCrosky, for example, remarks that "part of me will always be bitterly anti-American, but part of me loves the Declaration of Independence, and some of the early Supreme Court decisions; there is an immense value in some of it." He feels, however, that the country behaves often "like a mad dog ripping its guts out [in reference to political assassinations], killing the best and brightest of its own leaders, and scaring off the rest, heading to the catastrophic end of the civilization."[17] McCrosky has never doubted his decision to move north. Draft dodger Brian Linton agrees with McCrosky's sentiments, and makes it clear that evaders, such as himself, were not forced into exile, but chose to move to Canada. Interestingly, dodgers such as Jim Tarris claim that one factor which contributed to their decision to head north was their indoctrination and belief in core American principles. That suggests that the cherished concepts of liberty and individual rights, taught to them from the time they were children, actually helped mold them to do what they did. Says Tarris: "The country, ironically for me, taught me to *be* me. In America we were raised to be anything we set our hearts on. For me, and others, that was avoiding the draft and leaving the country."[18]

QUINTESSENTIAL AMERICANS?

Perhaps the most surprising—and ironic—aspect of the expatriates' stories is their allegiance to basic tenets of their old nation's ideology. Although estranged from the country, they have held fast to many values American society considers sacrosanct. Ideals of individualism, freedom and liberty were not peripheral, but central to their decisions to evade the draft by leaving the country permanently. Expatriate Jonathan Burke, for example, believes today that in many ways he was the quintessential American, a fact that contributed to his actions: "I think that we, all the northern-bound evaders, took that cult of individualism, and 'rags to riches' and the 'be all you can be,' and ran with it right across the border. It's almost like the country inadvertently created this group of monsters that turned against its maker, because they ended up training us too well."[19] Indeed, some observers voiced similar ideas at the time. In 1967 sociologist Mort Briemberg wrote that "though they condemn American society verbally, these boys epitomize the American cult of individualism. One of their strongest motivations against the draft was their rejection of the notion that a country could ask anyone to give up two years of his life to do something he didn't want to do. They see this as an external authority making intolerable demands on the individual."[20] The majority of expatriates felt that their move to Canada was shaped in part by a country that placed such an emphasis on individual liberty.

Draft evader Aston Davis remembers that "the whole idea of individual rights, as I recall, was even more emphasized in the South where I grew up. People were always talking about states' rights and all that. It was the culture I was immersed in. It's interesting that while I was rejected, and in turn rejected everything else there, this idea stuck."[21] Ron Needer remembers that "it was my old man that was always drilling into me what a great country it was as you could do what you wanted and make your own choices in life. It's ironic that that's exactly what I ended up doing, and my father and the rest of society condemned me for it."[22] Dodger Albert Caldwell believes that young men like him, because of their upbringing in the United States, received the tools and education necessary to make the move to Canada possible: "The United States of America raised me to do what I did. We were indoctrinated since we were young with the ideas of freedom of choice, to believe and trust in one's conscience, and not to blindly follow orders but to make your own way in life in a country where everything was possible."[23]

Caldwell hits upon a common theme among these draft dodgers. The boundless opportunities that the country afforded them in the 1950s and 1960s, and their sense of freedom and individuality, made the idea of conscription anathema to them. The mere prospect of forced military service, when bright futures awaited them, became unthinkable. Evader John Conway summed up the times and the choices draft evaders like himself faced:

I think it was coming at a time in history of great independence, and opportunity and privilege, because I'm typical of that. I had great opportunity and independence and privilege and maybe more so than other generations; freedom, as well. All things were possible. You had some talent, some privilege, some opportunities. The world was there, and America was feeding all of us all this grandiose view of one's life and encouraged us to take a challenge, and as an adolescent in particular you take this seriously.[24]

Others, such as Brandon Hockwald, agree that there were no limits on their futures: "We were brought up in the best economic conditions in history and with a country that boasted that fact and others since we were small. We truly believed that everything was possible. Going to the moon, becoming a surgeon, or a writer, or a world explorer, or a millionaire. It was all at our fingertips, yet we had the government sending us draft notices. The two things never fit together in my mind. I was brought up to do my own thing."[25] Martin Beech agrees saying that "most of the kids I went to college with were fast-tracking it to the good life. There were a lot of kids who hated the communities that they grew up in, and just at the conjuncture in their lives when they could do whatever they wanted and all possibilities could be realized, the government stepped in with the draft. I, for one, was not buying it."[26] Martin Strychuck resented the idea that the government had the power to take away two or three years of his life, without any real compensation, at a time in history when good "career opportunities were [his] for the taking."[27] Roger Neville Williams, in his 1971 study of draft dodgers in Canada, found that many of the Canadian-based draft dodgers he met were tired of having their lives dictated to them, and wished to enjoy all the opportunities that life offered them. Williams wrote that students no longer wanted to be "channeled" and wanted the freedom to do what they wished with their lives. They wanted the ability to relocate, to travel and to pursue higher education when they wished. This, according to Williams, was as important as their "objection to the Vietnam War, [and] is the reason that a very great many young men resisted the draft (especially in the case of those who chose Canada)."[28]

Resentment of the demands of the state, however, arose from more than just losing two years of their lives in college or the workforce; expatriates did not feel that the government had any right to demand they fight in a war they believed was wrong. While this book argues that the draft was not the prime reason for their departure to Canada, most expatriates were morally opposed to the war. Draft dodger Alan Kidd, for example, thought that the state should not force an individual to do anything against his will. "I didn't think they, the government, had any right to draft me into a war that I didn't agree with." While opposition to fight in wars for moral reasons is not unique to Vietnam, most expatriates believed the country had no right to be fighting in Southeast Asia. It was an example of what they believed was wrong with the country. Says Kidd: "Really what I was doing was washing my hands of the U.S. When I decided that the war was wrong, and when I left, I had no intention of returning. Basically I left the U.S. behind. We were parting company—I was going one way, and they were going another, and I basically still feel the same way, and that was the powerful thing: in one way I really wasn't trying to avoid the draft, but it was my feelings about the direction of the country, and I never intended to go back." The majority of the expatriates, like Kidd, believed that as individuals and Americans, they had the right to decline state servitude, especially when it asked for service they believed immoral and *unAmerican*.[29]

The idea that their actions were consistent with the true American character is apparent in other studies and interviews with expatriates. In 1968, draft dodger Stuart Byczynski told a reporter for *The Saturday Evening Post* that, "I believe in the freedom of the individual and big government in the United States is taking away all our freedoms. Even while I was still in high school, I decided no government was going to tell me I couldn't pursue my chosen profession and would have to sleep on cots with a lot of other people."[30] Draft dodger Oliver Drerup told James Dickerson "forgive me for being self-righteous, but I think that what I did was right and I think most Americans would agree with that."[31] Drerup and others point to the revolutionary forefathers for historical justification for their actions: "Good Americans fight when they have to, but don't when they don't have to. I'm convinced that Thomas Jefferson, had he been alive, would have been in that car [across the border to Canada] with me."[32]   Dodgers interviewed by Allan Haig-Brown also assert that their negative feelings about the United States and the Vietnam War were not inconsistent with true Americanism. Draft evader John Shinnick, for example, believed that concepts, such as justice, which he was taught as a child, shaped his views and his decisions. "Justice was an American concept as far as I was concerned. Justice was ingrained in who we were. We took the Pledge of Allegiance in school every morning, and I remember the phrase 'and justice for all.' I still believe it as an incredible concept." He, like other draft dodgers who grew up in the South, experienced the disturbing aspects of entrenched racism. He began to realize that while he had absorbed some of the positive aspects of his birth country's ideology, the daily injustices he saw did not allow him to support what the nation, in his view, was becoming.[33]

Any War but Vietnam?

The question of whether or not these draft dodgers would have willingly served in other wars is more difficult to determine. The Second World War saw the least resistance against the draft than any conflict in U.S. history. Several of the draft dodgers interviewed for this book say that they would most likely have accepted a draft notice and fought in World War II. Many suspect that they would have even volunteered after the attack on Pearl Harbor. Most thought that if the decision had been left up to them, they would have supported the war effort in some capacity. They admit, however, that if they had lived through that time they may have had different views. "It's hard to know," says Merrill Condel. "I'm a product of a different time. I would like to think that I would have served to defend the nation against the Nazis and the Japanese who attacked us. It was certainly a different thing being attacked, instead of attacking a small country like Vietnam, but America was different after the end of the war, with the Cold War, and I'm a product of *that* time, and it is hard to say what I would have done in 1941."[34] Ron Needer believes that even in World War II a citizen had a right to decide whether they wished to serve in uniform. "I think that [the reason] they had no real trouble getting people in the army was because it was seen as a just cause—America was not divided, the enemy was clear, and so was the mission. But people had choices then, if one thinks about it, and they could have evaded and didn't. I may have [gone], but I have the benefit of hindsight, knowing how it all came out."[35] Aston Davis agrees that it is difficult to say what he might have done in World War II given the perspective of today.

The era was so different, there was little opposition to our involvement once Pearl Harbor was attacked. And also there were few choices then for employment—the smart thing would have been to join up and get all the training one could get at that time if you had some smarts. There were lots of opportunities for home-front and rearguard action, support roles where one could train. Things were different in the 1960s. I'm sure that many of us thought, "who needs the military," and a terrible cause—what an awful combination if you think about it in those terms. World War II would have been different.[36]

Michael Shannon also notes that there were fewer choices for men in 1941, making them more inclined to serve in the military. "I'm sure that if I had been born in 1922, the opportunities in the army would have looked just right, especially if I had suffered through the Depression. But I was born after the war in the '50s. Who really knows? I would have been a different person, so I might have gone—but I'm sure I'd still believe that it would have been my choice to have served or to not have served."[37] Both Carl McCrosky and Alan Kidd believe they would have served in World War II, while others, such as Timothy Unger and Carroll Obline, say they would not have. Unger remarks:

Wars are terrible things. I think only a few people really have what it takes to do that job, and I really believe that the only ones who can really fight well for their country are the ones who volunteer to make that sacrifice. I really don't think, I could be wrong, that you can draft an effective fighting man into a war. I think that the mere fact that you have to draft him means that his heart is not in it, and he won't serve well. He will keep his head down and wait to leave. Volunteers are the only way. I think that is why WWII was so successful for our guys because they volunteered en masse. They wanted to serve to defeat the Japanese and the Germans, and that is what they did.[38]

Carroll Obline said that he hoped he would not have joined. He remembers that his father came back from that war a broken man.

The war was not right for my dad. He would have done more with an agriculture deferment than with a rifle in his hand. What I know from mom is that he spent the majority of his service in the Pacific in shell-shock, in deep trauma—his letters home, she said years later, were bizarre. No, I don't think I would have [gone], but I may have supported the war effort in another way, especially if I had been given a choice. I think that is the only way it really works for anyone.[39]

Although the expatriates believe that they may have served in an earlier conflict, their responses suggest that their participation would hinge on choice. These draft dodgers grew up in a different era, with distinct experiences and expectations. This combination of a sense of independence in a time of great economic opportunity, and their alienation from American society, made these draft dodgers resistant to any demands for their service—a trait that remains with them today. The ideal of individual choice on all matters vis-à-vis the state is paramount; that remains as true in their adopted home of Canada as it did in the United States. Draft dodger Jim Tarris, for example, admits that "as much as I like Canada, the prospect of fighting and dying for the country is not one I would be pleased about, especially if I was conscripted. I think I would recommend to my son that he not report should that unlikely scenario occur."[40] Michael Shannon agrees: "The entire concept of duty, honor, country has always been foreign to me. I don't believe that any government has that right to tell you that you must sacrifice yourself for it. It has to be a choice, and this goes for Canada as well as for the U.S."[41] David Ward remarks: "A country can't have it both ways. They can't tell you, yes, your future is yours, and you can do anything you want in your life, but first, young man, report for compulsory military duty in Southeast Asia."[42] Bill Warner points out: "A person, I would think, would have to grow up pretty patriotically inclined to report to a draft board in a time when everything else is at one's fingertips. I think the ones that went must not have had many other opportunities or had the Stars and Stripes stuffed you know where. It sure wasn't me."[43] Indeed, these types of attitudes were held by many on both sides of the border. Speakers at the National Student Congress in 1968 mirrored the ideology of dodgers, such as David Ward. The founder of the West Coast resistance, Dave Harris, compared the draft to involuntary servitude: "The most obvious assumption of military conscription is that the lives of young people in this country belong not to those young people; the lives of those young people instead are possessions of the state, to be used by the state when and where the state chooses to use them.[44] Draft dodger Bill Warner, like many others, agrees that he cannot remember feeling patriotic enough to sacrifice his time for the country in the military, and especially not in Vietnam. He believes that while the situation was different in the Second World War, even then it would have had to have been his choice to serve. These young men believed that as American citizens, they had the right to refuse state servitude.

The reality that some were unwilling to fight for their country was a natural point of recrimination for many in government. Former JFK press secretary Pierre Salinger called draft evaders "contemptible," adding during a trip to Toronto in 1968 that, "If Canada ever gets involved in a war, you won't find them any use to you either."[45]

THOSE WHO SERVED

Only a small minority of white middle- and upper-class young men with a college education served in Southeast Asia; conversely, they are the majority of expatriates in Canada. The great many of those who wore a uniform in Vietnam did not have the advantages of the Canadian-bound draft dodgers. As discussed in Chapter 4, the expatriates, for numerous reasons, had the best options and means not only to avoid induction, but remain in the country by finding loopholes out of induction lines. For everyone who avoided service, however, another was drafted in his place. It is interesting to hear the expatriates' thoughts on this situation, as they were the ones who invariably raised the issue. While they blame the U.S. government, and not themselves, the reality that others served in their place is a disturbing memory. Draft dodger Jonathan Burke, for example, doesn't wish to dwell too much about the ones who fought in the war as the thought still bothers him more than 30 years later: "At times I have nightmares about it. I can't imagine what it must be like for the ones who fought there, and died there. Sometimes I can imagine them calling my name—accusing me of running away from my duties, while they went."[46] Nick Theason states: "I didn't do anything wrong. It's not my fault that others couldn't get out or couldn't see that they had options and went there, losing limbs or their lives."[47] Carroll Obline states that it "was people like my father and grandfather who went into combat in the First and Second World Wars. It's always the poor suckers who get caught. Believe me, the war did not do my dad any favors. He was never the same when he returned, and it broke my mother's heart. I feel bad for all those inner-city black and Spanish kids who couldn't find a way out of the draft. It still bothers me, but what can you do about something like that? The war and the draft put a lot of people in a bad situation."[48]

Timothy Unger believes that the problem of who served should lie at society's door: "The poor, and the poorly connected, are always the ones who fight the wars. Even though they logically have the smallest slice of the pie, they often are called upon to make the largest sacrifice. I was born into a prosperous, if not happy, family, and I had choices. The choices I made were of course exacerbated by my upbringing, but I had the options. And for the poor people of that country, the draft grabbed them up like leaves in the wind."[49] Bill Warner simply states: "The war was not my fault! The people that fought and died there were not my fault! I should not be made to feel guilty for anyone who fought in my place because as far as I'm concerned, it wasn't my place. Nobody deserved to have that happen to them. Not me or the hundreds of thousands who went. I still think that I acted with personal honor."[50]

In the ensuing media frenzy that accompanied former Defense Secretary Robert McNamara on his book tour for *In Retrospect*, he was asked repeatedly about the anti-war demonstrators and draft dodgers who hounded him during his tenure in the Pentagon. There was considerable interest in McNamara's thoughts on the young men who avoided fighting in Vietnam, considering his reassessment of the war. McNamara's reply was that he felt that the men who protested and went to prison for their beliefs had acted with honor, and indicated with his silence that those who fled the country behaved somewhat less than honorably. Many expatriates are sensitive to any direct or indirect indictment of their personal honor. For these men, questions of honor appear inextricably linked to questions of guilt over the less fortunate men who served in Vietnam.

Ron Needer says: "How can anyone think that we acted dishonorably? Were we supposed to honor our country by dying for it? I did not grow up believing that one had to fight and die for your country to act honorably. Honor comes from within. It's how you treat yourself, your family, and your neighbors in your community. Interestingly, my family was not treated honorably in our community in the South when I was a kid, yet somehow our personal honor is questioned when we refuse to sacrifice ourselves." Needer does not think that he should be blamed for the poor blacks who went in his place: "It was [General William] Westmoreland's fault, and [President Lyndon] Johnson's but not mine for saving myself."[51] Draft dodger Jim Thomas told James Dickerson that he was troubled with the accusations that he acted dishonorably, as he, like others, needed to live his life in a manner consistent with his moral beliefs. This attitude is captured quite clearly in the words of draft dodger Carl McCrosky. McCrosky doesn't believe that he is responsible for the fate of those who served. He, like others, believes that he acted with honor because he did only what he was able to do given his perspective, experiences, and conscience:

Honor is very important to me, and I haven't the slightest qualms about what I did and never have. The argument against that is that poor blacks from South Carolina went in my place and died, and that is undoubtedly true. I don't take that as my personal sin. I was fighting the war the best I could. We were trying to make enough noise so maybe some of the poor blacks would have heard and not gone. But they didn't and they died, and I'm not very happy about that. But I don't want to say this too crudely, but it's not my fault! It's not my personal responsibility. I did what I could, and I acted honorably in my own sphere, and that's all that you can really be held responsible for.[52]

AMNESTY

The debate in the United States over clemency and eventually amnesty consumed much of the 1970s. As the war soured, debate on whether to pardon many of those who had committed draft violations began in earnest. Tens of thousands of young American men had run afoul of the law, collecting criminal records which threatened to perpetually shadow their lives. Concrete measures toward amnesty began with President Gerald Ford's clemency program in 1974 coinciding with his pardon of his predecessor, Richard Nixon. Ford's clemency took into consideration convicted draft violators, convicted deserters, convicted AWOLs, un-convicted Selective Service violators, and unconvicted veterans with less than honorable discharges.[53] While President Nixon was offered complete immunity for his involvement in the Watergate scandal, Vietnam War resisters and deserters were required under the clemency guidelines to perform two years of alternative service. Few dodgers or deserters took advantage of Ford's limited plan and calls soon followed for a more complete amnesty providing blanket coverage for draft offenders and deserters.

In 1977 new President Jimmy Carter, in an attempt to mend some of the wounds of the war and of recent scandals, proposed an unconditional amnesty that covered most draft resisters in Canada.[54] While the majority of deserters were available to apply for a more limited amnesty, not completely covering them in all instances, it was this group that more readily returned to live in the United States.[55] With amnesty, Canadian-based draft dodgers could safely reenter the United States. While Carter's plan was welcomed by the majority of the expatriates, it was not, however, celebrated as a victory over America, or a chance to renew their lives back home. Rather, it was viewed as a measure enabling them to visit their families without fear of arrest at the border. What amnesty did was to put to the test the expatriates' earlier claims that their move north was permanent, as nothing prevented their return. And while many were willing to return for visits, there was no exodus of white middle-class dodgers from Canada. As Surrey and others have pointed out, the U.S. media lined up at border crossings in anticipation of tearful reunions. The picture turned out to be somewhat different. "What they got instead, generally, were brief visits to Buffalo before the men returned to Canada to resume their lives."56

The groups who did return en masse were deserters; those who evaded the draft as a last resort; the underclass, blacks, and other racial minorities who found it difficult to assimilate into Canada without the necessary education and job skills. Joining them were the small core of men who saw themselves as revolutionary exiles—both draft dodgers and many deserters—who almost all returned.57 Ironically, the deserters, not completely covered in the amnesty, were the ones who more readily returned, suggesting that their inability to cope with military life, and not their feelings about America, was the primary reason for the move to Canada. Going north, for many, had been the course of last resort when things in their lives fell apart. These men simply followed the example set by older draft dodgers and fled north across the border. Deserters possessed the least skills and education and thus had fewer opportunities to find suitable employment in Canada.58 As a result, they turned out to be the most vocal of the exile community, actively working for amnesty.59 These deserters stand in sharp contrast with at least half the white middle-class evaders, who although completely covered in Carter's amnesty, elected to stay in Canada. As Surrey points out: "Dodgers, who could return to the United States with a clean slate, usually elected to remain in Canada."60 It was, of course, what many had planned when they left. Unlike most deserters, these expatriates knew what they wanted in life and began to plan for their futures from an early age. Draft dodger Jim Tarris, like many others, knew that his decision stemmed from his earliest days: "My mother always wanted me to make something of myself, and do all the things she thought she missed out on. I was a kid with a one-track mind: finish med school and start a successful practice. I know now that I was just a kid then, but I stuck to my personal beliefs and lived my life the way I wanted to—the way my mother raised me."61

Thirty years after the fact, the expatriates feel much the same about amnesty and returning home. Many bristle when the conversation turns to the subject. A good number recall that they weren't interested in the amnesty debate, and some were even unaware that the debate was taking place. Expatriates tend to find the subject insulting. They maintain that as draft dodgers, they did nothing that required a pardon, and always made it clear that they had no intention of returning.62 American journalists at the time also found that draft dodgers were insulted by the amnesty debate. Expatriates scorned the idea that they were guilty of anything, and that they were down-on-their-luck young men who regretted their actions. In 1972 draft dodger Warren Frederick told a reporter for *Time* that he didn't "think [he] did anything wrong." The *Time* reporter found that "many of the estimated 70,000 draft dodgers and deserters—concentrated mainly in

Canada and Sweden—profess to share Frederick's feeling that amnesty proposals are irrelevant and even insulting. Indeed, they believe that there is a prevalent misconception that those who have escaped from military service are a sorry breed of men without a country, steeped in expatriate misery, who want only to be exonerated and allowed to return to their native land."[63]

What Carter's plan did offer expatriates was the opportunity to visit their families. That they could not see friends and family members for a number of years was one issue that bothered most draft dodgers. Many intended to take advantage of the ability to travel across the border without fear of arrest. Draft dodger Bill Terry, for instance, said of amnesty at the time that "a lot of those guys [other evaders] will take amnesty just so they can go back and see their relatives. I can't believe that many of them will stay.[64] Another draft evader, originally from California, suggested that "freedom to travel in the States is more important to most of us than American citizenship."[65] In 1973, draft dodger Ed Starkins told a reporter from *Time* that he "wouldn't go back except to visit [his] family and friends." Like others, Starkins maintained that there were other, deeper reasons for leaving the United States than merely conscription: "The problem is not just the Vietnam War. It is the whole social structure that's screwed up."[66] Dodger Larry Johnson concurred at the time, saying, "If amnesty were declared in the next five years, I don't think I'd go back." Johnson said that the only reason he would return would be to attend an event, such as his grandmother's funeral.[67] As James Dickerson points out, most of the draft evaders had forged new lives and families and wanted little to do with the amnesty debate: "Obviously there were some resisters in Canada who benefited from Ford's amnesty, but most were like Oliver Drerup, who was too busy building a business to pay much attention to what was happening politically across the border."[68]

It is clear that the reason these middle-class expatriates had no desire to return after amnesty is that the war had not been the primary reason they left America. They did not feel that they belonged before leaving, and nothing they had witnessed in the intervening years made them reconsider their permanent move north. The fact that the war had ended, for most of these expatriates, was meaningless.[69] Such attitudes are a refrain throughout the expatriate narratives, indicating that the war and the draft played only a secondary role in their decision to leave America. As David Surrey points out, any question on the expatriates' commitment to their new home was less doubted once amnesty "failed to open the floodgates for returning resisters."[70] There was indeed surprise in the United States when these men did not all return. As pointed out earlier, one of the main reasons is that the U.S. media, for over a decade, had painted draft evaders in Canada as dispirited exiles, heartbroken over their choices, and longing to return. But most draft dodger accounts have always suggested otherwise. While the expatriates have always been clear on these points, few U.S. journalists have ever listened to them, believed them, or written it as such. "Most Americans have this misconception that we had been waiting all these years at the border, and would just go when the gate was lifted," said one draft dodger in Canada at the time. "They don't know Canada." Another expatriate blamed the media for the misconception. "American newspaper reporters who all had this idea that we are just aching to be back to our roots . . . that we were really suffering up here . . . they didn't believe it when I told them I didn't want to go back."[71] Indeed, as Baskir and Strauss observed, only 92 men requested certificates for a pardon from the Justice Department and a mere 85 returned permanently to the United States during the first six months of Carter's amnesty.[72]

Even some who decided to return to the United States following amnesty ended up going back to Canada as they were no longer able to tolerate the United States. Alan Kidd, for example, was hopeful that the country was about to change following the election of Jimmy Carter and his efforts to pardon draft dodgers. Kidd returned south to work in the aerospace industry, but soon found that his problem was still with the United States. "I thought maybe that things would change after Carter came in with amnesty but [President Ronald] Reagan decided that things were not going to change, and it was not long before I decided to return."[73]   For the rest of the expatriates, they "had established permanent homes outside the United States; they expected to visit their families now and then, but few had any intention of coming back permanently."[74]

While the expatriates' class position helped them find jobs and prosper in Canada, they could have just as easily returned south where the U.S. economy was stronger than in Canada in the late 1970s, and thus achieved more in their professional lives. While David Surrey concludes that many remained in Canada because they assimilated successfully, the bulk of the evidence suggests that their decisions to stay north were not so much due to their assimilation into Canada, but rather, to their failure to assimilate into America. It is a theme found throughout the expatriate narratives, and in the end it was what kept them above the 49th parallel, when the door opened for their safe return.

Amnesty had its benefits. After missing a decade's worth of family weddings, birthdays and funerals, Carter's program provided expatriates with the opportunity to visit parents, brothers, and sisters; mend family disputes; and bury skeletons from the past. Some families, originally against their sons' actions, have long since gotten over the events of the 1960s and early 1970s. If the draft is spoken of, it is usually in passing. The terrible legacy of the war has softened much of the rhetoric they once heard about duty, responsibility and honor. Alan Kidd remembers that some of his more right-wing Republican uncles held him in a negative view for some years. But when the war ended, and the years went by, attitudes changed and softened. There was "really no more bitterness left towards me," says Kidd.[75] Perhaps in the end—as Carl McCrosky remarks—the worst thing the draft dodgers did was to be "prematurely right."[76]

Today, Canada is home for these one-time American draft evaders. They now have lived more of their lives north of the border than south. For several years they held no papers of citizenship for either country, as many had neglected to obtain passports before their departures for Canada. They were not allowed to apply for their U.S. passports, once they left the country, and bench warrants were issued for their arrest. Most draft boards, however, allowed young men extended grace periods to return home and square themselves with their boards. These draft dodgers, however, knew they would never return to live in America and applied for landed immigrant status in Canada, which entitled them to become Canadian citizens after five years. With new lives and futures these men spread out across the country and staked out for themselves a place they could call home. These young Americans were also encouraged by some Canadians to establish roots in locales of which they were previously unaware. One man in Saskatchewan, for example, offered: "Land for draft dodgers, at $100 to $150 an acre."[77] The roots took hold. These draft evaders have remained north of the 49th parallel and have carried on with their lives with the same tenacity that had once sent them across that border—away from the Vietnam War and away from America. They, remain, however, products of the culture in which they were raised.

Ultimately, these draft dodgers are the fortunate sons of the Vietnam era. What they gained by going north was the ability to live without the demands of their country, however just or unjust those demands may have been. With their actions they spared themselves not only the horror of war, but their names will never grace the reflective, raven walls of the Vietnam Veterans Memorial.

Epilogue

On a crisp January day in 1961, President John F. Kennedy implored the nation's young: "ask not what your country can do for you, ask what you can do for your country." Few who heard those words during his inaugural address could have conceived what that call to duty and public service was to ultimately cost. Before the end of the decade, the president's bid to pass the "torch" to a new generation was rejected outright by thousands of young Americans on university campuses across the nation.

This decade-long discord called the Sixties raises some fundamental questions concerning an individual's duty to nation. What is the price of citizenship? What can any nation demand of its people? Kennedy's expectations of the next generation of young Americans to "pay any price, bear any burden, meet any hardship, support any friend, oppose any foe, to assure the survival and the success of liberty" raises an interesting conundrum. Rights, such as freedom and liberty, are only rights as long as a society is willing to protect them. This is true, not only for the majority, but for those unwilling or unable to join the preponderance of opinion. Among these dissenters to Kennedy's call were the expatriates in Canada. These young Americans, who sojourned north across the border in the 1960s and early 1970s, could not fathom the idea of forced military service in a country that taught them the rights of the individual are preeminent. Given that they never developed an allegiance to their nation of birth, their actions, in hindsight, should not surprise. Their disaffection from the United States and their heightened individualism led to their refusal to recognize any claim the country may have had on them. The nature of their country, however, taught them to do what they ultimately did.

In essence, these draft dodgers, in word and deed, evoked the literary father of their country, Thomas Jefferson, when he wrote that the

government derives its "just powers from the consent of the people"—
people who are entitled by *natural law* to "alter or abolish" whatever denied
them their "unalienable rights" to "life, liberty, and the pursuit of
happiness." Jefferson knew, undoubtedly, that his words meant more than
simply colonial freedom from the British Empire. He wrote that freemen—
citizens—had the right to refuse the blight of arbitrary rule. Jefferson, in
contrast to Kennedy 200 years later, knew that no one would "pay any
price" or "bear any burden," for to do so would, in many instances, corrupt
the very liberty one was trying to protect and preserve.

The draft dodgers' actions also raise issues concerning the divisiveness
of national boundaries and national ideals. The idea of what an "American"
is may soon bear redefinition. The world today is smaller, increasingly
interdependent, and more similar than disparate. Trade, commerce and
currency are more interrelated, and ancient divisions between countries and
cultures are blurring. This smaller world is also becoming faster, more
efficient and increasingly seamless. The English language is now almost
universal; it pervades commerce, science, and most forms of
communications. We are moving inexorably down this road, and as we
undergo this evolution of human geography, the need and want of the nation
state will be increasingly mutable.

Joining this increased fluidity of the tangible, is the intangible—the
ideals that have spawned great societies, ideals that venerate and dignify all
men and women. As the world fuses new challenges arise—those of
protecting and instituting standards, laws, morals, values and the ideals that
most people crave: justice and liberty. These abiding ideals on which
America was founded, are universal, and not constrained by borders, with
check points, staffed by vigilant sentinels. They are available to anyone who
wants to live by them, and this is becoming more true for each generation.
There is a massive coalescence taking place, and America, as a nation, is not
immune. More so, it is a development that the country, in thought and word,
helped engender. The ancient ideals that were given new voice and form
during the heady days of the American Revolution are not distinct to one
country nor were they intended to be. The Preamble to the U.S. Constitution
gave birth to an idea that cannot be contained: the revolutionary ideal that
"all men are created equal." That the Constitution failed to include women
and slaves mattered little to those who used these powerful words as a
weapon to end slavery a century later. The words have taken on a life of
their own; they have taken root and grown. As such, *America* connotes more
than a nation, but an experiment that has allowed people to rise above the
circumstance of birth, and concedes that one of the worst human failings is
low expectations in each other. In this larger sense, one of the things the
Vietnam draft dodgers did was to test the bounds of nation and national
ideals as we understand them to be. While disaffected from the United

States, as a country, these men held fast to the founding principles of America—principles and ideals they brought north as they lived the way they were raised to believe they could. Their actions also reveal that one does not have to live within particular borders to be "American." Two hundred years hence, the United States may be a nation no longer—at least in any way we now recognize or accept—but perhaps *America* will be recognized as a word that represents not a country, but the values that free people hold sacrosanct.

Instead of being traitors to America by dodging the draft, these expatriates are, in essence, quintessential Americans. In refusing conscription and plotting their own futures, they did not mock their nation's core ideals, but embraced them. In many respects they embody the best of what America has to offer: fortitude, optimism, determination, perseverance, and a strident individualism that carves its own path into the ever-expanding frontier of human autonomy. Their attitudes and actions as draft dodgers reflect much of the America they left behind. It is a nature unapologetic for its position, unrepentant for its stridency, unashamed of its resources and ability, and unafraid to stake out alone. After all, they were, and are, all American boys.

An editorial in *The Washington Post* once referred to the draft as "a generation-wide catastrophe." The schism that the war and the draft caused between generations and in families was revealed in many ways during the Vietnam era. In one memorable episode of the sitcom *All in the Family* a brusque Archie Bunker, played by Carroll O'Connor, sits down to Christmas dinner with his friend "Pinky" from work, and David, a college-aged friend of his son-in-law Michael, visiting from Canada. When Archie discovers his young dinner guest is a draft dodger, he becomes furious, demanding that David leave his house. Pinky, whose son went to Vietnam, tries to interject: "If my opinion is of any importance . . . " Archie bellows: "Certainly, your opinion is of importance. . . . Your opinion is more important than anyone else's in this room. And I want to hear that opinion, and I want all these young people to hear that opinion. Now, you tell 'em, Pinky. You tell 'em!

"I understand how you feel, Arch," says Pinky. "My kid hated the war, too. But he did what he thought he had to do. And David here did what he had to do. But David's alive to share Christmas dinner with us, and if Steve were here, he'd wanna sit down with him. And that's what I want to do." Pinky takes David's hand in his, and places his other hand on the young man's shoulder.

"Merry Christmas, David."

Appendix

Inductees from 1917 to the Draft's End in 1973

Year	Inductees
1917	516,212
1918	2,294,084
1940	18,633
1941	923,842
1942	3,033,361
1943	3,323,970
1944	1,591,942
1945	945,862
1946	183,383
1947	-----
1948	20,348
1949	9,781
1950	219,771
1951	551,806
1952	438,479
1953	471,806
1954	253,230
1955	152,777
1956	137,940
1957	138,504
1958	142,246
1959	96,153
1960	86,602
1961	118,586

Year	Inductees
1962	82,060
1963	119,265
1964	112,386
1965	230,991
1966	382,010
1967	228,263
1968	296,406
1969	283,586
1970	162,746
1971	94,092
1972	49,514
1973 (the draft ended on 7/1/73)	646

Source: U.S. Selective Service

Induction Statistics

The number of Americans who entered military service through the Selective Service System for major 20th century conflicts.

Conflict	Inductees
WWI (1917-1918)	2,666,867
WWII (1940-1945)	10,110,114
Korea (June 1950-June 1953)	1,529,537
Vietnam (Aug. 1964-Jan. 1973)	1,766,910

Source: U.S. Selective Service

U.S. Casualties in Vietnam by Volunteer, Drafted, or Enlisted

Status	Army	Marines	Navy	Air Force
Volunteer	16,374 (48.8%)	12,784 (91.9%)	1,764 (91.6)	808 (89.1%)
Drafted	16,964 (50.5%)	683 (4.9%)	--------------	-------------
Reserve	69 (.2%)	406 (2.9%)	148 (7.6%)	1 (0.1%)
National Guard	68 (.2%)	-------------	-------------	1 (0.1%)
Unknown	69 (.2%)	25 (0.1%)	13 (0.6%)	96 (10.5%)

Source: The American War Library

Vietnam War Casualties by U.S. region

Deaths per 100,000 population

South	17.6
West	16.5
North Central	14.5
Northeast	13.1

By State (Highest)

Hawaii	24.4
New Mexico	23.5
West Virginia	23.4
Maine	21.6
Arizona	20.8
Alabama	20.3
South Carolina	20.1
Oklahoma	20.0

By State (Lowest)

Rhode Island	9.6
Alaska	10.9
New Jersey	11.0
Connecticut	11.0
New York	11.6
Nebraska	11.7

Age	Percentage
17-19 years	31%
17-21	67%
17-22	81%
17-29	89%
30 and over	11%

Source: **American War Library**

Numbers Killed/Wounded, in America's Military Conflicts

Period	Event/Location	Killed	Wounded
1775-1783	War of Independence	4,500	8,445
1789	Indian Wars	6,125	2,156
1798-1800	Franco-American Naval War	20	42
1801-1815	Barbary Wars	35	64

Period	Event/Location	Killed	Wounded
1812-1815	War of 1812	2,260	4,505
1814	Marquesas Islands	4	1
1822-1825	West Indies	3	5
1832	Sumatra	2	11
1835-1836	Texas War Of Independence	704	138
1846-1848	Mexican War	13,283	32
1853	Japan	5	6
1855	Fiji	1	2
1859-1860	Texas Border Cortina War	5	18
1861-1865	U.S. Civil War, North	363,020	281,104
1861-1865	U.S. Civil War, South	199,110	137,102
1867	Formosa	1	0
1870	Mexico	1	4
1871	Korea	4	10
1898	Spanish-American War	2,893	1,637
1899-1902	Philippines War	4,273	2,840
1899	Samoa	4	5
1900	China Boxer Rebellion	53	253
1902-1913	Moro Campaigns	130	300
1904	Dominican Republic	1	0
1911-1919	Mexico	19	69
1912	Nicaragua	5	16
1915-1920	Haiti	146	26
1916-1922	Dominican Republic	144	50
1917-1918	First World War	116,708	204,002
1918-1919	Russia North Expedition	246	307
1918-1920	Russia Siberia Expedition	170	52
1921-1941	China Yangtze Service	5	80
1927-1932	Nicaragua	136	66
1941	N. Atlantic Naval War	141	44
1941-1945	Second World War	408,306	670,846
1945-1947	Italy Trieste	6	14
1945-1947	China Civil War	12	42
1950-1953	Korean War	34,246	103,284
1954	Matsu and Quemoy	3	0
1957-1975	Vietnam War	58,219	153,356
1962	Cuba	9	0
1964	Panama Canal Riots	4	85
1965-1966	Dominican Republic	59	174
1966-1969	South Korea	89	131

Period	Event/Location	Killed	Wounded
1967	Israeli Attack on USS Liberty	34	171
1980	Iran	8	0
1983	Grenada	19	100
1983	Lebanon/Terrorist Attack on Marine Barracks	241	100
1983-1991	El Salvador	20	0
1984-1989	Honduras	1	28
1986	Libya	2	0
1989-1990	Panama	40	240
1990-1991	Persian Gulf/ Operation Desert Shield/Storm	148	467
1991-1992	Somalia/ Operation Restore Hope	8	--
2000	Yemen/ Terrorist Attack on USS Cole	17	--

Sources: **American War Library/US Selective Service/US Navy/ US Department of Veterans Affairs**

Notes

INTRODUCTION

1. Henry Steele Commager, *Freedom Loyalty Dissent* (New York: Oxford University Press, 1954), pp. 152–54.

2. Roger Neville Williams, *The New Exiles* (New York: Liveright, 1971), p. 363; "For Americans: An Easier Life in Canada," *U.S. News and World Report*, October 28, 1968, p. 64.

3. The actual number of draft evaders who went to Canada, including those who returned, is difficult to assess. Neither government has specific records of draft dodgers, and the numbers vary from as low as 15,000 to as high as 100,000. Many accounts list deserters and draft dodgers together, which raises some estimates to 350,000. Some references even include all those who emigrated from the United States to Canada during the war years, taking the number up to 500,000. This number also includes countless women who went to Canada during the Vietnam era, by themselves or with draft dodgers and deserters. Most conservative estimates place the number of actual draft dodgers at 30,000, with at least 10,000 remaining in Canada. For references to numbers please see David S. Surrey, *Choice of Conscience: Vietnam Era Military and Draft Resisters in Canada* (New York: Praeger, 1982), p. 5; Lawrence Baskir and William Strauss, *Chance and Circumstance* (New York: Knopf, 1978), pp. 169, 180; "Men Who Cannot Come Home" *Time*, January 10, 1970, p. 15; "No Tears: Draft Evaders and Deserters in Canada, *Time*, February 12, 1973, p. 23; "Millions Who Avoided the Draft," *U.S. News and World Report*, March 1, 1971, p. 33; "For Americans: An Easier Life in Canada," *U.S. News and World Report*, October 28, 1968, p. 20; "If Draft Dodgers Come Home," *U.S. News and World Report*," December 6, 1971, p. 33; Williams, *The New Exiles*, pp. 27, 83, 399; James Dickerson, *North to Canada* (Westport, CT: Praeger, 1999), pp. xiii, 141, 169; John Cooney and Dana Spitzer, " 'Hell No We Won't Go!' Deserters and Draft Dodgers in Canada and Sweden," *Trans-Action*, 6

(September 1969), pp. 53–62, and Stewart Alsop "They Can't Go Home Again," *Newsweek*, July 20, 1970, p. 88.

4. The number of British Loyalists who went to Canada during the American Revolution is the only migration comparable to the exodus of young Americans to Canada during the Vietnam era in U.S. history. See Alicja Iwanska, *British American Loyalists in Canada and U.S. Southern Confederates in Brazil* (Lewiston, NY: E. Mellen Press, 1993).

Interestingly, while thousands of young Americans traveled north to avoid the war, thousands of young Canadians ventured south to join the U.S. military in Vietnam. Although some estimates run as high as 20,000 to 30,000, the actual number is probably closer to 6,000 to 12,000. Please see Fred Gaffen, *Unknown Warriors: Canadians in Vietnam* (Toronto: Dundurn Press, 1990).

5. Dickerson's *North to Canada*, for example, while providing absorbing insights into the experiences of six expatriates who evaded the draft (as well one draft dodger who returned, and one woman who emigrated to Canada due to objection to the war), does not offer a broader assessment of these individuals, nor longer-term examinations of events in their lives that may have contributed to their negative reaction to the draft and their permanent emigration from the United States. Dickerson, himself a draft evader, devotes a great deal of his book to the events of the war itself and the mechanics of the U.S. government and the military's war policy. While there are inferences that more than opposition to the war and the draft contributed to their actions, there is no direct focus on this idea, although many of their testimonies reflect clear detachment from their country, apart from attitudes about the war. Other studies, such as Allan Haig-Brown's, *Hell No, We Won't Go!* (Vancouver: Raincoast Books, 1996), presents interesting interviews with 20 Americans who for several reasons left the United States in the Sixties—twelve of whom were actual draft evaders. While valuable as a resource, Haig-Brown generally presents their unbroken narratives, with little analysis or examination of the historical context in which evaders reached their decisions. Please see Chapters 5, 6, and 7 for further discussion of implications of Dickerson's research and findings.

One study that presents a wider perspective of the Canadian-based draft dodgers, is Surrey's 1982 publication *Choice of Conscience.* His work draws upon the Vietnam Era Research Project (VERP), of which he was a member. VERP conducted interviews with 1,400 "age-eligible males" of the Vietnam era, including men who served in Vietnam, draft evaders in the United States, and 60 deserters and draft dodgers in Canada. His work provides a detailed, quantitative comparison of the Vietnam draft evasion with other conflicts in American history, and a thorough examination of the religious, ethnic, racial, political, and class backgrounds of these draft evaders. There is, however, little analysis on how these demographics may have shaped their decisions to avoid the draft and remain in exile. While he writes that successful assimilation explains why most of these draft evaders refused amnesty and failed to return, he concludes that many stayed in Canada because although "the war had ended, the United States, to them, had not changed substantially." In looking at the responses from VERP,

Surrey shows that these men not only had problems with the draft and the Vietnam War, but with the United States. Although he does not explore the implications of this, he concluded that "these men realized that the war was not the only thing wrong with America." Please see Surrey, *Choice of Conscience*, pp. 1, 103, 171.

6. The Notre Dame Survey was a survey conducted by Lawrence M. Baskir and William A. Strauss of 1,586 men who were of draft age during the Vietnam War. The results were published in their excellent study on the Vietnam draft, *Chance and Circumstance*. The 1978 book contains a great deal of primary research including interviews with draft dodgers in Canada and the United States. Also, please see previous note for a discussion on Surrey's book *Choice of Conscience* and VERP.

7. Racial minorities were also underrepresented in all surveys on the draft dodger population in the United States and especially in Canada. Blacks comprised a small minority of the draft dodgers who went to Canada and an even smaller percentage of the ones who remained following the 1977 amnesty. For further discussion of why this occurred, see Chapters 4 and 7; Surrey, *Choice of Conscience*, pp. 67–79, 135–52; Kenneth Fred Emerick, *War Resisters Canada* (Knox: Pennsylvania Free Press, 1972), pp. 11–38; Williams, *The New Exiles*, pp. 341–44, and Baskir and Strauss, *Chance and Circumstance*, p. 181.

8. For a thorough discussion please see Surrey, *Choice of Conscience*, pp. 67–86, and Baskir and Strauss, *Chance and Circumstance*, pp. 3–13, 28–61.

9. Baskir and Strauss, *Chance and Circumstance*, pp. 3–13. Statistics compiled by Baskir and Strauss reveal that higher-income bracket and better educated dodgers had much less chance of seeing combat in Vietnam.

10. In Dickerson's *North to Canada*, one of the draft dodgers interviewed says that it was easy to live out the American Dream across the border in Canada, where the economy and the customs were not unlike the United States.

11. Canadian immigration officials took a fairly benevolent view of refugees from the Vietnam War when they crossed the U.S.—Canadian border. Canada did not have a draft of its own, so evading the draft was not an extriditable offense, and a sympathetic Canadian Prime Minister, Pierre Elliott Trudeau, made it clear that he welcomed draft dodgers to Canada. The immigration policy was even more relaxed if draft dodgers brought with them essential job skills.

12. See Chapters 5 and 6 for more discussion on this issue, and Baskir and Strauss, *Chance and Circumstance*, pp. 190–92. The authors provide an interesting glimpse into the attitudes of some in the Canadian radical community toward the middle-class draft dodgers who failed to be radicals. Myrna Kostash's study of Canada's anti-war movement and counterculture also deals with some of the negative reaction to middle-class draft dodgers in Canadian activist circles. Please see Myrna Kostash, *Long Way from Home* (Toronto: James Lorimer & Company, 1980), pp. 66–67.

13. Baskir and Strauss touch on the phenomenon of the high level of American migration to Canada during the Vietnam era, as does James Dickerson in his introduction to *North to Canada*. The six draft evaders Dickerson interviewed appear to have a more general anti-American sentiment, rather than simply being opposed to the draft and the war in Vietnam. Interesting, as well, according to Dickerson's own numbers, draft dodgers comprised only a minority of those of draft age (including women) who came to Canada during the Vietnam era who voiced their general dissatisfaction with and disaffection from the country, suggesting further that there was much more taking place during this period than mere opposition to Vietnam. Dickerson's research and interviews provide interesting clues into deeper factors that motivated these men's actions that are not followed through. Please see Chapters 5, 6, and 7 for further discussion; Baskir and Strauss, *Chance and Circumstance*, p. 180; and David Harvey, *Americans in Canada* (Lewiston, NY: Edwin Mellen Press, 1991).

14. Please see John K. Galbraith, *The Affluent Society* (Boston: Houghton Mifflin, 1958); David Halberstam, *The Fifties* (New York: Villard Books, 1993), and Elaine Tyler May, *Homeward Bound* (New York: Basic Books, 1988).

15. Please see Theodore Roszak, *The Making of a Counter Culture* (New York: Dell, 1969); and for a look at the Beats, see William Burroughs, *Letters to Allen Ginsberg, 1953-1957* (New York: Full Court Press, 1982), and Jack Kerouac, *On The Road* (New York: The Viking Press, 1957).

16. Several of the draft dodgers became attached to influential writers of American political philosophy in their teen years. They took much of it to heart and used it to validate their emerging feelings and attitudes about the country and personal initiative. Please see further discussion in Chapters 3 and 7.

17. Baskir and Strauss found that most evaders could have dodged the draft, escaped conviction, and remained in the United States, without leaving for Canada, but were unaware, willfully or otherwise, of their legal deferments. See *Chance and Circumstance*, pp. 182–85.

18. Please see Oliver Clausen, "Boys Without a Country," *The New York Times Magazine*, May 21, 1967, p. 104; Williams, *The New Exiles*, p. 346, and Chapter 5 for more discussion of the reaction of the U.S. anti-war movement to draft dodgers in Canada.

19. Please see Williams, *The New Exiles*, pp. 34–90; Edmond Taylor, "Draft Dodgers in Canada," *The Reporter*, May 2, 1968, pp. 20–21; "Canada: Escape Hatch For U.S. Draft Dodgers," *U.S. News and World Report*, September 26, 1966, pp. 61–62; "The Real Story on Draft Dodging," *U.S. News and World Report*, December 4, 1967, p. 54. See also Chapters 5 and 6 for a detailed discussion.

20. See Emerick, *War Resisters Canada*, p. 9, and Surrey, *Choice of Conscience*, pp. 76, 164. See also Chapters 4 and 7 for discussion of blacks and other racial minorities, as well as draft dodgers from working-class and underclass backgrounds.

21. Baskir and Strauss, *Chance and Circumstance*, p. 91.

22. Surrey, *Choice of Conscience*, pp. 170–71. See also "For Americans," p. 64, and Williams, *The New Exiles*, pp. 341–49. Deserters comprised a large portion of the organized exile groups; many were mistaken for draft evaders, and were often the most vocal in condemning the war and working for amnesty. See Baskir and Strauss, *Chance and Circumstance,* pp. 182, 192, and Chapters 6 and 7 for further discussion of deserters and the exile community.

23. Ibid., p. 170; Baskir and Strauss, *Chance and Circumstance*, pp. 109– 258.

CHAPTER 1: THE DRAFT IN AMERICAN HISTORY

1. Thomas Jefferson to James Monroe (1782), quoted in Saul K. Padover, ed., *Thomas Jefferson on Democracy* (New York: Pelican Books, 1946), p. 14.

2. Francis P. Prucha, *The Sword of the Republic* (Bloomington: University of Indiana Press, 1977), pp. 6–7; Russell F. Weigley, *History of the United States Army* (New York: Macmillan, 1984), p. 81.

3. Lois G. Schwoerer, *"No Standing Armies!"* (Baltimore: Johns Hopkins University Press, 1974). See also, Lawrence D. Cress, *Citizens in Arms* (Chapel Hill: University of North Carolina Press, 1982).

4. There is a good discussion of this in Weigley's *History of the United States Army.*

5. Please see Howard H. Peckham, ed., *The Toll of Independence* (Chicago: University of Chicago Press, 1974).

6. John K. Mahon, *The American Militia* (Gainesville: University of Florida Press, 1960), pp. 14–24.

7. Theodore J. Crackel, "Jefferson, Politics, and the Navy" *Journal of the Early Republic,* II (Spring 1982).

8. C. Skeen Edward, *Citizen Soldiers in the War of 1812* (Lexington: University of Kentucky Press, 1999), pp. 2–4.

9. Cress, *Citizens in Arms.* See also John Whiteclay Chambers, *To Raise an Army* (New York: Free Press, 1987), p. 34; and Chambers, *Draftees or Volunteers* (New York: Garland, 1974), pp. 80–83.

10. James M. McPherson, *Ordeal by Fire* (New York: Knopf, 1982), pp. 149–83.

11. Herman Hattaway and Archer Jones, *How the North Won* (Urbana: University of Illinois Press, 1983), p. 14, and McPherson, *Ordeal by Fire*, pp. 181–96, 350–60. See also Albert Burton Moore, *Conscription and Conflict in the Confederacy* (New York: Hillary House, 1963); and Adrian Cook, *The Armies of the Streets* (Lexington: University of Kentucky Press, 1974).

12. Hattaway and Jones, *How the North Won*, p. 721.

13. Eugene Murdock, *One Million Men* (Madison: State Historical Society of Wisconsin, 1971), pp. 4–10, and "The Enrollment Act and the 37th Congress," *Historian* 46 (August 1984), pp. 550–90.

14. Chambers, *To Raise an Army*, p. 59.

15. Estimates of the deathtoll vary greatly, from one to two dozen, to over one thousand. Adrian Cook suggests that 119 people lost their lives in the New York riots. For more discussion, please see Cook, *The Armies of the Streets,* p. 194; Iver Bernstein, *The New York City Draft Riots* (New York: Oxford University Press, 1990), and Chambers, *To Raise an Army*, p. 53.

16. Chambers, *To Raise an Army*, p. 57; James W. Geary, *We Need Men* (Dekalb: Northern Illinois University Press, 1991), p. 173.

17. Chambers, *To Raise an Army*, p. 62.

18. Ibid., pp. 52–54.

19. Abraham Lincoln, "Opinion on the Draft," September 14, 1863, cited in Roy P. Basler, ed., *The Collected Works of Abraham Lincoln*, vol. 6 (New Brunswick, NJ: Rutgers University Press,1983), pp. 445–46.

20. James E. Hewes, Jr., *From Root to McNamara* (Washington. D.C.: Center of Military History United States Army 1975), pp. 3–21.

21. For a comprehensive discussion of this debate, please see John P. Finnegan, *Against the Specter of a Dragon* (Westport, CT.: Greenwood Press, 1974); and Richard Preston and Sydney F. Wise, *Men in Arms* (New York: Praeger, 1979), pp. 260–70.

22. Chambers, *To Raise an Army* p. 97.

23. Ibid., p. 184–85.

24. For an excellent discussion of this topic see H. C. Peterson and Gilbert C. Fite, *Opponents of War, 1771-1918* (Madison: University of Wisconsin Press, 1957). One of the more colorful and outspoken of the draft protesters during the First World War was Lithuanian immigrant Emma Goldman. Her work in organizing anti-draft campaigns led to several arrests, including her own.

25. Peterson and Fite, *Opponents of War.*

26. Chambers, *To Raise an Army*, p. 247.

27. Chambers, *Draftees or Volunteers*, pp. 267–76.

28. Chambers, *To Raise an Army*, pp. 246–48.

29. *Draftees or Volunteers*, pp. 301–7.

30. Ibid., pp. 305–7.

31. Please see John O. Sullivan, *From Voluntarism to Conscription* (New York: Garland, 1982); Albert A. Blum, *Drafted or Deferred* (Ann Arbor: Bureau of Industrial Relations, University of Michigan, 1967), and George Q. Flynn, *Lewis B. Hershey Mr. Selective Service* (Chapel Hill: University of North Carolina Press, 1985), pp. 170, 337n.

32. James M. Gerhardt, *The Draft and Public Policy* (Columbus: Ohio State University Press, 1971).

33. Please see Burton Ira Kaufman, *The Korean War* (New York: McGraw-Hill, 1986).

34. See U.S. Bureau of the Census, *Statistical Abstract of the United States* (Washington, D.C.: Government Printing Office, 1953), pp. 147: 148: 155; Chambers, *Draftees or Volunteers*, pp. 418–20.

35. Flynn, *Lewis B. Hershey*, pp. 192–93, 341n.

36. *Statistical Abstract of the United States*, pp. 147: 148: 155.

37. Ibid., 1973, Table 35, p. 31.

38. Please see Marvin E. Gettleman, ed., et al., *Vietnam and America* (New York: Grove Press, 1985), pp. 47–48.

39. Secretary of State Dean Acheson at a ministerial level meeting in Paris, May 1950. *U.S. Department of State Bulletin,* 22 (May 22, 1950), p. 821.

40. For a complete text of the SETO treaty, see *Background Information Relating to Southeast Asia and Vietnam* (revised June 16, 1965), *Report of the U.S. Senate Committee on Foreign Relations* (89th Cong. 1st sess., 1965, pp. 62–66. Please see also NSC 549212 (August 20, 1954) in Gareth Porter, ed., *Vietnam* (New York: New American Library, 1981), pp. 164–66.

41. Quote taken from a speech delivered to The Overseas Press Club in New York City on March 29, 1954. Please see U.S. *Department of State Bulletin, 30* (April 12, 1954), pp. 539–40.

42. Quoted in *The New York Times*, April 17, 1954.

43. For an excellent study on the American buildup in Vietnam please refer to James P. Harrison, *The Endless War* (New York: Free Press, 1982); Lloyd C. Gardner, *Approaching Vietnam* (New York: Norton, 1988); Stanley Karnow, *Vietnam* (New York: Viking, 1983); and George C. Herring, *America's Longest War* (New York: Wiley, 1979).

44. See appendix for year-by-year Selective Service inductee numbers.

45. See appendix for casualty statistics for all U.S. conflicts, including the Korean War.

46. There was a significant level of protest already by mid-1965, reported extensively by *The New York Times*, the *Washington Post*, and the major television networks. As early as August 1964, numerous rallies and peace vigils to protest U.S. bombing raids in North Vietnam were held across the nation. In September, one of the first major demonstrations against the war took place at the University of California at Berkeley, although polls at the time indicated that the majority of Americans still supported their nation's actions in Southeast Asia. In December 1964 a survey suggested that one-quarter of Americans did not know there was any fighting taking place in Vietnam. Please see Chapters 2 and 4 for more about the protests against the war. For an excellent overview of the lead up to the war, please refer to Karnow's *Vietnam*.

Republican opposition to America's deepening commitment was confined to the manner in which the Johnson administration was handling the war, not the fact that the United States was involved. The President was repeatedly criticized by former Vice President Richard Nixon for not prosecuting the war more vigorously, claiming that Johnson was "losing the war in Vietnam." There were only two dissenting votes against the Gulf of Tonkin Resolution, Senators Wayne Morse of Oregon and Ernest Gruening of Alaska.

47. Please see Karnow, *Vietnam*, p. 16.

CHAPTER 2: CHILDHOOD

1. Paul Goodman, *Growing Up Absurd* (New York: Random House, 1960), p. 11.

2. The reference to "Slouching towards Gomorra" comes from the title of Robert Bork's book: *Slouching Towards Gomorra: Modern Liberalism and American Decline* (New York: Harper Collins, 1996).

3. James Reston, Editorial, *The New York Times*, October 17, 1965.

4. *U.S. Congressional Record* (Washington, D.C.: Government Printing Office, October 18, 1965), p. 27251.

5. Ibid., p. 27218.

6. Ibid., p. 27252.

7. Ibid., p. 27253.

8. Ibid., pp. 27253–354.

9. Obline refers to then President Dwight Eisenhower.

10. Interview with Carroll Obline, March 20, 1995.

11. Interview with Ron Needer, August 14, 1995.

12. Interview with Michael Fischer, November 6, 1995.

13. Interview with Aston Davis, March 5, 1996.

14. Interview with Brian Linton, June 22, 1995.

15. Interview with Bill Warner, August 10, 1996.

16. For a complete discussion of this topic, please see Sara Evans, *Personal Politics* (New York: Vintage Books, 1980); Gerda Lerner, *The Grimke Sisters from South Carolina* (New York: Schocken Books, 1971), and Anne Firor Scott, *The Southern Lady* (Chicago: University of Chicago Press, 1970).

17. Interview with Bill Warner, August 10, 1996.

18. *The New York Times*, February 3–28, 1960.

19. Seth Cagin and Philip Dray, *We're Not Afraid* (New York: Macmillan,1988).

20. Doug McAdam, *Freedom Summer* (New York: Oxford University Press, 1988), p. 21.

21. Evans, *Personal Politics*, p. 60.

22. Please see McAdam, *Freedom Summer*, p. 4, *The Student Voice* 2, no.2 (February, 1961); Emily Stoper, *The Growth of Radicalism in a Civil Rights Organization* (New York: Carlson,1968); and Robert Weisbert, *Freedom Bound* (New York: Norton,1990). Weisbert provides an excellent overview of the movement in the South.

23. Interview with Albert Caldwell, May 9, 1996.

24. Interview with David Ward, June 27, 1996.

25. Haig-Brown, *Hell No, We Won't Go*, p. 111. See also the testimony of draft evader Roger Davies, pp. 120–21.

26. Interview with Carl McCrosky, September 10, 1995.

27. According to the research done by VERP, at least one-third of the men in that sample spoke of negative early family experiences. Please see Surrey, *Choice of Conscience*, pp. 80–81. Surrey found that the draft dodgers VERP

interviewed who experienced trouble forming close emotional childhood bonds with their families had "accelerated . . . independence."

28. Interview with Jim Tarris, March 8, 1995.

29. Interview with Bill Warner, August 10, 1996.

30. Interview with David Ward, June 27, 1996.

31. Interview with Martin Strychuck, March 21, 1996.

32. Interview with John Conway, August 26, 1996.

33. Interview with Michael Gillgannon, August 10, 1996.

34. Lerone Bennett, Jr., *What Manner of Man* (Chicago: Johnson Publishers, 1968), pp. 75–76, 82, 97–98; Martin Luther King, Jr., *I Have A Dream* (San Francisco: Harper, 1992), pp. 54–62.

35. *The New York Times*, July 19, 1955; Linus Pauling, *No More War!* (New York: Dodd, Mead, 1983), pp. 158–59.

36. Please see Charles Debendetti, *An American ordeal* (Syracuse NY: Syracuse University Press, 1990).

37. "Tract for the Times," *Liberation* I (March 1956), pp. 3–5.

38. Roy Finch, "The Liberation Poll," *Liberation* IV (November 1959), pp. 14–16. The VERP sample as well supports the fact that the parents of draft dodgers were well read, well informed, and took an active interest in the issues of the day. See Surrey, *Choice of Conscience*, p. 79.

39. Interview with Jonathan Burke, June 6, 1995.

40. Interview with Merrill Condel, November 18, 1995.

41. Interview with Brian Linton, June 22, 1995. Linton's parents would often talk about the possible effects of nuclear war in their son's presence.

42. Interview with Nick Theason, July 6, 1996.

43. Interview with Ron Needer, August 14, 1995.

44. Interview with Carroll Obline, March 20, 1995.

45. Gitlin provides an interesting discussion on childhood fears over the bomb, and the implications of those fears. Please see Todd Gitlin, *The Sixties* (New York: Bantam Books, 1993), pp. 22–23.

46. Michael Rossman, "Look, Ma, No Hope: A Memoir of the New Left," *Commonweal*, April 12, 1969.

47. Steven M. Spencer, "Fall Out: The Silent Killer," *The Saturday Evening Post*, August 29, 1959, pp. 26, 84–86; and September 5, 1959, pp. 25, 84–86.

48. Mike Broderick, *Nuclear Arms* (Jefferson, N.C.: McFarland, 1991), pp. 197—206.

49. *The New York Times*, November 15, 1957.

50. *Liberation* II, February 1958, pp. 4–6.

51. "Is There a Pacifist Revival?" *Liberation* III, May 1958. p. 3.

52. Interview with Timothy Unger, February 12, 1995.

53. Interview with Brandon Hockwald, March 21, 1996.

54. Interview with Michael Shannon, April 26, 1996.

55. Interview with Brian Anderson, October 10, 1995.

56. Interview with Martin Strychuck, March 21, 1996.

CHAPTER 3: ADOLESCENT PHILOSOPHERS

1. Roszak, *The Making of a Counter Culture*, p. 35.
2. Quotation taken from President Kennedy's Inaugural address of January 20, 1961.
3. Interview with Aston Davis, March 5, 1996 and June 10, 1998.
4. Interview with Bill Warner, August 10, 1996 and December 16, 1997.
5. Interview with Curt Erickson, July 15, 1996 and April 20, 1998.
6. Interview with Brian Linton, June 22, 1995 and July 14, 1996.
7. Interview with Dale Friesen, July 9, 1996 and August 17, 1998. See also, Nigel Hamilton, *JFK: Reckless Youth* (New York: Random House, 1992).
8. For an excellent discussion of this point see Noam Chomsky's *Rethinking Camelot* (Boston: South End Press, 1993).
9. Interviews with Carl McCrosky, September 10, 1995; Aston Davis, March 5, 1996 and June 10, 1998; Martin Strychuck, March 21, 1996 and February 18, 1998, and Ron Needer, August 14, 1995 and March 12, 1998.
10. For a detailed discussion on the effect of television on the American public, please refer to Erik Barnouw, *Tube of Plenty* (New York: Oxford University Press, 1990); David Potter, *People of Plenty* (Chicago: University of Chicago Press, 1954); Galbraith, *The Affluent Society*, and Halberstam, *The Fifties*.
11. Interview with David Ward, June 27, 1996 and May 14, 1997.
12. Interview with Michael Shannon, April 26, 1996 and September 20, 1998.
13. Interview with Albert Caldwell, May 9, 1996.
14. Interview with Merrill Condel, November 18, 1995 and January 16, 1998.
15. Interview with Nick Theason, July 6, 1996 and October 8, 1998.
16. Interview with Brandon Hockwald, August 21, 1995.
17. Interview with Ron Needer, August 14, 1995.
18. Interview with Michael Fischer, November 6, 1995.
19. Jack Kerouac, *On The Road* (New York: The Viking Press, 1957). Some of the draft dodgers interviewed by Allan Haig-Brown for his book, *Hell No We Won't Go*, also recounted their attraction to Kerouac's quintessential work. See Haig-Brown, pp. 25, 113, 144.
20. Interview with Albert Caldwell, May 9, 1996. Caldwell is referring to Beat writer William Burroughs and Kerouac character Neal Cassady.
21. Interview with Martin Strychuck, March 21, 1996.
22. Interview with Brian Linton, June 22, 1995.
23. Interview with Carroll Obline, March 20, 1995.
24. Interview with David Ward, June 27, 1996.
25. Interview with Jonathan Burke, June 6, 1995.
26. Interview with Jim Tarris, March 8, 1995.
27. Interview with Aston Davis, March 5, 1995.
28. Interview with Brian Linton, June 22, 1995 and July 14, 1996.

29. Interview with David Ward, June 27, 1996 and May 14, 1997.

30. Interview with Nick Theason, July 6, 1996 and October 8, 1998.

31. Interview with Merrill Condel, November 18, 1995 and January 16, 1998.

32. Interview with Michael Shannon, August 26, 1996 and September 20, 1998.

There is a rich collection of historical works and literature on American concepts of liberty and freedom applicable to the draft dodgers in Canada. Please consult the following books and articles for further reading: William T. Bluhm, *Force or Freedom?: The Paradox in Modern Political Thought* (New Haven: Yale University Press, 1984); Henry Steele Commager, *Freedom Loyalty Dissent* (New York: Oxford University Press, 1954); Clarence B. Carson, *The American Tradition* (Irvington-on-Hudson, N.Y.: Foundation for Economic Education, 1964); Richard N. Goodwin, *The American Condition* (New York: Doubleday, 1974); Joseph Hamburger, *John Stewart Mill on Liberty and Control* (Princeton, N.J.: Princeton University Press, 1999); Thomas Jefferson, *Writings* (New York: Literary Classics); Merwyn S. Johnson, *Locke on Freedom: An Incisive Study of the Thought of John Locke* (Austin, Tex.: Best Print. Co., 1978); Fred E. Katz, *Autonomy and Organization: The Limits of Social Control* (New York: Random House, 1968); Peter Augustine Lawler, *American Views of Liberty* (New York: Peter Lang, 1997); W. Von Leyden, *Hobbes and Locke, The Politics of Freedom and Obligation* (New York: St. Martin's Press, 1982); Michael McGiffert, ed., *The Character of Americans: A Book of Readings* (Homewood, Illinois: The Dorsey Press, 1964); Uday Singh Mehta, *The Anxiety of Freedom: Imagination and Individuality in Locke's Political Thought* (Ithaca: Cornell University Press, 1992); H. L. Nieburg, "The Ethics of Resistance to Tyranny," *American Political Review*, (December 1962); Saul K. Padover, ed., *Thomas Jefferson on Democracy* (New York: Pelican Books, 1946); Mulford Q. Sibley, *The Obligation to Disobey*, (New York: Council on Religion and International Affairs, 1970); Alexis de Tocqueville, *Democracy in America* (New York: Penguin, 1956), and Gordon Zahn, *War, Conscience and Dissent* (New York: Hawthorn, 1967).

33. Interview with Michael Shannon, April 12, 1996 and September 20, 1998. Several of the draft dodgers claim that if they would have been drafted in the Second World War they would have complied. They also claim that the country was much different then and their feelings about service and the nation's direction would have had an effect on their reactions and acceptance to conscription. Please see discussion in Chapter 7.

34. Interview with Michael Fischer, November 6, 1995 and December 12, 1997.

35. Interview with Carroll Obline, March 20, 1995 and August 23, 1997.

36. Interview with Michael Fischer, November 6, 1995.

37. Interview with Brian Anderson, October 10, 1995.

38. Interview with Carroll Obline, March 20, 1995.

39. Interview with Martin Beech, June 15, 1996.

40. Interview with Ron Needer, August 14, 1995.

41. Interview with Curt Erickson, July 15, 1996.

42. Interviews with Brandon Hockwald, August 21, 1995 and Jonathan Burke, June 6, 1995.

43. Interview with Brian Linton, June 22, 1995.

44. There was not only a significant rise in the numbers of college graduates between 1945 and 1960, but a rise in the percentage of the population that had completed post-secondary education.

45. Surrey, *Choice of Conscience*, pp. 67–86.

46. Interview with Nick Theason, July 6, 1996.

47. Interview with Merrill Condel, November 18, 1995.

48. Interview with Dale Friesen, June 27, 1996.

49. Interview with David Ward, June 27, 1996.

50. Interview with Carroll Obline, March 20, 1995. Obline refers to his father's service in the Second World War.

51. Interview with Dale Friesen, July 9, 1996.

52. Interview with Bill Warner, August 10, 1996.

CHAPTER 4: SELECTIVE SERVICE AND VIETNAM

1. Comment comes from former member of Students for a Democratic Society (SDS) at the University of Wisconsin, Jeffery Herf, now professor of history at Ohio University.

2. Baskir and Strauss, *Chance and Circumstance*, pp. 8–61.

3. Please see Karnow, *Vietnam*, p. 22.

4. John S. Bowman, ed., *The Vietnam War* (New York: World Almanac Publications, 1985), pp. 92–108; and Karnow, *Vietnam*, p. 416.

5. Karnow, *Vietnam*, pp. 416–26.

6. Baskir and Strauss, p. 7.

7. "Dodging the Draft: How Big a Problem?" *U.S. News and World Report*, October 25, 1965, p. 6.

8. *The Saturday Evening Post*, January 27, 1968, p. 22.

9. Quoted in Cooney and Spitzer, "Hell No We Won't Go," pp. 53–62.

10. Baskir and Strauss, *Chance and Circumstance*, p. 7.

11. "Dodging the Draft," p. 6.

12. Ibid., p. 6.

13. "Today's Draft Dodgers—How Big a Problem?" *U.S. News and World Report*, November 1, 1965, p. 32; "The ABC's of Draft Dodging," *Newsweek*, November 1, 1965, p. 32. See also Conrad J. Lynn, *How to Stay Out of the Army* (New York: Grove Press, 1967).

14. ' "Hell No!' at Harvard," *Newsweek*, January 29, 1968, p. 26.

15. "Needed: Community Draft Counseling Services," *The Christian Century*, April 24, 1968, pp. 510–11.

16. "Beating the Draft, 1970 Style," *Newsweek,* November 9, 1970, p. 27.

17. Interview with Jeffery Herf, May 1997.

18. It is unclear from the U.S. Army what "tests" were administered to potential inductees to determine if they were homosexual or not. Please see, "Today's Draft Dodgers—How Big a Problem?" p. 40.

19. Ibid., p. 41. Deferments for married men were also allowed between 1963 and 1966.

20. Sherry Gershon Gottlieb, *Hell No We Won't Go!* (New York: The Viking Press, 1991), p. 96.

21. Ibid., p. 93. See also Baskir and Strauss, *Chance and Circumstance*, p. 30. The authors cite statistics that indicate that 86,000 men were exempt from the draft for having "moral defects."

22. "Today's Draft Dodgers—How Big a Problem?" p. 40.

23. Ibid., p. 41.

24. Baskir and Strauss, *Chance and Circumstance*, p. 34.

25. Gottlieb, *Hell No, We Won't Go!*, pp. 144–45.

26. Ibid., pp. 162–63.

27. Ibid., p. 147.

28. Ibid., pp. 149, 169.

29. Interview with Jeffery Herf, May, 1997.

30. Gottlieb, *Hell No, We Won't Go!*, p. 53.

31. Ibid., p. 56.

32. Ibid., p. 59.

33. Ibid., p. 73.

34. David Sutter, *IV-F: A Guide to Draft Protection* (New York: Grove Press, 1970), pp. 66–74; Baskir and Strauss, *Chance and Circumstance*, pp. 36–48.

35. "The Draft: How to Beat it Without Really Trying" *Time*, March 15, 1968, p. 18. The famous New York Jets quarterback avoided military service by failing the standard medical exam with a problem knee, hence referred to as the "trick knee." Namath's problem, however, did not prevent him from winning a Super Bowl in 1969.

36. *U.S. vs. Seeger*, 380 U.S. 163.

37. Baskir and Strauss, *Chance and Circumstance*, pp. 40–43.

38. Ibid., pp. 50–51.

39. Gottlieb, *Hell No, We Won't Go!*, pp. 211–12.

40. Baskir and Strauss, *Chance and Circumstance*, p. 23.

41. "Today's Draft Dodgers—How Big a Problem?" p. 41.

42. Ibid., p. 41.

43. Baskir and Strauss, *Chance and Circumstance*, p. 36.

44. Curtis W. Tarr, *By the Numbers* (Washington, D.C.: National Defense University Press, 1981), pp. 145–47.

45. Ibid., p. 146.

46. *Life Magazine*, December 9, 1966.

47. Baskir and Strauss, *Chance and Circumstance*, pp. 47–8.

48. "Beating the Draft, 1970 Style," p. 28.

49. Racial minorities were underrepresented in all surveys on the draft dodger population in the United States and especially in Canada.   Blacks comprised a small minority of the draft dodgers who went to Canada and an even smaller percentage of the ones who remained following the 1977 amnesty. Please see Surrey, *Choice of Conscience,* pp. 67–79, 135–52; Emerick, *War Resisters Canada*, pp. 11–38; Williams, *The New Exiles*, pp. 341–44, and Baskir and Strauss, *Chance and Circumstance*, p.76.

50. Baskir and Strauss, *Chance and Circumstance,* pp. 3–13.

51. Williams, *The New Exiles*, p .41.

52. "Long Shot," *The New Republic*, February 21, 1970.

53. Stewart Alsop, "End of a Dreadful System," *Newsweek*, December 25, 1972, p. 34.

54. Baskir and Strauss, *Chance and Circumstance*, pp. 36–48.

55. Many of the less privileged young men, both black and white, who later ended up in Canada were not actually draft dodgers but military deserters. They often deserted once military life became unbearable; following the lead of earlier draft dodgers, they fled north to escape prosecution. Much like the small number of black inductees who went to Canada, these disadvantaged deserters (who were 75 percent white) had less education, fewer good job prospects, and also seemed less inclined to make firm decisions for their futures or had careers that they could resume easily across the border. American journalists covering the exile community in Canada at the time made similar observations. *Newsweek*'s Karl Fleming, for example, wrote "the deserters are different, usually poorer and less educated and they arrive in a panic with no preparation." Please see Karl Fleming, "America's Sad Young Exiles," *Newsweek*, February 15, 1971, p. 28. This view is supported by most accounts at the time, and in studies since the end of the war. For a complete breakdown on the class and educational backgrounds of the deserters, please see Baskir and Strauss, *Chance and Circumstance*, pp. 116–20, 180–83, 192; Williams, *The New Exiles*, pp. 90–127, 341, and Surrey, *Choice of Conscience*, pp. 69, 185. See Chapters 6 and 7 for further discussion of the differences between draft dodgers and deserters.

56. Williams, *The New Exiles*, p. 341. For more discussion please see Baskir and Strauss, *Chance and Circumstance*, pp. 134–39.

57. Gettleman, *Vietnam and America*, pp. 294–96, and Nancy Zaroulis and Gerald Sullivan, *Who Spoke Up?* (New York: Holt, Rinehart, Winston, 1985), pp. 80, 312, 379.

58. King's address can be found in its entirety in *Ramparts*, May 1967, pp. 33–37.

59. For an in-depth discussion, please see Harvard Sitkoff, *The Struggle For Black Equality, 1954-1980* (New York: Hill and Wang, 1981).

60. See Williams, *The New Exiles*, pp. 341–44.

61. Marshall is quoted in Baskir and Strauss, *Chance and Circumstance*, p. 8.

62. See Robert Coles, *The Middle Americans* (Boston: Little, Brown,1971), pp. 131–34.

CHAPTER 5: NORTHWARD BOUND

1. *Daily Cardinal*, University of Wisconsin-Madison, April 1967. Emphasis added.
2. Interview with Ron Needer, August 14, 1995.
3. Interview with Michael Fischer, November 6, 1995.
4. Interview with Aston Davis, March 5, 1996.
5. Interview with Carroll Obline, March 20, 1995.
6. Interview with Brian Linton, June 22, 1995.
7. Approximately 10,000 young men went underground in the United States during the war to avoid conscription.
8. Interview with Carl McCrosky, September 10, 1995.
9. Interview with John Conway, August 26, 1996.
10. Interview with Brandon Hockwald, August 21, 1995.
11. Baskir and Strauss, *Chance and Circumstance*, p. 182.
12. Ibid., p. 184.
13. Williams, *The New Exiles*, pp. 149–50.
14. At this point in the interview Timothy became visibly upset, and asked that we take a break for 15 minutes. He went out into his backyard and sat with his head in his hands for several minutes before we resumed. Interview with Timothy Unger, February 12, 1995.
15. Interview with Albert Caldwell, May 9, 1996.
16. Alice Lynd, *We Won't Go* (Boston: Beacon Press), p. 225.
17. "Canada: Escape Hatch for U.S. Draft Dodgers," p. 61.
18. Gettleman, *Vietnam and America*, p. 293.
19. *The New York Times Magazine,* May 21, 1967, p. 104.
20. Williams, *The New Exiles*, p. 346. Hayden said of the Canadian-based draft dodgers that it was essential that they politicize their movement in the United States. He believed that Canada should serve only as a "temporary sanctuary."
21. Interview with Nick Theason, July 6, 1996, and Curt Erickson, July 15, 1996.
22. Gettleman, *Vietnam and America,* pp. 315–16.
23. Interview with Carroll Obline, March 20, 1995.
24. Interview with Dale Friesen, July 9, 1996.
25. Interview with Timothy Unger, February 12, 1995.
26. Interview with Alan Kidd, September 18, 1995.
27. Interview with Jim Tarris, March 8, 1995.
28. Interview with Merrill Condel, November 18, 1995.
29. Interview with Brian Anderson, October 10, 1995.
30. See Williams, *The New Exiles*, p. 39.
31. Interview with Ron Needer, August 14, 1995.
32. Interview with Carroll Obline, March 20, 1995.
33. Interview with David Ward, June 27, 1996.
34. Interview with Albert Caldwell, May 9, 1996.

35. Baskir and Strauss, *Chance and Circumstance*, p. 201.

36. *The Saturday Evening Post*, January 27, 1968, p. 24.

37. Interview with Brian Linton, June 22, 1995.

38. Interview with Carl McCrosky, September 10, 1995.

39. Interview with Aston Davis, March 6, 1996. This view was shared at the time by several other draft dodgers after their arrival in Canada, as American newspaper correspondents found when traveling to Canada in the late 1960s and early 1970s to interview draft dodgers. See "No Tears," p. 23, and "Men Who Cannot Come Home," p. 15.

40. *The Saturday Evening Post,* January 17, 1968, p. 22.

41. "Trudeau Welcomes Draft Evaders," *The Christian Century,* April 8, 1970; interview with Carl McCrosky, September 10, 1995; see Williams, *The New Exiles*, p. 155.

42. Williams, *The New Exiles*, p. 50.

43. Robert S. Gilmour, and Robert B. Lamb *Political Alienation in Contemporary America* (New York: St. Martin's Press, 1975), pp. 133–34.

44. Please see the Introduction to Dickerson's *North to Canada.*

45. Interview with David Ward, June 27, 1996.

46. Allison is quoted in Baskir and Strauss, *Chance and Circumstance*, pp. 183, 185, 186.

CHAPTER 6: "BOYS WITHOUT A COUNTRY"

1. Oliver Clausen, "Boys Without a Country," *The New York Times Magazine*, May 21, 1967, pp. 25, 94, 104.

2. Ibid., p. 96.

3. Ibid., p. 94.

4. Williams, *The New Exiles*, pp. 45–89.

5. Clausen, "Boys Without a Country," pp. 95–96.

6. Ibid., p. 99.

7. Ibid., p. 96.

8. Ibid., p. 96.

9. Ibid., p. 104.

10. Interview with Nick Theason, July 6, 1996 and March 22, 1998.

11. Interview with David Ward, June 27, 1996 and January 21, 1998.

12. John Cooney and Dana Spitzer "Hell No We Won't Go," pp. 53–62.

13. Interview with Dale Friesen, July 9, 1996 and February 11, 1998.

14. Interview with Aston Davis, March 5, 1996 and April 17, 1998.

15. Dickerson, *North to Canada*, pp. 24, 32, 39.

16. Ibid., p. 39.

17. "For Americans: An Easier Life in Canada," *U.S. News and World Report*, October 28, 1968, p. 64.

18. Alsop, "They Can't Go Home Again," *Newsweek*, July 20, 1970 and Alsop, "The Need to Hate," *Newsweek*, July 27, 1970.

19. Gardner is quoted in "Men Who Cannot Come Home," p. 15.

20. Williams, *The New Exiles*, p. 324. According to figures compiled by VERP, only 27 percent of draft dodgers participated in any sort of exile activity. See Surrey, *Choice of Conscience*, p. 164.

21. Interview with Merrill Condel, November 18, 1995 and January 16, 1998; See Baskir and Strauss, *Chance and Circumstance*, p. 176.

22. "No Tears," *Time*, February 12, 1973, p. 23; and "Men Who Cannot Come Home," p. 15.

23. Dickerson, *North to Canada*, pp.135–36.

24. Ibid., p. 136.

25. *AMEX-Canada* was a magazine published in the exile community offering political commentary, information on services for draft resisters, and a forum for debate on amnesty. Most of the draft dodgers interviewed had either not heard of the magazine or were not particularly interested in it at the time. See Baskir and Strauss, *Chance and Circumstance*, p. 200.

26. In October 1970 Canada faced one of its most serious internal terrorist threats when members of the Quebec separatist Front de Liberation du Quebec (FLQ), a quasi-romantic revolutionary group, who were at their core terrorists, kidnapped British Trade Commissioner James Cross and Quebec's Minister of Labour Pierre Laporte. Quebec Premier Robert Bourassa, unable to stop the mounting crisis, asked Prime Minister Trudeau for help. In an unprecedented move, Trudeau proclaimed the War Measures Act, which effectively allowed arrest without charge. The civil liberties of Canadians were temporally suspended, while soldiers and armored vehicles patrolled the streets of Montreal. Homes were searched; dozens were arrested. Pierre Laporte was killed by his captors; they were later arrested and tried. While the majority of Canadians supported Trudeau's actions, the use of the War Measures Act in a domestic crisis was seen as an overstepping of federal power, a weakening of civil liberties, and a chance to settle political scores. For some draft evaders, the FLQ crisis was an unsettling episode for it caused them to ponder the political climate in their new country.

27. Interview with Timothy Unger, February 12, 1995 and August 16, 1997.

28. Dickerson, *North to Canada*, p. 146. See also Chapter 5 concerning whether draft evaders were anti-war activists.

29. Kostash, *Long Way From Home*, pp. 66–7.

30. Many draft dodgers, such as Michael Gillgannon, said that they were never joiners throughout their days growing up in America, and did not change their basic behavior once they emigrated north. It tended not to be in their nature to seek collective forms of activity.

31. Haig-Brown, *Hell No, We Won't Go*, p. 118.

32. Please see *AMEX-Canada*, 2, no.7, pp. 5–27, and Dickerson, *North to Canada*, pp. 135–36.

33. Interview with Jim Tarris, March 8, 1995.

CHAPTER 7: TRAITORS OR QUINTESSENTIAL AMERICANS?

1. Theodore Parker is quoted in Commager's *Freedom Loyalty Dissent*, p. 147.

2. Karnow, *Vietnam*, p. 17.

3. Surveys conducted with Americans in Canada and Canadians in the United States tell a tale of profound ignorance about the neighbor to the north. Few Americans, for example, realize that Canada is their largest trading partner. Lack of awareness concerning America's northern neighbor is not relegated to the general population. While George W. Bush was making his bid for the White House, a reporter asked him about the importance of America's relationship with Canada. The Texas governor explained that it was important to continue to foster good relations with Canada as the country is America's "*closest* neighbor to the north." Emphasis added.

4. Please see John McDermott, "Thoughts on the Movement: Who Does the Movement Move?" *Viet Report,* Sept/Oct, 1967; Baskir and Strauss, *Chance and Circumstance*, pp. 116–20, 180–83, 187, 192; Surrey, *Choice of Conscience*, pp. 69, 185, and Williams, *The New Exiles* pp. 90–126, 341.

5. Wealthier, skilled, and educated draft evaders often had an easier time crossing the border and receiving landed immigrant status than less-educated dodgers.

6. Dickerson, *North to Canada*, pp. 164, 170–71; Haig-Brown, *Hell No We Won't Go*! Haig-Brown's interviewees also report a life of above average incomes, higher education, suburban homes and satisfying advancements in their careers.

7. Interview with Brian Anderson, October 10, 1995.

8. Interview with Timothy Unger, February 12, 1995.

9. Interview with David Ward, June 27, 1996.

10. Interview with Carroll Obline, March 20, 1995.

11. Interview with Alan Kidd, September 18, 1995.

12. Interview with Michael Fischer, November 6, 1995.

13. Interview with Brian Linton, June 22, 1995.

14. Interview with Bill Warner, August 10, 1996.

15. Interview with Curtis Erickson, July 15, 1996. Erickson refers to Nixon's secret invasion of Vietcong garrisons in Cambodia. The expeditions were militarily successful, put politically disastrous at home when the public, through the release of the Pentagon Papers, discovered the truth. Some of the most heated protests against U.S. involvement in Southeast Asia occurred on college campuses, culminating in the shooting of four students at a protest at Kent State University in 1970.

16. Dickerson, *North to Canada*, p. 149.

17. Interview with Carl McCrosky, September 10, 1995.

18. Interview with Jim Tarris, March 8, 1995.

19. Interview with Jonathan Burke, June 6, 1995.

20. "Draft-Age Dilemma," *McCall's*, August 1967, p. 147.

21. Interview with Aston Davis, March 5, 1996.

22. Interview with Ron Needer, August 14, 1995.

23. Interview with Albert Caldwell, May 9, 1996.

24. Interview with John Conway, August 26, 1996.

25. Interview with Brandon Hockwald, August 21, 1995.

26. Interview with Martin Beech, June 15, 1996.

27. Interview with Martin Strychuck, March 21, 1996.

28. Williams, *The New Exiles*, p. 20.

29. Interview with Alan Kidd, September 18, 1995.

30. *The Saturday Evening Post*, January 27, 1968, p. 24.

31. Dickerson, *North To Canada*, p. 165.

32. Ibid., p. 150.

33. Haig-Brown, *Hell No, We Won't Go*, p. 112.

34. Interview with Merrill Condel, November 18, 1995 and January 16, 1998.

35. Interview with Ron Needer, August 14, 1999.

36. Interview with Aston Davis, March 5, 1996.

37. Interview with Michael Shannon, April 26, 1996 and September 20, 1998.

38. Interviews with Alan Kidd, September 18, 1995; Carl McCrosky, September 10, 1995; and Timothy Unger, February 12, 1995.

39. Interview with Carroll Obline, March 20, 1995 and August 23, 1997.

40. Interview with Jim Tarris, March 8, 1995.

41. Interview with Michael Shannon, April 12, 1996.

42. Interview with David Ward, June 27, 1996.

43. Interview with Bill Warner, August 10, 1996.

44. Mitchell Goodman, ed., *The Movement Toward a New America*, (New York: Alfred A. Knopf, 1970), p. 445.

45. *The New York Times Magazine,* May 21, 1967, p. 104.

46. Interview with Jonathan Burke, June 6, 1995.

47. Interview with Nick Theason, July 6, 1996.

48. Interview with Carroll Obline, March 20, 1995.

49. Interview with Timothy Unger, February 12, 1995.

50. Interview with Bill Warner, August 10, 1996.

51. Interview with Ron Needer, August 14, 1995. Needer refers to General William Westmoreland, who became one of the main targets of anti-war protesters and by more mainstream Americans as the war went south after the disastrous Tet Offensive in 1968. In the face of ever-growing casualties as the war progressed, Westmoreland continued to pressure President Lyndon Johnson for more troops to prosecute the jungle ground war.

52. Interview with Carl McCrosky, September 10, 1995.

53. Surrey, *Choice of Conscience*, p. 167.

54. Presidents Ford and Carter were not the first to offer amnesty to draft offenders in the twentieth century. Both Franklin Roosevelt and Harry Truman granted amnesty in certain situations, but nothing remotely similar to Carter's

blanket amnesty. See also Baskir and Strauss, *Chance and Circumstance*, pp. 203–46.

55. Surrey, *Choice of Conscience*, p. 170.

56. Ibid., p. 169.

57. Ibid., p. 170. Please see also Williams, *The New Exiles*, pp. 114–18; Baskir and Strauss, *Chance and Circumstance*, pp. 116–20, 180–83, 187, 192, and Chapter 6 for more discussion into the makeup of deserters in Canada.

58. See Baskir and Strauss, *Chance and Circumstance*, p. 109–92. An important point to remember is that deserters were still returning under a cloud, with few job prospects. But they still returned as they preferred to live in the United States, unlike the expatriates who had had enough of America. David Surrey points out that deserters actually suffered three times the unemployment rate as draft dodgers.

59. See Baskir and Strauss, *Chance and Circumstance*, pp. 182–92. According to the authors, four out of five deserters who went to Canada, returned, compared with one out of every two draft dodgers. Surrey's VERP study found that 55 percent of deserters compared with 35 percent of draft dodgers wished to return to the United States. See Surrey, *Choice of Conscience*, p. 165. Please see also Chapter 6 for more discussion of military deserters.

60. Surrey, *Choice of Conscience*, p. 170.

61. Interview with Jim Tarris, March 8, 1995.

62. The vast majority of the draft dodgers interviewed were not at all interested in amnesty other than it afforded them the opportunity to go home and visit family and friends. Some found the early amnesty proposals irrelevant or insulting since they suggested the dodgers had done something wrong. See also "Men Who Cannot Come Home," p. 15; and "No Tears," p. 23.

63. Quoted in "Men Who Cannot Come Home," p. 19.

64. Terry is quoted in Gilmour and Lamb, *Political Alienation in Contemporary America*, pp. 133–34.

65. Ibid., p. 132.

66. Starkins is quoted in "No Tears," p. 17.

67. Ibid., p. 17.

68. Dickerson, *North To Canada*, p. 157.

69. Some of James Dickerson's interviewees also report their problem was still with the nature of the United States, and they were therefore not interested in amnesty. Please see the interview with draft dodger Richard Deaton in *North to Canada*, p. 82.

70. Surrey, *Choice of Conscience*, pp. 165–66.

71. Both draft dodgers are quoted in Surrey, *Choice of Conscience*, p. 170.

72. Baskir and Strauss, *Chance and Circumstance*, p. 232.

73. Interview with Alan Kidd, September 18, 1995.

74. Surrey, *Choice of Conscience*, pp. 231–32.

75. Interview with Alan Kidd, September 18, 1995.

76. Interview with Carl McCrosky, September 10, 1995.

77. *The New York Times Magazine*, May 21, 1967, p. 104.

Bibliography

BOOKS

Bachman, Jerald G., and John D. Blair. *Soldiers, Sailors, and Civilians: The Military Mind and the All-Volunteer Force.* Ann Arbor: Institute of Social Research, University of Michigan, 1975.

Barnow, Eric. *Tube of Plenty: The Evolution of American Television.* New York: Oxford University Press, 1990.

Bartley, Numan V. *The Rise of Massive Resistance: Race and Politics in the South During the 1950s.* Baton Rouge: Louisiana State University Press, 1969.

Baskir, Lawrence M, and William Strauss. *Chance and Circumstance: The Draft, the War, and the Vietnam Generation.* New York: Alfred A. Knopf, 1978.

Basler, Roy P., ed. *The Collected Works of Abraham Lincoln.* 8 vols. New Brunswick, NJ: Rutgers University Press, 1983.

Bennett, Lerone Jr. *What Manner of Man: A Bibliography of Martin Luther King, Jr.* Chicago: Johnson Publishers, 1968.

Bernstein, Iver. *The New York City Draft Riots: Their Significance for American Society and Politics in the Age of the Civil War.* New York: Oxford University Press, 1990.

Bloom, Jack M. *Class, Race, and the Civil Rights Movement.* Bloomington: Indiana University Press, 1987.

Blum, Albert A. *Drafted or Deferred: Practices Past and Present.* Ann Arbor: Bureau of Industrial Relations, University of Michigan, 1967.

Bork, Robert. *Slouching Towards Gomorra: Modern Liberalism and American Decline.* New York: Harper Collins, 1996.

Bowman, John S., ed. *The Vietnam War: An Almanac.* New York: World Almanac Publications, 1985.

Branch, Taylor. *Parting the Waters: America in the King Years, 1954-1963.* New York: Simon and Schuster, 1988.

Bressler, Leo, and Marion A. Bressler. *Country, Conscience, and Conscription: Can They be Reconciled?* Englewood Cliffs, NJ: Prentice Hall, 1970.

Broderick, Mike. *Nuclear Arms: A Critical Analysis and Filmography.* Jefferson, NC: McFarland and Company, 1991.

Burroughs, William. *Letters to Allen Ginsberg, 1953-1957.* New York: Full Court Press, 1982.

Cagin, Seth, and Philip Dray. *We're Not Afraid: The Story of Goodman, Schwerner, and Chaney and the Civil Rights Campaign for Mississippi.* New York: Macmillan Publishing Company, 1988.

Canby, Steven L. *Military Manpower Procurement.* Lexington, MA: Lexington Books, 1972.

Capps, Walter. *The Unfinished War: Vietnam and the American Conscience.* Boston: Beacon, 1982.

Carson, Clarence B. *The American Tradition.* Irvington-on Hudson, NY: The Foundation for Economic Education, Inc., 1964.

Chafe, William. *The American Woman: Her Changing Social, Economic, and Political Roles, 1920-1970.* New York: Oxford University Press, 1972.

___.*The Unfinished Journey: America Since World War II.* New York: Oxford University Press, 1991.

Chambers, John Whiteclay. *Draftees and Volunteers: A Documentary History of the Debate over Military Conscription in the United States, 1787-1973.* New York: Garland Publishers, 1974.

___.*To Raise an Army.* New York: Free Press, 1987.

Chomsky, Noam. *For Reasons of State.* New York: Pantheon Books, 1973.

___.*Rethinking Camelot: JFK, the Vietnam War, and U.S. Political Culture.* Boston: South End Press, 1993.

Coles, Robert. *The Middle Americans.* Boston: Little, Brown & Company, 1971.

Commager, Henry Steele. *Freedom Loyalty Dissent.* New York: Oxford University Press, 1954.

Cook, Adrian. *The Armies of the Streets: The New York City Draft Riots of 1863.* Lexington: University of Kentucky Press, 1974.

Cress, Lawrence D. *Citizens in Arms: The Army and the Militia in American Society to the War of 1812.* Chapel Hill: University of North Carolina Press, 1982.

Curry, David G. *Sunshine Patriots: Punishment and the Vietnam Offender.* Notre Dame: University of Notre Dame Press, 1985.

Debendetti, Charles. *An American Ordeal: The Antiwar Movement of the Victorian Era.* Syracuse, NY: Syracuse University Press, 1990.

Dickerson, James. *North to Canada: Men and Women Against the Vietnam War.* Westport, CT.: Praeger, 1999.

Dicks, Shirley. *From Vietnam to Hell: Interviews with Victims of Post-traumatic Stress Disorder.* Jefferson, NC: McFarland, 1990.

Elder, Glen Jr. *Children of the Great Depression: Social Change in Life Experience.* Chicago: University of Chicago Press, 1974.

Emerick, Kenneth Fred. *War Resisters Canada: The World of the American Military-Political Refugees.* Knox: Pennsylvania Free Press, 1972.

Emerson, Gloria. *Winners and Losers: Battles, Retreats, Gains, Losses and Runs from the Vietnam War.* New York: Harcourt Brace Jovanovich, 1972.

Evans, Sara. *Personal Politics: The Roots of Women's Liberation in the Civil Rights Movement and the New Left.* New York: Vintage Books, 1980.

Ferber, Michael, and Saughton Lynd. *The Resistance.* Boston: Beacon Press, 1971.

Finnegan, John P. *Against the Specter of a Dragon: The Campaign for Military Preparedness, 1914-1917.* Westport, CT: Greenwood Press, 1974.

Flynn, George Q. *Lewis B. Hershey Mr. Selective Service.* Chapel Hill: University of North Carolina Press, 1985.

Friedan, Betty. *The Feminine Mystique.* New York: Dell Publishing Company, 1963.

Fullbright, William J. *The Crippled Giant: American Foreign Policy and its Domestic Consequences.* New York: Random House, 1972.

Gaffen, Fred. *Unknown Warriors: Canadians in Vietnam.* Toronto: Dundurn Press, 1990.

Galbraith, John K. The Affluent Society. Boston: Houghton Mifflin, 1958.

Gardner, Lloyd C. Approaching Vietnam From World War II through Dien Bien Phu. New York: W.W. Norton & Co., 1988.

Geary, James W. *We Need Men: The Union Draft and the Civil War.* Dekalb: Northern Illinois University Press, 1991.

Gerhardt, James M. *The Draft and Public Policy: Issues in Military Manpower Procurement, 1945-1970.* Columbus: Ohio State University Press, 1971.

Gettleman, Marvin E. ed., et al. *Vietnam and America: A Documented History.* New York: Grove Press, 1985.

Gilmour, Robert S., and Robert B. Lamb. *Political Alienation in Contemporary America.* New York: St. Martin's Press, 1975.

Gitlin, Todd. *The Sixties: Years of Hope, Days of Rage.* New York: Bantam, 1993.

Goodman, Mitchell, ed. *The Movement Toward a New America: The Beginnings of a Long Revolution.* New York: Alfred A. Knopf, 1970

Goodman, Paul. *Growing Up Absurd: Problems of Youth in the Organized System.* New York: Random House, 1960.

Gottlieb, Sherry Gershon. *Hell No We Won't Go! Resisting the Draft During the Vietnam War.* New York: The Viking Press, 1991.

Goulden, Joseph C. *Truth is the First Causality: The Gulf of Tonkin Affair, Illusion and Reality.* Chicago: Rand McNally, 1969.

Haig-Brown, Allan. *Hell No, We Won't Go!* Vancouver: Raincoast Books, 1996.

Halberstam, David, *The Best and the Brightest,* New York: Random House, 1969.

___.*The Fifties*. New York: Villard Books, 1993.

Harrison, James P. *The Endless War: Fifty Years of Struggle in Vietnam*. New York: Free Press, 1982.

Harvey, David. *Americans in Canada: Migration and Settlement Since 1840*. Lewiston, NY: Edwin Mellen Press, 1991.

Hattaway, Herman, and Archer Jones. *How the North Won: A Military History of the Civil War*. Urbana: University of Illinois Press, 1983.

Heineman, Kenneth J. *Campus Wars: The Peace Movement at American State Universities in the Vietnam Era*. New York: New York University Press, 1993.

Helmer, John. *Bringing the War Home: The American Soldier Before Vietnam and After*. New York: Free Press, 1974.

Herring, George C. *America's Longest War: The United States in Vietnam, 1950-1975*. New York: Wiley, 1979.

Hewes, James E., Jr. *From Root to McNamara: Army Organization an Administration, 1900-1963*. Washington, D.C.: Center of Military History United States Army, 1975.

Hirschman, Albert O. *Exit, Voice and Loyalty: Responses to Decline in Firms, Organizations, and States*. Cambridge: Harvard University Press, 1970.

Iwanska, Alicja. *British American Loyalists in Canada and U.S. Southern Confederates in Brazil: Exiles from the United States*. Lewiston, NY: Edwin Mellen Press, 1993.

Jones, Landon Y. *Great Expectations: America and the Baby Boom Generation*. New York: Ballantine Books, 1991.

Karnow, Stanley. *Vietnam: A History*. New York: The Viking Press, 1983.

Katona, George. *The Mass Consumption Society*. New York: McGraw-Hill Book Company, 1964.

Kaufman, Burton Ira. *The Korean War: Challenges in Crisis, Credibility and Command*. New York: McGraw-Hill Companies, 1997.

Kendall, David, and Leonard Ross. *The Lottery and the Draft: Where do I Stand?* New York: Harper & Row, 1970.

Kerouac, Jack. *On The Road*. New York: The Viking Press, 1957.

King, Martin Luther, Jr. *I Have A Dream: Writings & Speeches that Changed the World*. Ed. by James Melvin Washington. San Francisco: Harper, 1992.

Klein, Michael, ed. *The Vietnam Era: Media and Popular Culture in the U. S. and Vietnam*. Winchester, MA: Pluto Press, 1990.

Kostash, Myrna. *Long Way from Home: The Story of the Sixties Generation in Canada*. Toronto: James Lorimer & Company, Publishers, 1980.

Leinwand, Gerald. *The Draft*. New York: Pocket Books, 1970.

Lemboke, Jerry. *The Spitting Image: Myth, Memory, and the Legacy of Vietnam*. New York: New York University Press, 1998.

Lerner, Gerda. *The Grimke Sisters from South Carolina: Pioneers for Women's Rights and Abolition*. New York: Schocken Books, 1971.

Lynd, Alice. *We Won't Go*. Boston: Beacon Press, 1968.

Lynn, Conrad J. *How to Stay Out of the Army: A Guide to Your Rights Under the Draft Law*, 2d ed., rev. New York: Grove Press, 1967.

Mahon, John K. *The American Militia*. Gainesville: University of Florida Press, 1960.

Matusow, Allen J. *The Unraveling of America: A History of Liberalism in the 1960s*. New York: Harper & Row, 1984.

May, Elaine Tyler. *Homeward Bound: American Families in the Cold War Era*. New York: Basic Books, 1988.

McAdam, Doug. *Freedom Summer*. New York: Oxford University Press, 1988.

McNamara, Robert S. *The Essence of Security: Reflections in Office*. New York: Harper & Row Publishers, 1968.

___.*In Retrospect: The Tragedy and Lessons of Vietnam*. New York: Random House, 1995.

McPherson, James M. *Ordeal by Fire: The Civil War and Reconstruction*. New York: Knopf; Distr. by Random House, 1982.

Mehnert, Klaus. *Twilight of the Young: The Radical Movements of the 1960s and their Legacy*. New York: Holt, Rinehart and Winston, 1976.

Moore, Albert Burton. *Conscription and Conflict in the Confederacy*. New York: Hillary House Publishers, 1963.

Morrison, Wilber H. *The Elephant and the Tiger: The Full Story of the Vietnam War*. New York: Hippocrene Books, 1990.

Moss, George Donelson. *Vietnam: An American Ordeal*. Upper Saddle River, NJ: Prentice Hall, 1998.

Murdock, Eugene. *One Million Men: The Civil War Draft in the North*. Madison: State Historical Society of Wisconsin, 1971.

Murphy, Jeffrie, G., ed. *Civil Disobedience and Violence*. Belmont, CA: Wadsworth Publishing Company, 1971.

Padover, Saul K., ed. *Thomas Jefferson on Democracy*. New York: Pelican Books, 1946.

Pauling, Linus. *No More War!* New York: Dodd, Mead, 1983.

Peckham, Howard H., ed. *The Toll of Independence: Engagements and Battle Causalities of the American Revolution*. Chicago: University of Chicago Press, 1974.

Peterson, H. C., and Gilbert C. Fite. *Opponents of War, 1771-1918*. Madison: University of Wisconsin Press, 1957.

Phillips, Michael J. *The Dilemmas of Individualism: Status, Liberty and American Constitutional Law*. Westport, CT: Greenwood Press, 1983.

Porter, Gareth, ed. *Vietnam: A History in Documents*. New York: New American Library, 1981.

Potter, David. *People of Plenty: Economic Abundance and the American Character*. Chicago: University of Chicago Press, 1954.

Preston, Richard, and Sydney F. Wise. *Men in Arms: A History of Warfare and its Interrelationships with Western Society* IV ed. New York: Praeger, 1979.

Prucha, Francis P. *The Sword of the Republic: The United States Army on the Frontier, 1783-1846.* Bloomington: University of Indiana Press, 1977.

Rapson, Richard L. *Individualism and Conformity in the American Character.* Boston: D.C. Heath and Company, 1967.

Roszak, Theodore. *The Making of a Counter Culture.* New York: Dell Publishing Company, 1969.

Rupp Leila J., and Verta Taylor. *Survival in the Doldrums: The American Women's Movement, 1945 to the 1960s.* New York: Oxford University Press, 1978.

Sanders, Jacquin. *The Draft and the Vietnam War.* New York: Walker, 1966.

Schuyler, Foster H. *Activism Replaces Isolationism: U.S. Public Attitudes, 1940-1975.* Washington: Foxhall Press, 1993.

Schwoerer, Lois G. *"No Standing Armies!" The Anti-Army Ideology in Seventeenth Century England.* Baltimore: Johns Hopkins University Press, 1974.

Scott, Anne Firor. *The Southern Lady: From Pedestal to Politics 1820-1920.* Chicago: University of Chicago Press, 1970.

Sitkoff, Harvard. *The Struggle for Black Equality, 1954-1980.* New York: Hill and Wang, 1981.

Skeen, C. Edward. *Citizen Soldiers in the War of 1812.* Lexington: University of Kentucky Press, 1999.

Spector, Roland H. *After Tet: The Bloodiest Year in the War.* New York: Free Press, 1993.

Starr, Paul. *The Discarded Army: Veterans after Vietnam.* New York: Charterhouse, 1973.

Stewart, Walter. *As They See Us.* Toronto: McCelland and Stewart, 1977.

Stoper, Emily. *The Growth of Radicalism in a Civil Rights Organization.* New York: Carlson Publishers Inc., 1968.

Sullivan, John O. *From Voluntarism to Conscription: Congress and the Selective Service, 1940-1945.* New York: Garland, 1982.

Surrey, David S. *Choice of Conscience: Vietnam Era Military and Draft Resisters in Canada.* New York: Praeger, 1982.

Sutter, David. *IV-F: A Guide to Draft Protection.* New York: Grove Press, 1970.

Tarr, Curtis W. *By the Numbers: The Reform of the Selective Service System, 1970-1972.* Washington, D.C.: National Defense University Press, 1981.

Weigley, Russell F. *History of the United States Army.* New York: Macmillan, 1984.

Weisbert, Robert. *Freedom Bound: A History of American Civil Rights Movement.* New York: W.W. Norton & Company, 1990.

Wells, Tom. *The War Within: America's Battle Over Vietnam.* Berkeley: University of California Press, 1994.

Williams, Roger Neville. *The New Exiles: American War Resisters in Canada.* New York: Liveright Publishers, 1971.

Wirtz, James J. *The Tet Offensive: Intelligence Failure in War.* Ithaca: Cornell University Press, 1991.
Zaroulis, Nancy, and Gerald Sullivan. *Who Spoke Up? American Protest Against the War in Vietnam, 1963-1975.* New York: Holt, Rinehart, and Winston, 1985.

ARTICLES

"A Youth's Reason for Spurning the Draft—A Judge's Answer" *U.S. News and World Report*, 8 June 1970.
Alexander, Shana. "Amnesty, Agony and Responsibility" *Newsweek,* 19 March 1973.
Alsop, Stewart. "End of a Dreadful System" *Newsweek,* 25 December 1972.
___."They Can't Go Home Again" *Newsweek,* 20 July 1970.
___."The Need To Hate" *Newsweek,* 27 July 1970.
"An End to Most Draft Deferments?" *U.S. News and World Report*, 16 February 1970.
"Bald Case in Point: Pro Football's Magic Immunity" *Life*, 61 (December 9, 1966).
"Beating the Draft, 1970 Style" *Newsweek,* 9 November 1970.
"Behind the Campus Protests Over Draft and Vietnam" *U.S. News and World Report*, 25 October 1965.
Bell, Joseph N. "I'm Not Coming Home" *McCall's* (February 1975).
Boulanger, Raymond P. "The Undesirable Veteran" *Commonweal*, 21 September 1973.
"Canada: Escape Hatch for U.S. Draft Dodgers" *U.S. News and World Report*, 26 September 1966.
Clausen, Oliver. "Boys Without a Country" *The New York Times Magazine,* 21 May 1967.
Commager, Henry Steele "The Case for Amnesty" *The New York Review of Books*, 6 April 1972.
Cooney, John, and Dana Spitzer "'Hell No We Won't Go!' Deserters and Draft Dodgers in Canada and Sweden" *Trans-Action* VI (September 1969).
Crackel, Theodore J. "Jefferson Politics and the Navy: An Examination of the Military Peace Establishment Act of 1802" *Journal of the Early Republic* II (Spring 1982).
"Dodging the Draft: How Big a Problem?" *U.S. News and World Report,* 25 October 1965.
"Draft Age Dilemma" *McCall's* (August 1967).
Fallows, James "What Did You Do in the Class War, Daddy?" *Washington Monthly* (October 1975).
Fiedler, Leslie "Who Really Died in Vietnam?" *Saturday Review*, 18 November 1972.
Finch, Roy "The Liberation Poll" *Liberation* IV (November 1959).
Finn, James "The Amnesty Issue" *Commonweal*, November 3, 1972.

Fleming, Karl "America's Sad Young Exiles" *Newsweek*, 15 February 1971.

Fliegel, Dorian, J. "Forgotten History of the Draft" *The Nation*, 10 April 1967.

"For Americans: An Easier Life in Canada" *U.S. News and World Report*, 28 October 1968

"Good-by Grad School?" *Newsweek*, 18 December 1967.

Gooding, Richard "An Exile in My Own Country" *Look*, 24 February 1970.

"Gone With The Draft?" *Newsweek*, 15 April 1968.

"Hell No! at Harvard" *Newsweek,* 29 January 1968.

"How the New Draft Rules Will Work. . . .Who Will Be Hit" *U.S. News and World Report*, 26 February 1968.

"How Two Allies Fare with Volunteers" *U.S. News and World Report*, 1 March 1971.

"If Draft Dodgers Come Home" *U.S. News and World Report*, 6 December 1971.

"If U.S. Tries an All-Volunteer Army: Survey by Military Experts" *U.S. News and World Report*, 1 March 1971.

"Is There a Pacifist Revival?" *Liberation* III (May 1958).

Levitas, Mitchell "2S—Too Smart to Fight?" *The New York Times Magazine*, 24 April 1966.

"Long Shot" *The New Republic*, 21 February 1970.

"Lottery Draft—How It's Working" *U.S. News and World Report*, 19 January 1970.

McDermott, John "Thoughts on the Movement: Who Does the Movement Move?" *Viet Report* (Sept/Oct 1967).

"Men Who Cannot Come Home" *Time,* 10 January 1970.

"Millions Who Avoided the Draft" *U.S. News and World Report*, 1 March 1971.

Musil, Robert K. "The Truth about Deserters" *The Nation*, 16 April 1973.

"Needed: Community Draft Counseling Services" *The Christian Century,* 24 April 1968.

"No Tears: Draft Evaders and Deserters in Canada" *Time,* 12 February 1973.

"Real Story on Draft Dodging: A Survey Shows This…" *U.S. News and Word Report*, 4 December 1967.

Reston, James Editorial *The New York Times,* 17 October 1965.

Spencer, Steven M. "Fall Out: The Silent Killer" *The Saturday Evening Post*, 29 August and 5 September 1959.

Swomley, John M., Jr. "Draft Exiles in Canada" *The Christian Century*, 30 October 1968.

Taylor, Edmond "Draft Dodgers in Canada" *The Reporter*, 2 May 1968.

"The ABC's of Draft Dodging" *Newsweek*, 1 November 1965

"The Draft: How to Beat it Without Really Trying" *Time*, 15 March 1968.

"The Draft: Man Without a Country?" *Newsweek*, 30 March 1970.

"The Draft. Thanks, But No Thanks" *Time*, 3 March 1967.

"The Enrollment Act and the 37th Congress" *Historian,* 46 (August 1984).

"The Vietnam Dodgers" *Newsweek*, 3 October 1966.

"Today's Draft Dodgers—How Big a Problem?" *U.S. News and World Report* 1 November 1965

"Tract for the Times" *Liberation* I (March 1956).

"Trudeau Welcomes Draft Evaders" *The Christian Century*, 8 April 1970.

"Who Has Been Fighting in Vietnam" *U.S. News and World Report*, 1 March 1971.

Willard, William "The Coming War on Women" *San Francisco Chronicle*, 8 February 1945.

Zetlin, Maurice, Kenneth Lutterman, and James Russell. "Death in Vietnam Class, Poverty, and the Risks of War" *Politics and Society,* III (Spring 1973).

U.S. GOVERNMENT DOCUMENTS

U.S. Bureau of the Census *Statistical Abstract of the United States.* Washington, D.C.: Government Printing Office, 1953, 1973.

U.S. Congress. Senate. *Report of the U.S. Senate Committee on Foreign Relations.* 89th Cong., 1st sess., 1965.

___.U.S. *Congressional Record.* Washington, D.C.: Government Printing Office, October 18, 1965.

U.S. Department of State. *Bulletin,* 22 (May 22, 1950).

___.*Bulletin,* 30 (April 12, 1954).

FILMS

"America Love it or Leave it" National Film Board of Canada (November 1995), Narrated by Peter Gzowski.

INTERVIEWS

All of the author's interviews were conducted between February 12, 1995 and September 28, 2000.

Index

About the Author

FRANK KUSCH is a journalist and historian currently working on a second book on the anti-war movement in the United States during the 1960s.